Police Ethics

and

Catholic Christianity

Police Ethics

and

Catholic Christianity

Lying and Related Ethical Issues within Policing

PAUL DIXON

KENRYCUDDEN PRESS

Nihil Obstat
Fr Michael Wheaton
Censor Deputatus

Imprimatur
+ Rt Revd Mark O'Toole,
Bishop of Plymouth, United Kingdom
March 28, 2019

The *Nihil Obstat* and *Imprimatur* are official declarations that a book or pamphlet is free of doctrinal or moral error. No implication is contained therein that those who have granted the *Nihil Obstat* and *Imprimatur* agree with the contents, opinions, or statements expressed.

Published by KenryCudden Press, United Kingdom
Email: enquiries@kenrycuddenpress.com

Copyright © Paul Dixon 2019

The moral rights of the author have been asserted

First Edition published in 2019

This book is protected by copyright law. All rights reserved. Apart from any fair dealing for the purposes of criticism, review or private study, no part of this book may be reproduced, stored in a retrieval system, or transmitted in any form or by any means, without the prior written permission of the publisher.

British Library Cataloguing-in-Publication Data

A catalogue record for this book is available from the British Library

ISBN 978-1-9162046-1-4

The content of this book (ISBN 978-1-9162046-1-4) is identical to the previously printed version of the same title (ISBN 978-1-9162046-0-7).

Grateful acknowledgement for permission to reprint:
Paul Dixon, 'Police Lies and the Catechism on Lying'. *Irish Theological Quarterly* 78 (2), 162–178. Copyright © [2013] (Copyright Holder). Reprinted by permission of SAGE Publications. https://journals.sagepub.com/doi/full/10.1177/0021140012472633.

Scripture quotations are from the New Revised Standard Version Bible: Catholic Edition, copyright © 1989, 1993 National Council of the Churches of Christ in the United States of America. Used by permission. All rights reserved.

For Letitia

and

police officers of yesterday, today and tomorrow

At a time of acute concern among professionals that the demands of their work may require compromise or even repudiation of their Christian beliefs, this book offers a timely intervention. Unsurprisingly, police too find themselves today in unprecedented situations of moral uncertainty and challenges to their integrity that cry out for sound teaching and practical advice. This book does the business. It is addressed to police men and women on the ground; it offers clear explanations of essential elements of Christian belief and practice; it initiates discussion of difficult cases in which these things are put to the test . . .
Dr Susan Frank Parsons, Editor of *Studies in Christian Ethics*

It's not often that a professional ethics book is written by a member of the profession rather than by an ethicist, and it's always welcome. Paul Dixon brings to this book his experience as policeman as well as his theological expertise, to produce a thorough and thoughtful account of police ethics viewed from a standpoint within Catholic faith, written in an accessible idiom. He goes behind practical norms and principles to their bases, his concern always being to show how Catholic teaching and thinking can illuminate some key concrete problems in police work. A fine piece of work.
Patrick Hannon, Emeritus Professor of Moral Theology, Maynooth College, Ireland

Acknowledgements

This book has taken more years to write than I care to remember. I am indebted to all who have helped along the way. You know who you are, and I am most grateful.

A special mention must be made to my wife, Letitia, who, over many years, has patiently endured the many hours I have joyfully spent in my writing cave.

To all good police officers, past, present and future, thank you for your service.

All glory be to God.

Contents

Preface   xi

  1. Introduction   1

  2. Policing: Culture and Code   9

  3. Catholic Christian Ethics   31

  4. Lying: an Analysis   65

  5. Lying: and Tradition   92

  6. Discreet Language   111

  7. Perjury and Oaths   125

  8. Virtuous Policing   147

  9. Conclusion   160

Appendices
    1. Natural Law – an outline   165
    2. Situation Ethics – an outline   167
    3. Proportionalism – a context   170
    4. Judaism and Lying   172
    5. Reality of Perjury   173

Abbreviations   175
Bibliography   177
Index   193

[C]omplex ethical problems are an inherent part of policing.
—Newburn[1]

Preface

Why this book? Policing presents various moral challenges, and the fact of the matter is that there is very little published moral guidance on police ethics from the Catholic Christian tradition. This book offers a Catholic Christian perspective on several ethical issues within policing.

Hopefully others, too, in due course, will contribute to this area of moral concern, thereby building up a corpus of material that brings together issues within policing with further insights and teachings from the Catholic Christian tradition.

The author, a former police officer who served in the United Kingdom, resigned from the police service with an exemplary certified condition of service. He subsequently taught religious studies in further education for over ten years. He has earned three degrees: a BA in Philosophy, a Pontifical MA in Catholic Theology and a PhD in Catholic Studies. He has previously published in the *Irish Theological Quarterly* and *The Heythrop Journal*.

This book is for all who have an interest in how Catholic Christianity might contribute to the development of police ethics. It has particular relevance for Catholic police officers and all other Christian police officers. The book will also be of service to academics within criminal justice ethics, offering them new material, insights and perspectives that have not so far illuminated the world of policing.

Additionally, this book will be of use to the Catholic layperson and Catholic ethicist too, since it offers a fresh perspective on the ongoing, unsettled debate within Catholicism concerning the ethics of lying.

Ironically, this book should also prove to be of benefit to those within policing who think that Catholic Christianity has little to offer the police; and those within Catholic Christianity who believe that ethical issues within policing have little to teach them.

---

[1] Newburn, *Literature review – Police integrity and corruption*, 3. Throughout this book, short citations are used for all references. Full citations are provided in the bibliography.

1) dangerous people, victims not in right mind, people bent on evil, people who are not in their right mind

> *All truth passes through three stages:*
> *First, it is ridiculed.*
> *Second, it is opposed.*
> *Third, it is accepted as self-evident.*
> —Schopenhauer[1]

1

INTRODUCTION

Sherman asks whether a Christian can be a police officer?[2] The answer, in principle, is yes, given the fact that police officers are peace officers and police for the good of society. Indeed, the Christian Police Association (CPA) states that there is no conflict between Christianity and policing.[3] Christianity complements and enhances the policing role, but there are significant moral challenges facing police officers. Policing requires officers to confront ethical issues that would not usually be experienced by the public, at least not to the same degree or frequency. What help can the Catholic Christian tradition offer to these areas of moral concern?

It is pleasing to see significant efforts in recent years to improve the professionalism and ethics within policing. In the United Kingdom (UK), for example, the Police and Criminal Evidence Act of 1984 introduced significant changes to legislation to improve police practice in England and Wales.[4] Then in 2014, the College of Policing's Code of Ethics was introduced in England and Wales to improve police behaviour.[5] Also, in recent years (c.2015+) body cameras are increasingly being worn by both UK and United States (US) police.[6] Yet it would be naive to think that

started wearing them b/c citizens complaints abt policing

---

[1] These words/thoughts are often attributed to the German philosopher Arthur Schopenhauer (1788–1860), though their true origins appear uncertain.

[2] Sherman, *Ethics in Criminal Justice Education*, 38.

[3] See the Christian Police Association (CPA) website.

[4] The National Archives, Police and Criminal Evidence Act 1984.

[5] College of Policing, *Code of Ethics*.

[6] Between 2014–2015 a year-long research study (led by the University of Cambridge's Institute of Criminology) of nearly 2000 police officers across the UK and US has revealed that when the police used body-worn cameras (BWCs) it led to a 93% reduction in complaints against the police. The study's researchers say this may be due to the 'observer effect' of BWCs on modifying behaviour of both police and public (University of Cambridge, 'Use of body-worn cameras').

not cure unethical behavior b/c the underlying causes of the behavior remain

deontological - duty to do certain things

teleological - consequences
  └ problematic : only thinking abt end

these and other laudable measures to change police practice have cured all the problems that led to the need for such changes in the first place. Human nature being what it is, there will always be the temptation to err away from the straight path. We must also keep in mind that our police officers are drawn from the communities they serve. As such, the moral values and standards held by our police officers, reflect the moral values and standards dominant within society.

Put simply, ethics, one might say, is about working out what are and are not morally upright ways of behaving.[7] There are two basic approaches: deontological and teleological. A deontological approach to ethics focuses on one's duty to do certain acts and avoid others; the rightness or wrongness coming from the actions themselves, whose moral status is determined by reference to some moral authority. A teleological approach to ethics, on the other hand, focuses on what comes after the acts, in other words, the consequences. Here, rightness or wrongness is respectively linked to what helps or harms others. Most people within society take a teleological approach towards much of their ethical decision making. They will still, as might be expected, adopt at times a deontological approach too and accept that certain acts are just wrong and unacceptable because these acts violate another's human rights, regardless of what good consequences may also come about from such actions. A teleological approach to ethics is a problem within policing when good and desirable ends are seen to justify what others consider to be wrongful acts. It is a problem for society in general too.

The rule/norm against lying, for example, both in society generally and specifically within policing, is sometimes thought to admit of exceptions when a lie helps not harms others. The permitting of some lies is a problem for those, such as Catholics, whose religious-based moral principles require that they adhere to an absolute proscription of lying. In contrast, the rule against perjury—lying under oath—is treated as an absolute by society's law; so this should not be a problem for those adhering to an absolute proscription of lying since their position embraces lying under oath too. Even so, there are many within society, and some within the police also, who justify (at least to themselves) the breaking of the rule prohibiting perjury. For the police, this can manifest itself in the unofficial committing of perjury to help secure the conviction of those they believe to be factually guilty. It is one form of what is called noble-

---

[7] In this book, unless otherwise stated, 'morality' and 'ethics' are used as interchangeable terms.

cause corruption whereby, contrary to Catholic teaching, the corrupt means (perjury) is used to achieve the good end (noble cause) of protecting society. ↳ occurs when law enforcement things they are achieving a good end through the wrong means

The purpose of this book is *not* to surmise as to how often police officers act corruptly and fail to perform their duties according to approved police procedures and the letter of the law. Police behaviour will, nevertheless, be contextualised by reference to numerous scholarly works in this area of moral concern. We shall proceed on the assumption that most police officers are law-abiding, honest and act with integrity. Yet we shall not ignore the fact that some police officers do at times bend the rules and operate beyond what their role requires of them; as well as the fact that police procedure and legislation does allow police officers to use falsehood with intent to deceive ('lie') in certain areas of their police work. The dishonesty of some New York City Police Department (NYPD) police officers has undoubtedly been exposed, as discussed in a recent series of three articles in *The New York Times* (2018).[8] It is no doubt the case that the use of police deception and the issue of cooperating in the evil/wrongdoing of others (topics discussed later in this book), will resonate to some degree in the hearts and minds of all police officers—and maybe a little more than some may care to admit.

In respect of the medical profession, there exists a wealth of published material explaining the Catholic perspective on various medical issues, in addition to ethical guidance offered by the medical profession itself. By comparison, there is very little Catholic Christian academic attention given to the field of police ethics. It is time for this to change. The Catholic Christian tradition has a rich source of moral guidance, but one needs to apply it to the various ethical issues within policing. This book enters this reality and makes some first steps in articulating specific Catholic Christian guidance on some ethical issues within policing.

In Chapter 2, we look at police culture within the broader context of societal values. Preliminary consideration is given to the topics of lying, deception, corruption, loyalty, and perjury. We note the tension that exists between a due process mentality (i.e. sticking to the rules) and a due justice mentality (i.e. breaking the rules to help ensure those believed to be

---

[8] The three articles, whose full titles capture the flavour of their content, were all written by Joseph Goldstein, a reporter at *The Times* since 2011. Note: 'Testilying' is a euphemism, referring to the practice of lying under oath (perjury). The articles are: (i) Goldstein, '"Testilying" by Police', (ii) Goldstein, 'Promotions, Not Punishments', (iii) Goldstein, 'Police "Testilying" Remains a Problem'.

factually guilty are convicted). We also consider the College of Policing's Code of Ethics in England and Wales (2014). Its secular basis is acknowledged as well as the absence of any explicit ethical underpinning for the nine principles and ten standards within the Code, other than that they conform to public expectations, beliefs and aspirations. An argument is proffered to show how the Code of Ethics' principles and standards can be supported and underpinned by Christian ethics. By focussing on two of the Code's standards of behaviour: (i) Honesty and Integrity, and (ii) Challenging and Reporting Improper Behaviour, it is illustrated how the understanding of these standards can be enhanced by recourse to moral guidance from within Catholic Christianity.

In working out what are and are not morally acceptable ways of behaving, police officers engage in ethics. In discussing various issues within policing, this book takes as a given that we are dealing with people with sincerely held beliefs; yet these beliefs differ at times as to what constitutes a morally upright response in any given situation. Using one's conscience is a fact of life facing all of us. Chapter 3 presents an exposition of Catholic Christian ethics (CCE) within the backdrop of ethical decision making in general and from within the broader Christian tradition. In exploring the nuts and bolts underpinning CCE, our main point of reference is the *Catechism of the Catholic Church* (CCC), also referred to as the *Catechism*. All Christians try to hear God's voice, respond to His call, and thereby do God's will. Put another way, they try to live by the Christian mantra: 'what would Jesus do (WWJD)?' The problem, indubitably, is in ascertaining what exactly Jesus would do in response to the various moral issues life presents. Sometimes the answer is obvious, at other times, less so. Some Christians take a liberal approach, while others take a more conservative one.

Catholic Christian police officers are expected to be guided by the magisterial teaching of the Catholic Church: teaching that includes the concept of intrinsically evil acts (acts deemed as always wrong regardless of circumstances, such as lying and perjury, and essentially anything that is perceived to attack the dignity of human beings). The consciences of other Christians, including some individual Catholics, do not, however, always agree with the Magisterium's teaching. We shall consider some dissenting voices within the Christian tradition: namely the ethical theory of situation ethics, the ethical theory of proportionalism, as well as the recent call by a leading Catholic moral theologian, Joseph Selling, for a reframing of the way the Catholic Church approaches ethics. We shall also consider the Magisterium's teaching concerning how to inform and act upon a good conscience.

Certainly, when non-religious police officers use their consciences to discern what is the morally right thing to do, they will not be seeking to conform to 'God's will' since, as far as they are concerned, God does not exist. That, in itself, is interesting as it raises the question of how non-religious police officers inform and use their consciences to discern what they consider to be morally upright behaviour within police work, in addition to acting in accord with the relevant police code of ethics.

We do not live in a perfect world: society, the police, all of us are imperfect. How then should a Catholic police officer or indeed any police officer respond to the challenge of working in an inevitably flawed police service? In light of the strong sense of loyalty that pervades the ranks of the police, this is a considerable issue. Her Majesty's Inspectorate of Constabulary (HMIC) reported thus:

> When speaking to probationers at different stages of their training programme, the Inspection Team found a clear mismatch between the virtues extolled during their training and the views and attitudes of tutor constables and other experienced colleagues. A view was expressed that, '*new starters go with the flow, it's part of the police culture*', and it is clear new staff are heavily influenced by events going on around them.[9]

What should one do when a fellow police officer acts in a way one perceives to be wrong and/or immoral (evil)? Does one report it (whistle-blow) or do something else? To help with this, we explore the Church's teaching on when it is and is not morally acceptable to cooperate in the evil of another. Closely linked to this, and discussed too, is the issue of causing scandal.

The use of police deception, including lying, can be both legal and illegal, immoral and possibly moral. The reason for using such behaviour and whether it occurs at the investigative, interrogatory or testimonial stages of police work, determines, to a large extent, the legal and moral status of such behaviour. Furthermore, police corruption is likely to involve deception to cover up such practices. The issue of lying is the main topic in this book; as such, two chapters are devoted to it. Two subsequent chapters then deal with the associated topics of discreet language (mental reservation), and perjury and oaths.

---

[9] HMIC, *Police Integrity*, 29 (5.3).

In Chapter 4, in relation to the contexts of lying within society and police practice, the Catholic Church's upholding of the absolute proscription of lying is analysed and evaluated alongside its definition of lying. The Catholic police officer is required by his religion never to lie, even though society does not expect such an absolute proscription from its police officers. This chapter interprets Catholic teaching in several ways to accommodate the need for police officers at times to utter falsehoods with intent to deceive ('lie') in the course of their legitimate police work. This analysis provides a rationale and ethical underpinning to help better discern the ethics of the police use of deception and 'lies'. Its significance will also be of benefit to others outside the policing context who struggle to reconcile the desire to uphold the absolute proscription of lying with the harsh realities of life when, in certain circumstances, to 'lie' seems to be the morally correct thing to do, such as to avoid serious harm to others.

In Chapter 5, there is a selective and chronological overview of the treatment of lying within the Christian tradition, to see what light this might shed on the use of 'lies' within police work. Elements within Catholic Christianity will be seen to permit exceptions to the norm against lying, despite this not being the official position of the Catholic Church. Also, one draws analogies between the use of lies, the just war tradition and pacifism. These comparisons add further insight for interpreting the College of Policing's Code of Ethics' principle and standard concerning honesty and integrity.

In the process of catching criminals, the police from time to time will inevitably need to engage in deceptive tactics, which will include the need to 'lie'. While this is probably not an issue for those who are open to the justification of exceptions to the norm against lying, it is a problem for those who uphold an absolute proscription of lying. What alternative methods to lying can one use when there is a need to hide the truth from those who have no right to it? The *Catechism of the Catholic Church* merely suggests keeping silent or using a discreet language, but does not develop this point further. What is discreet language? In Chapter 6, we explore the concept of mental reservation: an old, to some extent neglected, though not obsolete Catholic Christian doctrine (teaching). Mental reservation is, arguably, what the term 'discreet language' means. Mental reservation comes in two basic formats, strict and wide, and one explores the legitimacy of both as valid alternatives to lying. If the concept of mental reservation is found wanting, this poses a challenge to the teaching of the Catholic Church as to how it proposes one ought to protect the truth, without lying, from those who have no right to the truth. In addition, how the concept of mental reservation might legitimately be employed by the police to hide the truth from those who have no right to it is considered, including the possibility of its use within the context of a court of law.

Police officers are required to give evidence in a court of law. In Chapter 7, we highlight the pervasiveness of perjury by witnesses in general within the criminal justice systems of both the UK and US. In addition to clarifying the reasons behind the Church's absolute proscription of perjury, we investigate how an 'end justifying the means' mentality can cause some police officers to be led astray at times and engage in perjury to help ensure the conviction of those believed to be factually guilty. And linked to the clandestine topic of police perjury (the worst form of police deception) is the issue of taking an oath as a way of assuring to the court that one is speaking 'the truth, the whole truth and nothing but the truth'. Oath-taking, as we shall see, is not in itself contrary to Catholic teaching, nor is it contrary to the teachings of most Christian denominations, though some do object to its use. We will look at the reasoning behind these differing positions. We shall argue that given the disrepute oath-taking has fallen into within our courts nowadays by witnesses in general, it might be more appropriate for Christian police officers not to take the oath at all. As an alternative, despite their religious commitment—in point of fact, because of it—Christian officers might be better off taking an affirmation instead (i.e. a solemn promise to be truthful, without using a sacred text and calling upon God).

In this book, we will have considered the concept of ethics, the issues of conscience, loyalty and the cooperation in the evil of another. Also, we will have looked at the issues within policing of corruption, lying and the need to protect the truth, as well as perjury and the taking of oaths. In doing all this, we will have variously engaged in the moral analysis of human acts. We will have used an act-centred focus; an approach associated with both a deontological assessment and a teleological assessment of the ethics of human acts. In Chapter 8, we take a different though not unrelated approach via a consideration of the virtues. A virtue is an excellent human quality. Virtue ethics is rooted within ancient Greek society in the writings of those such as Plato and Aristotle and has been adopted and developed by others both within and outside the Christian tradition. We will explore through the lens of Catholic Christianity, some of the virtues police officers need in order to perform their duties effectively and ethically. These virtues will help police officers make the right decisions in response to the various moral challenges they face, particularly concerning the use of police deception. Via engagement with the various stages of the case study offered, the reader also has the opportunity to test his or her ethical viewpoint(s) and associated moral reasoning in a policing context.

In Chapter 9, a brief overview of the book is given, with further guidance offered to Catholic Christian police offers.

2

POLICING: CULTURE AND CODE

This book contextualises police practice via the sourcing of numerous scholarly works and anecdotal evidence. Our consideration of police culture has a United Kingdom (UK) and United States (US) focus, in which no attempt is made to distinguish between the police practice of the two countries, other than to say that, as a UK citizen, one believes the US has much more of a problem with its police culture than does the UK. Still, that is not to deny there is a problem with UK police culture too. In the UK the Police and Criminal Evidence Act 1984 and other measures such as the introduction in 2014 of the College of Policing's Code of Ethics in England and Wales have, for sure, contributed towards the betterment of policing.[2] It may very well be the case that the changes made to policing over recent years have largely eliminated a great deal of the problems of police malpractice and corruption. We are probably not there yet and, of course, long-lasting change for the better can only come about through police officers embracing the appropriate values. In 2016, the House of Commons Home Affairs Committee commented: 'Change to the culture and structure of policing in England and Wales will not happen overnight. Progress is being made but, as Alex Marshall recognises, there is a long way to go.'[3] Legislation and ethical codes are a great help, but they can only do so much.[4]

---

[1] Peel, *Principles of Law Enforcement*.

[2] Many police forces throughout the world will, no doubt, have some form of code of ethics. In this book we use as our exemplar the 2014 College of Policing's Code of Ethics.

[3] House of Commons Home Affairs Committee, *College of Policing: three years on*, 27. Chief Constable Alex Marshall was the College of Policing's Chief Executive between 2013–2017.

[4] A reduction in police corruption does not necessarily mean the values of police officers have improved. By analogy, not speeding in the vicinity of a speed camera, yet speeding when no camera is present, reduces instances of speeding but one's driving attitude remains unchanged.

[handwritten: police culture - police come from society + are influenced by society's values]

When considering police culture, we need to keep in mind the values of society. Our police come from the community, and as such will reflect in varying degrees the values common to society. In the UK, much of Western Europe and the US too, secularism and a non-religious mindset continue to assert themselves over a declining religious influence. Arguably, a non-religious approach to ethics with its earthly considerations is more likely to champion a consequential approach to moral decision making than would a religious approach to ethics.[5] Much less so nowadays do moral absolutes such as those of the Ten Commandments motivate people to conform to an ethic that finds its ultimate justification in one's relationship with God and one's post-mortem existence. If the moral fabric of the police is not up to the standards society expects, society itself shares the blame and responsibility to change as a prerequisite to making such improvements.[6] To a large extent, society gets the police service it deserves.

2.1 POLICE CULTURE

2.1.1 Lying and Deception[7]

Increased scrutiny of the use of force by the police and the constraints put in place to reduce the misuse of such force has resulted, it would seem, in the police's increased reliance on deceptive practices. Writing in 1996, Kleinig noted that 'over the past forty years police investigators have placed an ever greater reliance on deception as a means of accessing both material and verbal evidence'.[8] In addition, Ashworth notes that there has been a trend in the US for the police to move away from coercion to deception in police practices and that 'in 1992 leading police

---

[5] Without wishing to be pedantic, an *earthly* consequential approach would be a more accurate expression here, since the deontological approach within theistic moral structures contain a post-mortem teleological (aka consequential) consideration too: that is, does an act ultimately lead one after death to or away from God.

[6] The College of Policing's Code of Ethics is the result of a wide consultation process that ascertained what was to be included in the Code, including very importantly what the public wants. See College of Policing, 'How we developed the Code of Ethics'.

[7] This section is a reworking of material from Dixon, 'Police Lies', 165–166. Used by permission (see p. 65, fn. 2). For more details on lying and deception, see Chapter 4, in particular sec. 4.1 Lying Within Society And The Police.

[8] Kleinig, *Ethics of Policing*, 123.

researchers wrote that "contemporary police interrogation is routinely deceptive".[9] This view is also shared by Khasin, who notes that sociological studies confirm that police use of 'lies and trickery essentially have replaced physical brutality as the favored technique to secure confessions'.[10] Indeed, Villiers informs us that '[a] favourite interrogation technique, as used by many interviewers (and not just in the context of police work) is to lie and note the reaction.'[11]

From the masses of published material discussing the police use of lying and deception, that which is referred to here is but a sample. Alpert and Noble state that '[t]o perform their job effectively, police officers lie.'[12] The use of informants and sting operations are two of the various approved police methods of crime detection, in addition to the use of lying in general as part of their investigative work, particularly as part of undercover operations. Furthermore, the courts have even condoned the use of police officers posing as contract killers to catch those planning to commit murder.[13] Klockars adds that:

> The work of the police requires them to learn to lie skilfully and in doing so exposes them to its seductions . . . Whether or not police lie more frequently than persons in any other occupation is an unanswerable empirical question. What is certain is that the coercive responsibility of their vocation obliges them to lie regularly and supplies them with a variety of moral justifications when they do.[14]

Skolnick states that '[d]eception is considered by police—and courts as well—to be as natural to detecting as pouncing is to a cat.'[15]

---

[9] Ashworth, 'Should the Police', 108. Ashworth cites Skolnick and Leo, 'The Ethics of Deceptive Interrogation', *Criminal Justice Ethics* 11 (1992) 3.

[10] Khasin, 'Honesty Is the Best Policy', 1036.

[11] Villiers, *Better Police Ethics,* 80.

[12] Alpert and Noble, 'Lies, True Lies', 237.

[13] Maguire and John inform us that:

> In *R v. Gill and Nanuana* [1989] Crim LR 358, CA, the court deemed admissible conversations with officers (introduced to the defendant by an informant) who had posed as IRA members willing to kill for money. Likewise, in *R v. Dixon* and *R v. Mann* (Court of Appeal Criminal Division, 20 December 1994; (1995) NLJ [45, 6684) recordings were allowed of conversations with undercover officers posing as contract killers.

(Maguire and John, 'Covert and Deceptive Policing', 327, footnote 42).

[14] Klockars, 'Blue Lies and Police Placebos', 542–543.

[15] Skolnick, 'Deception by Police', 40.

[handwritten: increase in the use of deception = greater Scrutiny of the use of force]

In this section, our reference to lying and deception by the police is fundamentally in respect of its lawful use. However, any misconduct by police officers, unlawful or lawful, is also likely to involve lies and deception when attempting to cover up such misdemeanours.

2.1.2 Corruption[16]

Any organisation is open to corruption; the police service is no exception. Writing in 1999, Newburn comments that: 'Police corruption is not new, it has been part of policing for as long as we have had policing. It is also pervasive.'[17] In 2012, The Independent Police Complaints Commission (IPCC) report into corruption in England and Wales had this to say:

> The overriding message that comes out of this report is that corruption is not widespread, or considered to be widespread, but that where it exists it is corrosive of the public trust that is at the heart of policing by consent.[18]

Thankfully, it is not the purpose of this book to engage in debate as to the prevalence of police corruption, whether it be in the UK, the US or some other country. One works on the basis that it exists, whatever the degree, and as such needs to be addressed in one way or another.

What is corruption? The IPCC acknowledged that 'there is clearly some confusion about what should be defined as corrupt, as opposed to a breach of conduct'.[19] Newburn too acknowledges that corruption is not easy to define, but says it can be understood to involve the abuse of position and can be for private and/or organisational gain.[20] We do not need to delve into the intricacies of this; for our purposes, we only need to acknowledge that there are two basic types of police corruption: bent-for-oneself and bent-for-the-job, the latter often referred to as 'noble-cause corruption'. Being bent-for-oneself is the worst kind since, in seeking personal gain of some sort, it involves abusing the position of trust society has placed in the police. Obvious examples would be the taking of bribes and lying to cover up what might be construed as the

---

[16] For more details see secs. 7.1 Perjury Phenomenon and 7.3 Bent-For-The-Job Police Perjury.

[17] Newburn, *Understanding and preventing police corruption*, 45.

[18] IPCC, *Corruption in the police service*, 4.

[19] IPCC, *Corruption in the police service*, 6.

[20] Newburn, *Literature review – Police integrity and corruption*, 3–6.

excessive use of force when executing an arrest.[21] The other type of corruption, being bent-for-the-job, is also an abuse of the trust society has placed in the police to uphold the law. Within police ranks in varying degrees, there is an unofficial culture which advocates breaking the rules in the cause of furthering justice (the so-called noble cause) to help ensure perceived factually guilty persons do not escape justice. This might occur, perhaps, to avoid a technicality of law, to hide some police irregularity that occurred during the investigation, or simply due to a lack of sufficient admissible evidence to meet the high requirement of the court that a person's guilt be beyond all reasonable doubt—despite the police's confidence that such a person is guilty.

This book takes the view that most police officers are decent, honest, hard-working people, serving society by doing a difficult job to the best of their ability—and, to boot, deserving of our utmost respect. So, hopefully, let us all agree that our police service is fundamentally made up of decent men and women doing a noble job.[22] Yes, for sure, there will always be a few rotten apples in an otherwise healthy barrel, be it the police or some other organisation.[23] In truth, as we all know, corrupt individuals are to be found in many organisations, such as politics, the Church and within society generally.

Nevertheless, the police barrel contains within it—in varying degrees—an element of the end justifying the means mentality to police

---

[21] For some, it seems silly that others classify such things as a police officer receiving a free cup of tea as constituting the corruption of receiving gratuities or the lesser misdemeanour of misconduct. And notwithstanding the overt use of force, some officers may also consider it unfair that they face potential punishment for their actions when apprehending violent persons where, through human weakness, they might have been slightly overly zealous in their use of force.

[22] Her Majesty's Inspectorate of Constabulary (HMIC) concluded that: 'Generally speaking though, the Inspection confirmed the vast majority of men and women working in the 44 police forces are honest, industrious and dedicated.' (HMIC, *Police Integrity*, 1)

[23] In March 2018: 'An investigation by The New York Times has found that on more than 25 occasions since January 2015, judges or prosecutors determined that a key aspect of a New York City police officer's testimony was probably untrue.' (Goldstein, '"Testilying" by Police') The report informs us that these lies included: falsely claiming suspects were carrying guns, falsely denying searches had taken place, and falsely claiming to have witnessed drug deals. Furthermore, the report adds that in many of the cases it was clear to see that the motive to lie was to avoid 'constitutional restrictions against unreasonable searches and stops', and, in different cases, with the apparent aim of 'convicting people—who may or may not have committed a crime—with trumped-up evidence'. (Ibid)

work. In other words, at times, in the pursuit of justice (the *end*), some police officers will bend the rules (the *means*). Bending the rules in this way is sometimes referred to as the Dirty Harry problem.[24] It can manifest itself in small ways as well as large. Even Barker and Carter, two leading academics in criminal justice and former US police officers speak of themselves when as police officers as having 'been cajoled into writing creatively to put a "known criminal" in jail'.[25] Quite clearly, the end justifying the means mentality can sometimes involve the police operating outside the law to bring to justice the perpetrators of crime.[26] Newburn comments that while few would openly endorse noble-cause corruption 'it is clear from studies of policing in practice that some officers, and some in supervisory or managerial roles, occasionally tacitly endorse such conduct'.[27] Does noble-cause corruption within the police surprise you? Does it shock you? Would you be any different in similar circumstances? Hopefully, you would. What are your principles/values?[28]

---

[24] The name comes from the 1971 film *Dirty Harry* in which the fictitious character US detective Harry Callaghan, played by Clint Eastwood, uses unlawful means to bring offenders to justice. The term Dirty Harry problem was coined by Carl Klockars in 'The Dirty Harry Problem'.

[25] Barker and Carter, *Police Deviance*, 431.

[26] For a thorough study of noble-cause corruption, see Caldero and Crank, *Police Ethics: The Corruption of Noble Cause*. They comment:

> Our view, stated simply, is that police work is too "ends" focused. Our police sense of identity is bound up in the achievement of law and order. We tend to believe that there are ends so noble, so right, that sometimes it's okay to bend the rules a bit. Sometimes we end up bending the rules a lot. (9)

It would appear that things are much better in the UK. HMIC state:

> Whilst the Inspection Team concluded any bending of the rules is largely an activity of the past, broadly, it is seen by those still guilty of it as not being for personal gain but to protect society, and therefore not at the worst end of corruption. This is sometimes referred to as 'noble cause corruption'…

(HMIC, *Police Integrity*, 21, para. 4.13).
Whatever the amount of noble-cause corruption in UK police forces nowadays, one notes that HMIC's comment implicitly endorses the reality of noble-cause corruption, both past and present.

[27] Newburn, *Literature review – Police integrity and corruption*, 9.

[28] Identify the moral principles/values you live by (or you believe you live by). Make a list of them. Later in this book you will be asked to refer back to them. As you read through this book, add to and change your list as you see fit.

2.1.3 Loyalty[29]

In the nineteenth-century novel, *The Three Musketeers*, the musketeers lived by the motto: 'All for one and one for all.' Much the same can be said about the police service too. An early impression one encounters when joining the police is of the strong bond that exists amongst police officers. Given the fact that police officers depend on each other for support in dealing with challenging situations, sometimes life-threatening, it is hardly surprising that this bond of loyalty exists. Loyalty is necessary for survival and a good thing. That said, loyalty, this 'band of brothers' mentality, can go astray—even for the best of motives.

The combination of the end justifying the means mentality, together with a sense of loyalty to look after one's own, has over the years spawned the phenomenon known as the Blue Wall of Silence whereby there is a reluctance by police officers to report or give evidence against fellow police officers should they break the rules. There also exists a strong expectation for them not to do so. For most of the time, it is hopefully the case that a due process approach to policing holds sway over a due justice approach.[30]

The public is probably of the view that society would be better off overall if the police stuck 'religiously' to the rules all of the time. By analogy, the same might be said too for road safety if drivers kept to the rules of the road all of the time, such as observing speed limits and parking restrictions. The reality, as we all know, is very different. All road users will probably break the rules of the road from time to time as they go about their daily lives, and do so without any intention of causing harm to others. Similarly, some police officers will break the rules from time to time in the pursuit of justice (bent-for-the-job), and there is something of an expectation (though perhaps less so nowadays) that fellow officers will back each other up and keep quiet about such misdemeanours—and if need be 'lie'. Bok comments:

> Thus police officers often maintain secrecy about mistakes in arrest, excesses in interrogation, and illegal actions by fellow officers. Indeed, rookie officers are often

---

[29] For more details see sec. 3.8.1 Misplaced Loyalty.

[30] The due process approach means following the correct procedural routes within the criminal justice system. The due justice approach means the end of securing justice in terms of detecting and preventing crime, including the conviction of those believed to be factually guilty, is believed to justify the means of not following these correct procedural routes.

told that one of the most fundamental rules for police officers is that they must never betray other officers, least of all by testifying against them in court.[31]

Moreover, quite recent research led by Dr Louise Westmarland, Senior Lecturer in Criminology at the Open University, suggests that police forces still have a culture of silence within their ranks.[32] A culture of silence ought not to surprise us, as a closing of ranks mentality is probably common across most, if not all, institutions.

One is not denying that whistle-blowing occurs within the police, though it is probably the case that whistle-blowing is more likely to manifest itself in respect of bent-for-oneself police corruption. Most will be aware of the well-known New York City Police Department (NYPD) officer Frank Serpico who blew the whistle on corruption in the NYPD during the late 1960s and early 1970s.[33] The police corruption exposed by Serpico is, as might be expected, an extreme version of being bent-for-oneself. Another example of whistle-blowing is ex-rookie New Jersey State law enforcement officer Justin Hopson, who refused to testify in support of his training officer who had made an illegal arrest. In his account of what happened, he describes both the bullying and harassment that went on against officers who refused to cooperate with police corruption, its associated secrecy, and the way he stood up to this challenge and made a difference.[34]

2.1.4 Perjury[35] *perjury is not frequently prosecuted*

It is a sad fact of life that perjury, in general, is a common phenomenon in both the UK and US criminal justice systems.[36] Way back in 1968, Henry Cecil, a UK County Court judge of eighteen years, said that in his opinion:

---

[31] Bok, *Secrets*, 266.

[32] See Westmarland and Rowe, 'Police ethics and integrity: can a new code', and Westmarland, 'Police Ethics and Integrity: Breaking the Blue Code'.

[33] See Mass, *Serpico*. See also the 1973 film 'Serpico' based on this book, where Al Pacino plays Serpico. In 2017, Director Antonino D'Ambroso made a new film version, 'Frank Serpico'.

[34] Hopson, *Breaking the Blue Wall*. In his book, he asserts that while some names have been changed to protect privacy, facts can be checked and verified via Hopson v. State of New Jersey, et al. (Case#1:03-cv-5817).

[35] For more details see secs. 7.1 Perjury Phenomenon and 7.3 Bent-For-The-Job Police Perjury.

phenomenon of perjury may very well be prevalent in most, if not all societies.

[M]any lawyers and laymen do not treat it [perjury] seriously enough. A man charged with a crime is pretty well given a free licence to commit as much perjury as he likes in his attempts to be acquitted of the crime with which he's charged. The amount of perjury committed in criminal trials is tremendous.[37]

Also, David Pickover, a former police officer and commandant of the West Yorkshire Police Training School, comments that the UK judicial system 'is increasingly perceived as being nothing more than a game, perjury is sometimes seen as nothing more than a "professional foul"'.[38] Furthermore, in the US, Judge R. Duncan informs us that: 'Lying under oath is an accepted element of most trials. . . . all of us who have been around the court system for a while know that perjury is almost never prosecuted'.[39]

In respect of police perjury, Slobogin comments concerning the US that: 'Few knowledgeable persons are willing to say that police perjury about investigative matters is sporadic or rare, except perhaps the police, and . . . even many of them believe it is common enough to merit a label all its own [i.e. testilying]'.[40] Nicholas Zales comments: 'The evidence is clear, that police perjury is, if not pervasive, at least a serious cancer invading our criminal justice system.'[41] Writing in 2018, Goldstein reports that over seventy police officers in the last five years have left the NYPD due to perjury or false statements.[42]

Furthermore, the IPCC (2012) informs us in its report on the police in England and Wales that: 'Irregularity in relation to evidence/perjury (3,758 allegations) is the most prevalent form of corruption allegations recorded by the police.'[43] Also, that 33% of cases of corruption by the police referred to the IPCC from 2008/9 to 2010/11 concern 'perverting the course of justice including falsification of records, perjury at trial, falsification of witness statements, and tampering with evidence'.[44] Finally, one notes that the Mollen Commission (1994), which investigated police misconduct in New York, concluded that [police] perjury is 'widely

---

[37] Cecil, *Brief Tales*, 43.
[38] Pickover, 'False Witness', 26.
[39] Duncan, 'Lying in Court'.
[40] Slobogin, 'Testilying: Police Perjury', 1042.
[41] N. Zales, 'Reasonable Doubts: The O.J. Simpson Case and the Criminal Justice System', 69 WIS. LAW. 37 (Dec 1996) book review), as cited in Cunningham, 'Taking on Testilying', 28–29.
[42] Goldstein, 'Promotions, Not Punishments'.
[43] IPCC, *Corruption in the police service*, 8.
[44] Ibid., 33, Fig. 4.1.

tolerated by corrupt and honest officers alike, as well as their supervisors'.[45]

2.2 POLICE CODE OF ETHICS

Some years ago (2010c.), a former police sergeant from the UK was asked whether he thought police officers needed better training in ethics. His reply was a simple but interesting one. He said, "No," adding that he knew the difference between right and wrong because he was human. His answer based on one's 'humanity' has merit for sure. Policing in England and Wales and in other countries too has, nevertheless, despite our shared humanity, seen the need to formulate and articulate a code of ethics to help guide its officers in the path of righteousness.[46]

In 2014, the College of Policing for England and Wales published its Code of Ethics (Code). It is a code of practice setting out the principles and standards of behaviour expected from the policing profession in England and Wales. In short, all police officers and those associated with policing within the forty-three police forces in England and Wales are required to adhere to this code. The Code aims to raise the professionalism and ethics within policing. In this section, we use this Code as one example of the ethical codes used within policing more widely. We consider aspects of the Code through the lens of the Catholic Christian tradition. This Code of Ethics is a much-needed document, and, one assumes, Christian police officers, indeed most police officers, will have welcomed it. One will not be seeking to criticise the Code, but merely using it to help illustrate how police ethics and Catholic Christian ethics (CCE) can work in harmony.

Police forces within England and Wales will have set out their values before the 2014 Code. One notes, however, that a 2012 survey by the Independent Police Commission reported that only 22% of respondents

---

[45] 'Mollen Commission', at 40, as cited in Chin and Wells, 'The "Blue Wall of Silence"', 249.

[46] By way of comparison, Catholic Christianity teaches that the moral law as derived from God's will can be discerned via reflection on our human nature (aka the natural moral law); but in addition and to support humanity in this endeavour, God also and crucially revealed his will through revelation, e.g. the Bible, which includes the Ten Commandments, details about the life and teachings of Jesus, as well as other moral guidance. One might say that God's Revelation of His will in the Bible is humanity's code of ethics.

said that they felt closely aligned with their respective force's stated values.[47] The House of Commons Home Affairs Committee (2016) reported that there is a reluctance by some police forces to embed the 2014 Code of Ethics:

> We welcomed the introduction of a Code of Ethics for the police forces of England and Wales as an important and necessary step forward for the police service and we expect it to be taken seriously by Chief Constables. We agree with Her Majesty's Inspectorate of Constabulary (HMIC) that it is unacceptable that police forces in England and Wales are failing to embed the College of Policing's Code of Ethics. If policing is to move on from controversies and scandals such as Hillsborough and undercover policing then reassuring the public of the integrity of those involved must be the first priority. The College and the National Police Chiefs' Council must work harder to ensure that the Code is instilled "in the DNA" of serving officers.[48]

The Code contains nine policing principles and ten standards of professional behaviour. It also promotes the use of the National Decision Model (NDM) 'to help embed ethical reasoning in accordance with policing principles and expected standards of behaviour'.[49]

2.2.1 Christians and the National Decision Model (NDM)

The NDM consists of a series of five stages of decision making, all rooted in and guided by the Code of Ethics.[50] The centrality of the Code to all police decision making is illustrated in diagrammatic form in the said

---

[47] Independent Police Commission, *Results of a survey*, 2. In the survey,14,167 police officers responded, which is one tenth of all police officers in England and Wales up to Chief Superintendent. This report was two years prior to the College of Policing's *Code of Ethics*. Furthermore, HMIC inform us that:

> Most forces have their own sets of values and have used these instead. Some forces have amended their values better to reflect the code; others have not. Where both the code and the forces' values are used, there is often confusion about which takes priority. This variation in approach to a code which is issued under statute is unacceptable.

(Her Majesty's Chief Inspector of Constabulary, *the State of Policing: The Annual Assessment of Policing in England and Wales* 2015 (London: HMIC, 24 February 2016), as cited in House of Commons Home Affairs Committee, *College of Policing: three years on*, 7).
[48] Ibid., 28.
[49] College of Policing, *Code of Ethics*, 17.
[50] For the NDM, see College of Policing, *Code of Ethics*, 18.

document by a pentagon symbolising the Code of Ethics, around which the five staged decision-making process revolves.[51]

The Christian police officer must, and will surely want to, embrace the Code of Ethics into his policing role. For the Christian police officer, it is also crucial that the moral centre of his policing goes deeper than the Code since he has placed God's will (Jesus) at the heart of all he does. It is the Christian police officer's relationship with Jesus that underpins and is at the centre of his adherence to the Code of Ethics and his subsequent police decision making. We are to have a 'mature adult faith', which is one 'deeply rooted in friendship with Christ'; for such a friendship 'gives us a criterion by which to distinguish the true from the false, and deceit from truth'.[52]

In respect of police officers who do not infuse their moral sense with a religious commitment, Christian or otherwise, one wonders what ethical foundation underpins their motivation, drive and commitment to adhere to the Code, other than it is *the* Code of Ethics? One recalls Kleinig's comment that: 'With some frequency their job [police officers] places them in situations for which they have been ill-prepared by the ordinary processes of moral nurture and the habits of moral response that develop therefrom.'[53] Humanity is, of course, capable of discerning moral principles—*good* moral principles to boot. Even so, if moral goodness is only a social construct based on what society deems is useful for society, there appears to be no objective morality (a source of moral authority outside humanity's own decision making) other than the quasi-objective character of the subjective human law. Arguably, an absence of an objective moral reference point is a cause of moral confusion.[54]

Are non-religious police officers by their lack of religiosity less likely to abide by the Code of Ethics? One would be reluctant to say yes out of respect for the no doubt many highly moral atheist and agnostic police officers, many of whom may very well be far more moral than some

---

[51] The five stages of the NDM are: 'Gather information and intelligence' → 'Assess threat and risk and develop a working strategy' → 'Consider powers and policy' → 'Identify options and contingencies' → 'Take action and review what happened'. (Ibid.)
[52] Ratzinger, 'Mass Pro Eligendo'. These terms were used by, the then, Cardinal Ratzinger to challenge relativism; which, in the same homily, he referred to as a 'dictatorship of relativism'.
[53] Kleinig, 'Ethical Questions', 213.
[54] In fairness, one acknowledges that many atheists and agnostics would, no doubt, wish to challenge this point, though it is not within the purpose of this book to enter such a debate.

religious police officers. One cannot, all the same, ignore the dramatic effect the police use of body-worn cameras (BWCs) appears to have had on modifying behaviour for the better, of both the police and the public.[55] The point here is that from a Catholic Christian and general theistic perspective, there has always existed what one might call a God-worn ~~support to behave~~ camera (GWC) since, for them, God is omniscient (all-knowing). The ~~correctly~~ effect BWCs appear to have had in improving police behaviour (albeit via the quasi-objective moral reference point of subjective society) does lend support to the view that those who possess a GWC have added support to behave correctly. For Christians, Jesus is the sure foundation, the rock, upon which to build; it is only the foolish who ignore His voice and build on sand (Mt 7:24–27).

One would not, however, want to give the impression that Christians think God is like some overzealous celestial police officer. Rather, motivated by their love of God do they seek to do the right thing. Christians love in response to God's love for them. Love, not fear, is the mature Christian motivation to do good and avoid evil. Catholic teaching states that contrition for one's sins (i.e. being sorrowful for sins committed and having a detestation for them, with sincere intention not to sin again) can be either imperfect (being contrite out of fear of punishment such as eternal damnation and/or the detestation of one's sin) or perfect (being contrite because one has offended the God whom one loves above everything).[56]

The Code of Ethics makes clear that the principles within the Code reflect public expectations.[57] Reflecting public expectations ties in, naturally, with the fundamental Peelian philosophy of policing by consent. However, other than the reference to public beliefs, aspirations and expectations, the Code does not refer to any specific ethical

---

[55] See Introduction, 1, fn. 6.

[56] See John Paul II, *Catechism* (2000), CCC 1451–1453. Unless otherwise stated, all references to the *Catechism* (CCC) are in respect of its definitive edition (CCC2). The use of reference CCC2 is only used when there is a need to emphasise the difference between the definitive edition (John Paul II, *Catechism*, 2000 [based on the 1997 Latin definitive edition], CCC2) and the provisional edition (John Paul II, *Catechism*, 1994, [based on the 1992 French provisional edition] CCC1). Ironically, at the time of writing, a search with the term 'Catechism' or 'Catechism of the Catholic Church' on the Vatican's website, 'Holy See' takes one to the provisional edition of the *Catechism*, not the definitive edition. The reader may wish to note, however, that one way to access the English translation of the 1997 Latin definitive edition of the *Catechism* on the Vatican website is to use the following: http://www.vatican.va/archive/ccc_css/archive/catechism/ccc_toc.htm.

[57] College of Policing, *Code of Ethics*, 3, sec. 2.1.2.

underpinning of the principles and standards within the Code.[58] In other words, there is no reference to any moral authority other than society itself.[59] The will of the people is, of course, central to the concept of policing by consent, but one ought not to forget that the will of the people is not always synonymous with that which is morally upright, whether it be the will of an individual or the will of a group. Nero's thumb may well have reflected the will of the people, as did Pilate's sentencing of Jesus to death, but in both cases, their decision-making lacked the approval of an adequate moral authority. Arguably, in the absence of an objective moral authority, public moral opinion rests on shifting sands.

2.2.2 Christianity and Policing Principles

The Code of Ethics sets out nine policing principles. The Code (2.1.2) explains that seven of these nine policing principles are taken from the Committee on Standards in Public Life (CSPL) publication on the Principles of Public Life, while the further two principles of fairness and respect were also added to the Code because they are essential for the public's confidence in the police.[60] The principles are:

Accountability: You are answerable for your decisions, actions and omissions.
Fairness: You treat people fairly.
Honesty: You are truthful and trustworthy.
Integrity: You always do the right thing.
Leadership: You lead by good example.
Objectivity: You make choices on evidence and your best professional judgement.
Openness: You are open and transparent in your actions and decisions.
Respect: You treat everyone with respect.
Selflessness: You act in the public interest.[61]

Motivator for Christian to do Good → love God
Perfect contrition → one loves God above all else + has offended God
imperfect → fear of punishment

[58] Ibid., secs. 2.1.2, 2.1.3 and 4, sec. 3.1.1. That is not, in itself, a criticism, merely an observation.

[59] By 'society' one means either one's own society's derived and legislated man-made rules/laws/principles and/or those of another man-made group or society, including the notion of a secular foundation of human rights. One does acknowledge, nevertheless, that the material referred to in the development of the Code of Ethics is both exhaustive and impressive (See College of Policing, *Code of Ethics – Reading list*). Within this array of material there appears to be an absence of any material from specifically religious sources, Christian or otherwise.

[60] Committee on Standards, *The 7 principles of public life*.

[61] College of Policing, *Code of Ethics*, 3.

Shame → motivator to do the right thing

22

Our police are, as we have acknowledged previously, the products of—distillations from—the societies they serve. As Sir Robert Peel reminds us, 'the police are the public and the public are the police'.[62] It is then somewhat hypocritical if society expects from holders of public office, police or otherwise, ethical values (as, for example, those manifested in the Code's principles and standards) that society itself does not uphold. That is not to say holders of public office should not uphold these values, but it is to point out that society has a responsibility to live by these values too if that is what it deems fit for its public servants. The Code also states that the personal beliefs and aspirations reflected in these policing principles will 'in turn serve to guide behaviour and shape the policing culture'.[63] When both society and the police live by the same values the influence of these policing principles will indeed be enhanced.

Excellent though these principles are, they raise questions, such as: What constitutes 'fairness' when police officers are dealing with those who seek to harm society? What exactly does being 'truthful and trustworthy' require from police officers? What is the 'right thing' to do in the many and varied situations police deal with, and on what basis is something deemed to be the 'right thing'? Being 'open and transparent' is fine, but to whom and by how much exactly? What police action truly constitutes acting in the 'public interest'? The point of these questions is not to criticise the principles themselves but to illustrate their general nature and, therefore, acknowledge that they are open to interpretation.

Before the publication of the 2014 Code of Ethics, what were the values that guided policing within England and Wales? By that one means the values held by police officers going about their day-to-day policing; not the values enshrined within the separate codes of ethics of individual police forces or those written in various police training manuals. Over the years there have been serious misgivings about aspects of police culture within policing in the UK, especially in the US and no doubt affecting policing globally too.[64] The values prevalent within society will have shaped such a police culture; a culture which the 2014 Code of Ethics is admirably seeking to change. Old habits die hard, so it is probably naive and overly optimistic for anyone to think the publication of the Code of

---

[62] Peel, *Principles of Law Enforcement.*

[63] College of Policing, *Code of Ethics,* 3, sec. 2.1.3.

[64] For example, the so-called Blue Wall of Silence, the excessive use of force, the use of perjury, lying and deceptive tactics, the end justifying the means mentality in terms of being bent-for-the-job, not to mention an element of being bent-for-oneself.

Ethics landmarks a complete paradigm shift in police practice—though it is certainly a move in the right direction and to be hugely welcomed and supported by all.

The nine policing principles, regardless, do fit well with Christian ethical teaching and belief. The following table gives some indication of this consonance:

Policing Principle	Related Christian Teaching/Belief
Accountability	In addition to being answerable to the public, one is also ultimately accountable to God at the end of life.
Fairness	Golden Rule: 'In everything, do to others as you would have them do to you'. (Mt 7:12)
Honesty	Eighth commandment: 'You shall not bear false witness against your neighbor.' (Ex 20:16) Determining what this commandment (and principle) permits/prohibits is the subject matter of Chapters 4, 5, 6 and 7.
Integrity	Do good and avoid evil. Our fundamental option (orientation in life) must be to live in ways that are pleasing to God. It might have been better regarding the principle of integrity if the Code had stated: 'You always *try to* do the right thing' rather than 'You always do the right thing', since nobody is perfect and all will make mistakes from time to time.
Leadership	Virtue ethics acknowledges the importance of role models in educating and fostering the appropriate virtues in others. Christian saints are role models, Jesus being the perfect role model. Christians seek to imitate Jesus and become 'Christ' for others.
Objectivity	Christians are called to act rationally, transcend bias and discrimination, and thereby choose to love all equally since God has no favourites, so neither must they.
Openness	For those up to no good, St Ignatius of Loyola's thirteenth rule of discernment applies, where he states that the devil behaves like a licentious lover who wants secrecy, not transparency. One also notes that: 'Truthfulness keeps to the just mean between what ought to be expressed and what ought to be kept secret: it entails honesty and discretion.' (CCC 2469)
Respect	We are all made equally in the image of God and possess a dignity that must always be respected. 'There is no longer Jew or Greek, there is no longer slave or free, there is no longer male and female; for all of you are one in Christ Jesus.' (Gal 3:28)
Selflessness	Acting in the public interest is in accord with the Church's social teaching on working for the common good. In addition, agape is the unconditional, selfless love God has for humanity; and humanity is expected to respond likewise to God and neighbour.

Christian police officers in England and Wales should, therefore, have no problem in embracing the principles in this Code of Ethics. That said, it still leaves open to interpretation the application of these principles. In the next section, we consider this in more detail in our consideration of the Code's Standards: these standards closely link to the said principles.

2.2.3 Christianity and Standards of Professional Behaviour

The Code of Ethics sets out ten standards of professional behaviour. These are: 'honesty and integrity; authority, respect and courtesy; equality and diversity; use of force; orders and instructions; duties and responsibilities; confidentiality; fitness for work; conduct; challenging and reporting improper behaviour'.[65] We shall focus on two of these standards, namely: honesty and integrity, and the challenging and reporting of improper behaviour.

Standard 1 (Honesty and Integrity) states: 'I will be honest and act with integrity at all times, and will not compromise or abuse my position.'[66] This standard embraces the two principles of honesty and integrity referred to earlier. Under this standard, we are also told: 'To achieve legitimate policing aims, it is sometimes necessary to use covert tactics. This is recognised in law.'[67] The Code gives some examples of meeting this standard, such as when you 'are sincere and truthful' and when you 'do not knowingly make false, misleading or inaccurate oral or written statements in any professional context'.[68] What is not mentioned anywhere in this standard concerning honesty is the requirement *never* to deceive or lie. Indeed, the standard does not even use the words 'deception' and 'lie'. But obviously, covert tactics are deceptive and will involve the use of making false and misleading statements of one kind or another ('lie'); how else could an undercover officer, for example, hide his true identity and carry out covert investigations?

---

[65] College of Policing, *Code of Ethics*, 4. The brief comment that accompanies each standard in the Code has been omitted from this citation.

[66] Ibid., 5.

[67] Ibid., sec. 1.5. And in the US, in its efforts to detect dishonest police officers, the NYPD's integrity-testing unit apparently uses undercover operations in which investigators pass themselves off as victims of crime, witnesses and suspects to see how officers respond to them (See Goldstein, 'Promotions, Not Punishments'). Clearly, and somewhat ironically, lies and deception are being used by the NYPD integrity-testing unit in their search for the truth.

[68] College of Policing, *Code of Ethics*, 5, sec. 1.7.

Furthermore, neither do the examples given of meeting this standard suggest that deception, falsehoods or lying are prohibited absolutely. The point is that what the Code of Ethics seems to be claiming (wishing to allow) is that an officer can use false or misleading statements within covert policing (and presumably at other times that are deemed appropriate) without compromising his honesty and integrity. How else is one to square this principle with and make sense of the scholarly evidence that demonstrates the legally approved use of lies (and other deceptions) by the police?[69]

During the public consultation process of the Draft version of this Code of Ethics between 24 October and 29 November 2013 (before the publication of the Code's revised version in July 2014), I wrote to the Integrity Programme at the College of Policing to offer feedback on the Draft. I suggested more clarity was needed to the 'Honesty and Integrity' standard so that it would become abundantly clear when police officers are authorised to lie during their work. I also suggested they define what they take to be a 'lie'. Some changes were subsequently made to the wording and layout of this standard, though one does not know whether the feedback referred to above was the reason or part of the reason for the change. What one can certainly say is that the change did not, as far as one can tell, succeed in adding the clarity sought.[70]

---

[69] See secs. 2.1.1 Lying and Deception and 4.1 Lying Within Society And The Police. Even though the legal position in the US about the use of police deception is more lenient than in the UK, one wonders whether the value of honesty embedded within US and UK society and their police officers is that much different from each other?

[70] To view the changes made to the draft and revised editions of the Code of Ethics, see College of Policing, 'How we developed the Code of Ethics'. Note in passing the following related comments made by the Interdisciplinary Ethics Research Group at Warwick University, headed by Professor Tom Sorell and Katerina Hadjimatheou about Standard 1: Honesty and Integrity in the feedback they made during the consultation process for the Draft Code of Police Ethics:

Covert policing is included under this standard. This is presumably because it entails deception and thus constitutes an exceptional departure from the requirement to be honest. Given the recent scandals in relation to undercover policing, some more detailed reference to the extent of deception permitted and the justifying reasons might be appropriate.

It may also be relevant to include under this standard any other exceptions to the requirement for honesty. For example, it may be the case that deception is justified if necessary to protect vulnerable individuals from harm or if used in interrogations designed to elicit information that will prevent serious harm.

One suggests that, given the explicit mention of the lawful use of covert policing tactics within Standard 1, it might have been better, more transparent and clearer, if the principle of 'Honesty' which underpins Standard 1 had qualified itself by adding that one will be truthful *to those who have a right to the truth*. It further seems reasonable to suggest that Standard 1 could profitably include the following wording found within Standard 4 about the use of force, replacing the word 'force' with 'deception'. The relevant text reads: 'I will only use force [deception] as part of my role and responsibilities, and only to the extent that it is necessary, proportionate and reasonable in all the circumstances.'[71] The principle of 'Honesty' and Standard 1 is not demanding an absolute proscription of all deception (including lies) for police officers (whatever might be their understanding of the definition of a lie). With Catholic Christianity (as will be explained in Chapter 4), the Magisterium of the Catholic Church does, however, teach the absolute proscription of lying. Others, however, within the Christian tradition, while endorsing the importance of veracity, do permit exceptions to the norm against lying, essentially when it is to help not harm others. Furthermore, in the subsequent discussion on lying in Chapters 4 and 5, the reader will discover how the circumstance of 'a right to the truth' has significant relevance to the definition of a lie, and also the occasion for using non-lying methods of protecting the truth from those who have no right to it, as discussed in Chapter 6.

Finally, in making ethical decisions following the NDM, the Code of Ethics advises that one should ask oneself specific questions, such as: 'Would I be prepared to defend this action or decision in public?'[72] Such transparency is in harmony with Christian principles. It is very important here concerning the police use of deceptive tactics (including lying) to remember that the public to whom one should be prepared to defend one's action or decision is a public who, on consequential grounds, is highly likely to deem it morally upright to allow exceptions to the norm against lying when such deceit helps not harms others. One is not, in other words, defending one's actions and decisions to those who uphold an absolute proscription of lying; though this is the case with the Magisterium of the Catholic Church.

(Warwick University Interdisciplinary Ethics Research Group, 'College of Policing Draft Code of Ethics: Comments', sec. 9.1 Honesty and Integrity).

[71] College of Policing, *Code of Ethics*, 8.

[72] Ibid., 17, sec. 4.1.7.

Standard 10 (Challenging and Reporting Improper Conduct) states: 'I will report, challenge or take action against the conduct of colleagues which has fallen below the standards of professional behaviour.'[73] This standard is the antithesis of the Blue Wall of Silence phenomenon: the unwritten and informal code not to report on the wrongdoing of other police officers. We have touched on this matter previously in our introduction, and we will come back to it again in subsequent chapters. This standard, though, requires that 'you must never ignore unethical or unprofessional behaviour by a policing colleague, irrespective of the person's rank, grade or role'.[74] The standard goes on to make clear that one's response may be to question or challenge the misbehaving colleague directly, and/or report the matter, and that '[t]he policing profession will protect whistleblowers according to the law.'[75]

'Then the Lord said to Cain, "Where is your brother Abel?" He said, "I do not know; am I my brother's keeper?".' (Gen 4:9) For a Christian, we certainly are our brother's keeper. In other words, we have a responsibility for others; we must have concern for their welfare. It is through this lens, the lens of fraternal love, brotherly love, should Christian police officers in England and Wales approach their adherence to Standard 10 of the Code of Ethics. Precisely what response one makes will be affected by the severity of the wrongdoing, and it is not our purpose to enter discussions on that matter. Nevertheless, Pope Benedict XVI has told us that 'brotherly love also involves a sense of mutual responsibility'.[76] So while it is fully compliant with Christian principles that the so-called Blue Wall of Silence is knocked down, one's motivation to report, challenge and act against the substandard conduct of police colleagues needs to be done out of and in a way consonant with fraternal love, brotherly love.

Pope Benedict refers us to Jesus words concerning a brother who sins.[77] The full biblical text reads:

If your brother sins against you, go to him and show him his fault. But do it privately, just between yourselves. If he listens to you, you have won your brother back. But if he will not listen to you, take one or two other persons with you, so that 'every accusation may be upheld by the testimony of two or more witnesses' as the scripture

[73] Ibid., 15.
[74] Ibid., sec. 10.1.
[75] Ibid., secs. 10.3 and 10.4 respectively.
[76] Benedict XVI, 'Angelus'.
[77] Ibid.

says. And if he will not listen to them, then tell the whole thing to the church . . . (Mt 18:15–17).

What we see here is a gradual approach within a fraternal correction; and a gradual approach is also present in the College of Policing's Code of Ethics at Standard 10.[78] Moreover, this duty of police officers to challenge and report improper conduct is, for the Christian, part of his or her mission of living the Christian life. Pope Benedict XVI stated that 'we are responsible for each other in the journey of Christian life; each person, aware of his own limitations and shortcomings, is called to accept fraternal correction and to help others with this specific service [too]'.[79] In this book our focus is not on bent-for-oneself police corruption; instead, it is on those police officers who break the accepted codes of conduct from time to time with the best of motives or, conceivably, simply through human weakness. Saying that is not to condone their action, but it is to acknowledge that we are dealing with ethical, otherwise honest police officers even though they may get misled from time to time.

The guidance to the public within the Code of Ethics is that one has 'the right to make a complaint if you feel that someone within policing has behaved unprofessionally'.[80] That is an important right. Even so, just because one has a right to something does not mean one should always exercise it. Perhaps a little more understanding and appreciation is needed at times in respect of the difficult situations police officers find themselves in during their police work: police officers doing their best for society. If there is a real need, based on fraternal love, to make a complaint against the police then, certainly, such a complaint needs to be made. Still, before one does, it may be beneficial to first ponder Jesus' teaching on judging others. Jesus said:

> Why do you see the speck in your neighbor's eye, but do not notice the log in your own eye? Or how can you say to your neighbor, 'Let me take the speck out of your eye,' while the log is in your own eye? You hypocrite, first take the log out of your own eye, and then you will see clearly to take the speck out of your neighbor's eye. (Matt 7:3–5)

---

[78] We are told that not all breaches of the Code involve misconduct or the need for disciplinary measures to be taken (College of Policing, *Code of Ethics*, 19, sec. 5.1.1). In addition, a suitable response can range from 'self-regulation' of 'your own behaviour and that of your immediate peers and teams' to 'local management action and formal assessment and investigation'. (Ibid., 20)

[79] Benedict XVI, 'Angelus'.

[80] College of Policing, *Code of Ethics*, 22, sec. 5.2.1.

In other words, as the saying goes: 'When you point a finger, remember that three fingers point back at you.'

2.3 SUMMARY

Police culture includes the use of lying and deception, both legally and illegally. This deceit can sometimes involve the police committing acts of perjury too. The end justifying the means mentality is the logic used by some officers in their attempt to justify so-called noble-cause corruption. Strong bonds of loyalty exist within police ranks, and it can lead to the Blue Wall of Silence whereby police wrongdoing is covered up by other officers. Societal values influence police values. The introduction in 2014 of the College of Policing's Code of Ethics in England and Wales aims at improving the ethics of police culture. The principles and standards within the Code are presented within a secular framework and without any explicit reference to an ethical underpinning other than public expectations, beliefs and aspirations. It has been shown, all the same, that the principles and standards of the Code can be seen to be in harmony with Christian ethical principles. Christian police officers need to ensure that they underpin their adherence to the Code with their motivation to do God's will, Jesus being the Christian's ethical norm. This chapter has focussed on the standards dealing with honesty and integrity, and the challenge to and reporting of improper behaviour. In the next chapter, we explore Catholic Christian ethics in detail

3

CATHOLIC CHRISTIAN ETHICS

In this chapter, the main aim is to set out the Catholic approach to morality and ethical decision making. The Catholic approach will be situated within the broader context of ethics generally and more specifically, Christian ethics. Most police officers are not Christian, and even less are Catholic Christian. Still, all sincere and morally decent officers, religious and non-religious, will use their consciences in the endeavour to think and act in a morally upright way. While working within a strong culture of police loyalty, this will include deliberation on how to deal with the wrongdoing they may encounter from other officers.

3.1 ETHICS

In our consideration of police ethics, the assumption is that we are dealing with people who are sincerely seeking to live morally good lives. While there will always be some immoral people in every walk of life who do not try to live ethically, the people we are focussing on are those who are trying to follow their consciences.

Sometimes an absolutist stance is taken on a moral issue, at other times a relativist one. An absolutist position means that if something is considered wrong, then it is always wrong for everyone, everywhere, regardless of the circumstances. A relativist stance, in contrast, means that the same action could be right in one set of circumstances but wrong in another. Take the example of lying. An absolutist stance to lying claims it is wrong in all situations, whereas a relativist stance might approve of lying in circumstances when it helps not harms, especially if one can avoid serious injury.

Ethics can be classified as deontological (concerned with actions) or teleological (concerned with the consequences of actions). A

---

[1] CCC 1756. This approach is key to Catholic ethics. See also Rom 3:8.

Catholic teaching maintains that Natural law is a moral law discoverable by drawing upon our shared human nature

deontological approach focuses on obeying a law, rule or norm because that is thought to equate to moral rightness. In contrast, a teleological approach focuses on the consequences of actions since it is these consequences, such as happiness or the most loving result, that are deemed to determine the moral rightness of actions.

One thing to note, and it is an obvious point: non-religious ethics does not involve God—at least not explicitly.[2] To paraphrase the words of the Ancient Greek philosopher, Protagoras, man is the measure of what is good and bad. We all participate, all the same, in shared humanity, and Catholic teaching maintains that humanity qua humanity—religious and non-religious—can draw upon our shared human nature to discover a moral law that we ought to follow. Discovering the moral law is possible whether we explicitly acknowledge the existence of it or not. It is called the natural law. At its simplest, natural law is the sense/insight we get from human nature that we ought to be good and not do evil. What constitutes good or bad ethical behaviour is at the core of all ethical debate. Catholic moral theology, as we shall see later, maintains that one's moral sense, *when working correctly*, reflects God's will (God's law)—non-religious people, of course, would not interpret it like this.[3]

Some may argue that morality is primarily about obeying society's laws.[4] These laws do often reflect the values dominant in society—though morality and society's laws are not synonymous. It is not a good idea for an individual to *limit* his moral sense to what society's laws require. For example, in the not too distant past, British law permitted slavery, but few nowadays would consider this as morally acceptable and, of course, never was. Similarly, abortion is legal nowadays provided specific criteria are met—yet, Catholics and others remain morally opposed to abortion despite its approval by society's law as well as the moral claim by some that a woman has a human right to abortion. While adherence to society's laws is necessary for sustaining civilised society (and will often result in ethical behaviour), the moral claim on every one of us transcends mere adherence to society's laws. This is not, however, a charter for anarchy.

Others might claim that morality is about doing what feels right. We are all, no doubt, familiar with the sense that some acts 'feel' right while

---

[2] By secular ethics, one means ethical reasoning based solely upon human faculties, without reference to God.

[3] See *Appendix 1* for a brief overview of natural law thinking. See also CCC 1954–1960.

[4] Loosely speaking, within the term 'society's laws' one might also include the various policies and procedures that organisations develop to help foster appropriate conduct of its members, e.g. a police code of ethics.

others 'feel' wrong. A police officer, for example, might feel good about catching a burglar but feel bad about his use of excessive force when arresting the villain. Paying attention to our emotions is, for sure, an indicator of what is or is not morally upright: it is part of our moral awareness. Be that as it may, feelings are never enough in themselves to form the basis of good ethical decision-making.

Notwithstanding one's sense of human rights, it seems fair to say that a consideration of the consequences of one's actions is a crucial feature, though certainly not the only element, in how many people decide what behaviour is or is not morally acceptable. Consequences are a necessary factor to consider in one's moral decision making, but to what extent should our decisions be influenced by the consequences? When faced with a moral problem, is there not a human tendency/weakness to focus on the consequences of one's actions at the expense of compromising one's moral principles, these principles thereby fading into the background, though never perhaps totally going away? How will the consequences affect others, those I care about, me? These are the sorts of consequential considerations people make when trying to make ethical decisions, both in non-religious and religious circles.

Even when one approves of the moral norm against lying, if to lie in a particular situation brings about the avoidance of serious harm to others, some/many will believe it is acceptable. Consider the following example. A police officer stumbles upon a young person intent on committing suicide by jumping off the top of a multi-storey car park. The person threatens to jump if one attempts a rescue. Unable to get too close, the officer strikes up a conversation in the hope of talking the person away from the edge and his intention to kill himself. After some time, the officer cunningly manages to convince the person that he sadly, though reluctantly, accepts his decision to commit suicide, and offers his hand in a farewell handshake. Once both hands meet, the police officer does what he had always planned to do: pull the person to safety. This person subsequently says how grateful he is to have been saved. The act of lying saved this person's life?[5]

1) Morality is primarily obeying Society's laws
2) Morality is about doing what feels right
3) Consequential considerations determine the moral
   acceptability of a behavior

[5] This example was inspired by a similar scenario in one of the episodes from the NBC western television series *Bonanza*, that ran from 1959 to 1973.

3.2 CHRISTIAN ETHICS

Christian ethics is about trying to do God's will. Christians believe that Jesus Christ is God Incarnate in human flesh. Jesus is, therefore, the perfect expression of God's will, and hence the role model for Christians. In working out what is the morally correct action to take in any situation, Christians are trying to imitate Christ. The following of Jesus flows out of the Christian's relationship with God: God calls us in love, and through God's help (grace) we respond in love. God's plan is for this loving relationship between Creator and creature to end with our union with Him in Heaven for eternity.

Working out what to do to conform to God's will is not always easy, even though, quite simply: God is love. Christians will sometimes disagree on what they believe the love of God requires of them. Nobody has a hotline to God, so we are left to use various sources to work out what God requires of us, such as the Bible, Church teachings, our human nature and our ability to reason (think). Christians also believe that God empowers and guides them through the workings of the Holy Spirit. For Christians, working out what God's will requires is an exercise of conscience and prayer.

All Christians treat the Bible as the Word of God, although they do, at times, interpret it differently. Both the Bible's Old and New Testament provide ethical guidance for Christians. In the Old Testament (which is essentially the Hebrew (Jewish) Bible), immoral behaviour is viewed as damaging one's relationship with God: 'Against you, you alone, have I sinned, and done what is evil in your sight'. (Ps 51:4) The central ethical guidance in the Old Testament is the Decalogue (Ten Commandments) (Ex 20:1–17). For example: 'You shall not make wrongful use of the name of the Lord your God', (Ex 20:7) and 'You shall not bear false witness against your neighbor.' (Ex 20:16) It is a summary of both Jewish and subsequent Christian morality. It is worth remembering too that Jesus was a Jew. Christians are the followers of Jesus, Jesus-the-Jew, accepting, of course, that Jesus posed various challenges to Jewish belief and practice.

In the New Testament, Jesus, in his loving example and teachings, is the centre of all Christian ethical teaching. In the Sermon on the Mount (Mt 5–7), we have a summary of Jesus' ethical teaching, which includes the Beatitudes (Mt 5:3–12) such as: 'Blessed are those who are persecuted for righteousness' sake, for theirs is the kingdom of heaven.' (Mt 5:10) Moreover, Jesus taught that the two greatest commandments are, first, to love God with all your heart, soul and mind, and second, to love your

Catholic Church embraces an approach to ethics which allows one to justify an act if it leads to the most loving outcome = FALSE

neighbour as yourself (Cf. Mt 22:37–40). Immoral behaviour is also viewed in the New Testament within the context of one's relationship with God; as in the Parable of the Prodigal Son, we hear the words: 'I will get up and go to my father, and I will say to him, "Father, I have sinned against heaven and before you"'. (Lk 15:18) Jesus did not replace the Ten Commandments but reinterpreted and fulfilled them by showing us that following the spirit of the law is far more important than following merely the letter of the law. So, for example, the spirit of the commandment not to murder contains within it the call to rid oneself of the anger that could lead to murderous acts.

A desire to avoid the extremes of legalism (fanatical rule-following) and antinomianism (the absence of rules), led to the emergence within Christianity in the 1950–1960s of the ethical approach of situation ethics. Situation ethics has not won favour with the main Christian traditions—especially not Catholicism—but it had several exponents, one of the most notable being Joseph Fletcher in his book *Situation Ethics* (1966). Although many would conclude the approach of situation ethics to ethical decision making is flawed, its intention to bring about love is, definitely, laudable.

The basic idea of situation ethics is that the morally correct action to take in any situation is whatever brings about the most agape love. *All* rules (norms) are understood to be guides only; *all* rules—at least in principle—are permitted to be broken if love is better served.[6] For some, situation ethics might seem a reasonable approach, given the fact that God is love. It is no doubt correct that most people, religious or non-religious, would be approving of an ethic of love—loving consequences—in ethical decision making.

Situation ethics is a form of Christian relativism because even though doing the most loving thing is an *absolute* requirement of this approach, the determination of what is the most loving thing to do is *relative* to every situation, and that right and wrong are always measured relative to the yardstick of love. Arguably this consequential logic of love is not a million miles away from the noble-cause corruption mentality of some police officers: again, another misguided method but one having a laudable intent (justice). Situation ethics can potentially justify any act if it leads to the most loving outcome. It could, for example, justify an act of noble-cause corruption if it was deemed the most loving thing to do, maybe by helping to secure the apprehending and prosecution of dangerous criminals and thus protecting society from much harm.

---

[6] See *Appendix 2* for an outline of situation ethics.

legalism = all abt rules   antinom35ianism = abandoning rules

All moral laws are relative to the situation

noble cause = action I am taking is moral

The Magisterium of the Catholic Church has explicitly condemned situation ethics.[7] As we shall see in more detail in the next section, ethical relativism, in general, has been condemned by the Catholic Church. The Church maintains that situation ethics is a denial of God's revealed will in biblical teaching and what we come to discover through natural law. Quite simply, the Church teaches that some moral rules must never be broken since to do so would offend against our human dignity; made as we are in the image and likeness of God. We are to follow the instructions of our maker, God. In a perfect world, there would not, in a sense, be any need for laws (norms) since love rules supreme—the law of love being the only 'law' we need. However, in this imperfect world in which we live, we need laws to help keep us on track. For Christians and other theists, moral laws and society's laws are, in principle, signposts pointing the way to God.

In their ethical reasoning, Catholics share much in common with other Christians, but they will differ too. For example, following what the Pope says (part of Church teaching) is far more important to Catholics than what it is for other Christians. Significant also is that Catholics hold an absolutist stance on some issues while some non-Catholic Christians and non-religious people on the same issues will take a relativist stance.[8]

3.3 CATHOLIC ETHICS

Catholics are, of course, Christians, and like all Christians believe that Christian morality is the lived-out implication of being in a faith relationship with Jesus. Indeed, as Pope Benedict XVI reminds us: 'Christian faith is not only a matter of believing that certain things are true, but above all a personal relationship with Jesus Christ'.[9]

We shall focus on some of the specifics of Catholic fundamental moral theology—the basis of Catholic ethics. We shall use the *Catechism of the Catholic Church* as our primary reference point, though we will also refer

---

[7] Pope Pius XII, in forbidding that situation ethics be taught or approved, claims that it denies the objective moral law of God as manifested in the natural law (Pius XII, 'Instruction Of The Holy Office', in Neuner and Dupuis, *The Christian Faith*, 794–796, nos. 2022–2025. See also Ratzinger's attack on the 'dictatorship of relativism' as discussed in sec. 2.2.1 Christians and the National Decision Model (NDM).

[8] Clearly, Christians in general and non-religious people will hold absolutist views on certain issues as well.

[9] Benedict XVI, 'Message of His Holiness', sec. 2.

serves to assist in informing his conscience

to other key Church documents.[10] Pope John Paul II stated that the *Catechism* is 'a sure and authentic reference text for teaching Catholic doctrine'.[11] Therefore, the *Catechism* needs to be used by Catholics to inform their consciences. The *Catechism* has authority for Catholics, and it should be given its due respect.[12] Kelly comments that the *Catechism* must possess a high level of authority by the very fact that the promulgation of the text was delivered via an Apostolic Constitution.[13] So while the *Catechism* qua catechism does not possess infallibility status, '[f]rom the pastoral and catechetical point of view, therefore, the *Catechism* represents a unique and highly authoritative synthetic presentation of the Christian mystery'.[14] The *Catechism*'s Latin definitive edition of 1997 supersedes the French provisional edition of 1992. On the publication of the *Catechism*'s definitive edition, the then Cardinal Ratzinger (later to become Pope Benedict XVI) said of it that 'the official version must be definitive, and cannot be subject to changes'.[15]

it contains infallible teaching but not by itself + therefore unique + highly authoritative synthetic presentation of the Christian mystery

3.3.1 Human Act: Traditionalist Approach (Magisterium's Approach)

The relevant parts of the *Catechism* here are paragraphs 1749 to 1761 where it discusses the morality of human acts. The *Catechism* states that there are three parts to a complete understanding of a human act. These are called the sources of morality (*fontes moralitatis*) and consist of what is

---

[10] See, for example, John Paul II, *Veritatis Splendor* (VS), Part II: Conscience and Truth, paras. 54–64.

[11] John Paul II, Apostolic Constitution *Fidei Depositum*, sec. 4.

[12] That is certainly not to say everything in the *Catechism* is of infallible status. Cardinal Ratzinger had this to say as regards the authority of the *Catechism* in terms of how binding the work was to be. He stated that the *Catechism* is a collegial work that is also a papal work in the sense that:

> [I]t has been transmitted by the Holy Father to Christendom by virtue of his specific magisterial power.… The individual doctrines that the catechism affirms have no other authority than that which they already possess. What is important is the catechism in its totality: it reflects the Church's teaching; anyone who rejects it overall separates himself unequivocally from the faith and teaching of the Church.

(Ratzinger, '*Catechism* . . . optimism of the redeemed', 478–479). These same points are echoed in Ratzinger and Schönborn, *Introduction to the Catechism*, 26–27).

[13] Francis D. Kelly, '*The Catechism*', 405.

[14] Ibid., 406.

[15] Ratzinger's comment was made in a press conference on the 9 September 1997, as cited in John Paul II, *Catechism . . . Corrigenda*, back page.

Morality = lived out implications of being in a faith relationship w/ Jesus

called the object (the act performed), the intention (why the act is done) and the circumstances (the context within which the act is done, which include the consequences resulting from the act) (CCC 1750).[16] These are the criteria for evaluating the morality of human acts (CCC 1750).[17] According to Catholicism, if the above considerations are dealt with correctly, one will have worked out just how it is that man relates to the objective moral order that is God's will.

All three elements (object, intention, circumstances) need to be good for the complete human act to be good, i.e. what you do, why you do it and in the appropriate circumstances (CCC 1755). For all that, and—crucially—it is the object (what is done), in and of itself, independent of intention and circumstances which is the primary and fundamental element in evaluating the morality of an act. Janet Smith uses the analogy of the building of a house to help explain the functioning of these three elements within a human act, where the foundations equate to the object, the frame to the intentions, and the trimmings such as colour to the circumstances.[18]

The object of an act is, quite simply, what is done. The Church teaches: 'The morality of the human act depends primarily and fundamentally on the "object" rationally chosen by the deliberate will'.[19] The object determines whether the act is fundamentally morally good or morally evil.[20] The object is not merely a physical act (e.g. falsehood with intent to deceive—aka 'lie'); the object is what a person chooses to do with his will. As such, it affects the moral character of the person acting since the object 'determines the act of willing on the part of the acting person'.[21] In choosing to lie, for example, one has made oneself into a liar. The Magisterium teaches that an intrinsically evil act (an act whose object is evil) is said to involve 'a disorder of the will, that is a moral evil'.[22] 'Lying' is one example of an act deemed intrinsically evil. The Magisterium

---

[16] The terms object and moral object mean the same. The term moral object is a fuller way to refer to the object of an act: it constitutes what the act amounts to morally speaking.

[17] Hughes points out that the *Catechism*, in its dealing with the issue of the morality of human acts, in general, follows Aquinas (Hughes, 'Our Human Vocation', 345).

[18] Smith, 'Moral Terminology', 138.

[19] John Paul II, *Veritatis Splendor*, 78.

[20] The object of an act can be morally neutral too, e.g. the act of drinking tea rather than coffee.

[21] Ibid.

[22] Ibid.

teaches that an intrinsically evil act, in itself (i.e. independent of intention or circumstances), can never be ordered to God because it, 'radically contradict[s] the good of the person made in his [God's] image'.[23]

As regards the intention of a human act, the *Catechism* states that it 'indicates the purpose pursued . . . the goal . . . the good anticipated from the action undertaken'. (CCC 1752) In short, the intention concerns why a person wills the object of the act. There can exist more than one end to an act in that one can have several reasons why one does what one does (CCC 1752). For example, a defendant in a criminal court may commit perjury (object) to avoid being found guilty for a crime he has committed (intention) because he wants to avoid paying a fine (another intention). The relationship of *intention* to *object* is also considered. The *Catechism* states: 'A good intention (for example, that of helping one's neighbour) does not make behaviour that is intrinsically disordered, such as lying and calumny, good or just. The end does not justify the means.'[24] (CCC 1753) This teaching that some acts are always wrong is, indubitably, an attack on the ethical relativism common in modern-day society. The end justifying the means mentality is what lies behind the phenomenon of being bent-for-the-job within the police (noble-cause corruption). Interestingly, one notes that the College of Policing's Code of Ethics states that one should 'do the right thing in the right way'.[25] Despite that, one ought not to conclude from this that the Code endorses the *Catechism*'s teaching on lying and intrinsically evil acts, if for no other reason that the Code does explicitly endorse the use of lawful covert tactics within policing,[26] which will, of course, involve the use of lies (falsehoods with intent to deceive).

In respect of the circumstances surrounding an act, the *Catechism* states:

> The *circumstances*, including the consequences . . . contribute to increasing or diminishing the moral goodness or evil of human acts . . . can also diminish or increase the agent's responsibility . . . [but] of themselves cannot change the moral quality of acts themselves; they can make neither good nor right an action that is in itself evil. (CCC 1754)

In other words, while circumstances can never justify doing an intrinsically evil act (i.e. always wrong), they can affect the overall moral

---

[23] Ibid., 80.
[24] Footnote cf. reference in original text made to Mt 6:2–4.
[25] College of Policing, *Code of Ethics*, 3, sec. 2.1.1.
[26] Ibid., 5, sec. 1.5.

goodness of an act and the moral accountability of the person acting. Take, for example, a police officer's act of committing perjury to ensure a prolific drug dealer does not escape conviction on a technicality of law. The act is morally unjustifiable—it should not be done, period. If the defendant's factual guilt is known and that he or she will almost certainly continue to go on reoffending if not convicted, this diminishes the evilness of the act as a whole. Furthermore, if the police officer concerned is acting under pressure from senior officers to secure a conviction and, perhaps, feels an overwhelming imperative to protect society from this prolific drug dealer, then these factors can diminish the police officer's responsibility further—but not eradicate it. All said and done, perjury is, nonetheless, deemed an intrinsically evil act (as well as being illegal), so can never be morally justified according to magisterial teaching.

3.3.2 Human Act: Proportionalist Approach

Lying and perjury are two critical issues in this book. The morality of lying and perjury is affected by the approach one takes to the moral evaluation of human acts. We have seen above that the Magisterium teaches that the object is the fundamental element in the moral evaluation of a human act. Although the ethical theory of proportionalism is an ethical approach that emerged from within Catholic Christianity, it differs from magisterial teaching in its method of evaluating the morality of human acts.[27] Essentially, the difference boils down to how one construes the object of a human act, in respect of morally relevant circumstances.[28]

In a different text, McCormick uses the issue of lying to illustrate two different ways the object of an act may be construed. He states:

> The Augustinian-Kantian approach holds that every falsehood is a lie. Others would hold that falsehood is morally wrong (a lie) only when it is denial of the truth to one who has a right to know. In the first case the object of the act is said to be falsehood (=lie) and it is seen as *ex objecto* morally wrong. In the second case the object is

doesn't look at act in isolation + see what they are doing in the 1st place

---

[27] It is important to note the distinction between these two schools of thought. Key proportionalist (revisionist) Catholic theologians include: P.Knauer, L. Janssens, J. Fuchs, B. Schüller, T.E. O'Connell, P.S. Keane, R. Gula, C. Curran, R.A. McCormick and Joseph A. Selling. Key traditionalist Catholic theologians, headed by John Paul II, include: G. Grisez, J. Finnis, W.E. May, J. Boyle, Martin Rhonheimer and Robert P. George.
[28] McCormick, 'Notes: 1981', 84–86.

"falsehood to protect an important secret" and is seen as *ex objecto* morally right (*ex objecto* because the very end must be viewed as pertaining to the object).[29]

The point McCormick is making here in this example of lying is that in the Augustinian-Kantian approach to lying (the approach, as it turned out, endorsed in the *Catechism*'s definitive edition), the utterance of falsehood with intent to deceive (lie) has been given its moral character independent of the circumstances of its occurrence. By contrast, in the second case (the approach, as it turned out, endorsed in the *Catechism*'s provisional edition), the reason for using falsehood with intent to deceive enters one's deliberation before the moral character of the falsehood with intent to deceive is ascertained.[30] In other words, these two different definitions of lying help illustrate the proportionalist's point that in seeking to morally evaluate human action 'we must look at all dimensions (morally relevant circumstances) before we know what the action is and whether it should be said to be "contrary to the commands of the divine and natural law"'.[31]

Also, proportionalists reject the traditionalist teaching of the existence of what is known as concrete negative moral norms; that is, they reject the absolute proscription of particular types of acts (intrinsically evil acts), such as lying, without consideration of the circumstances in which these acts might occur.[32] While there are differences within the views of proportionalist theologians, McCormick captures the fundamental difference between traditionalists and proportionalists as follows:

[Proportionalists] share a certain bottom line, so to speak: individual actions independent of their morally significant circumstances (e.g., killing, contraception, speaking falsehood, sterilization, masturbation) cannot be said to be intrinsically morally evil as this term is used by tradition and the recent magisterium.[33]

---

[29] McCormick, 'Killing the Patient', 1410. The full relevance of this to lying is made clear in 5.1.5 Proportionalism and the *Catechism*. Note: this current page uses reworked material taken from Dixon, 'Police Lies', 170–171. Used by permission (see p. 65, fn. 2).
[30] Not that McCormick specifically referred to the definition of lying found within the *Catechism*.
[31] Ibid., 1411. McCormick's citation of 'contrary to the commands of the divine and natural law' is taken from VS 76. Note the text of VS actually uses the word 'commandments' not 'commands', though the meaning appears the same.
[32] See *Appendix 3* for a contextual overview of the proportionalist challenge to the traditionalist evaluation of human acts.
[33] McCormick, 'Notes: 1981', 84.

With the proportionalist approach, the object (what you do morally speaking) comes from the totality of the act—a totality that embraces the intention why you do what you do in the pertaining circumstances. McCormick points out that proportionalists criticise the Magisterium when, at times, it does not always take a teleological assessment of acts into account when it conceives the moral object.[34]

The year 2016 saw the publication of *Reframing Catholic Theological Ethics* by the well-known Catholic moral theologian, Joseph A. Selling.[35] He has long been an advocate of the proportionalist approach to the moral evaluation of human acts. Although a detailed study of Selling's recent work is beyond the scope of this book, we can still note its rejection of the traditionalist approach to morally evaluating human acts where the object (as the Magisterium understands it) is the starting point and fundamental criterion of an act's moral evaluation. Selling argues it is better if one's moral evaluation begins with the end/goal (intention for acting) and work backwards via the circumstances to the act done.[36] His point, simply put, is that without first considering the intention with which an act is performed and the particular set of circumstances within which an act occurs, one cannot properly morally evaluate the moral rightness of such an act. Selling says that 'beginning with an analysis of a mere physical action is very awkward, for what may look like something evil from the beginning may indeed be justified in certain circumstances, given an upright intention'.[37]

We shall consider Selling's work a little further in section 8.4. concerning the following of the spirit of the law rather than the letter of the law, as well as how this might apply to the use of lies by the police within the various stages of their work.

---

[34] Ibid., 85.

[35] Selling, *Reframing*.

[36] Ibid., 24–25.

[37] Ibid., 26. Speak of the 'physical action' here is referring to what traditionalists treat as the object, but crucially, traditionalists maintain it does not merely constitutes a physical act due to the self-reflective nature of what one does, e.g. by choosing to lie, one turns oneself into a liar. See sec. 3.3.1 Human Act: Traditionalist Approach (Magisterium's Approach).

3.4 VIEWS ON CONSCIENCE

Police officers, like all people, have a conscience, what one might call an inner sense of what is morally right and what is morally wrong.[38] A police officer's moral sense exists prior to the observance of any police code of ethics, and one hopes this moral sense motivates them to carry out their policing role by such a code. Of course, individual people's consciences will differ at times, as well as there being differences in moral awareness (conscience) between societies, cultures and religions. It seems fair to say that the moral sense of police recruits and established police officers is, in no small way, influenced by their upbringing. 'Police conscience' is also influenced by the shifting sands of public opinion. Furthermore, a police officer's conscience is likely to be associated with feelings of guilt for doing what one perceives to be morally wrong and a sense of peace for doing what one perceives to be morally right. Conscience, some might say, is like an internal moral compass, providing moral orientation.

In what he describes as the 'socialization' of the 'rookie' police officer, Sherman recognises a moral dilemma for individual police officers when the informal rules and attitudes within police culture are at odds with the formal rules and expectations of society.[39] For the Christian police officer, there is a further challenge if and when these informal rules and attitudes conflict with one's religiously-based moral principles. Sherman speaks of a police officer's moral career, during which most officers, but not all, will have moral experiences (pangs of conscience). These moral experiences, he argues, lead to apologia whereby officers resolve the moral conflict by denying the validity of the principle they flout, or somehow reconcile their behaviour with the principle that is causing them bother.[40]

For some Christians, conscience is the voice of God, meaning that God gives direct moral guidance, something like a direct prompting/call to act or not to act in certain ways. One might think of it like an internal moral satnav. For others, conscience is understood to be more like the voice of reason, meaning that God gives humans the ability to discover for themselves, by using their reason, what is morally good. Here one might think of it like a moral map used to work out which way to go as one makes moral decisions. For a theist, conscience is linked, crucially, to doing God's will, which for a Christian involves adhering to divine

Catholics - natural law = more inclined to hold any act as a moral absolute

---

[38] Cf. sec. 3.1 Ethics, in respect of its reference to the natural law.
[39] Sherman, 'Learning Police Ethics', 11.
[40] Ibid., 17–18.

Non-religious = knows there is right or wrong but doesn't look to God, gets it from society

commands such as those of the Ten Commandments. For Catholic Christians, this is closely associated with God's will as manifested in the natural law: a law which humanity discovers within its human nature.

Non-religious views, in contrast, do not believe that conscience involves God. Sigmund Freud, for example, gave a purely psychological explanation for the conscience. For some non-religious people, conscience might equate with obeying the commands of society as expressed through the laws of the land. Others might say one can intuit (have a kind of direct awareness) of what is morally good or bad; that is to say, you know the ethically right action to take when one experiences any given situation. Some people (religious and non-religious) think that conscience comes from within our human nature, usually understood as from birth (innate), while others say it is acquired from the influences upon us from society; a combination of both is also possible and perhaps more likely too. The use of reason is also particularly important within non-religious understandings of conscience since the belief is that humanity decides itself (not discovers) what is or is not morally good or bad.

Sir Robert Peel tells us that policing requires society's consent.[41] Our police, as we have acknowledged, are drawn from society and are imbued with its values. Arguably, a secular society, one that has lost its awe, wonder and fear (love) of God, where the ends are often, though not always, thought to justify the means, is one in which the societal conscience is less inclined to uphold the acts of lying and perjury as moral absolutes, never to be committed. Society reaps what it sows.[42]

3.5 CATHOLIC TEACHING ON CONSCIENCE

The Catholic Church's teaching on conscience is set out in the *Catechism* within paragraphs 1776 to 1802. We also need to relate this to paragraphs 2032 to 2040 in which the role of the Magisterium (teaching office) in one's moral life is discussed. The *Catechism* teaches that man is said to 'hear' (discern) God's voice/call in his conscience, and that conscience is man's ability to use reason to discover what God's will is, as manifest in

MUST inform conscience

[41] Peel, *Principles of Law Enforcement*.
[42] Consequential logic also applies, as we have seen, to the approach of situation ethics. One does not have to be a Christian to follow the principle that in any situation the morally correct action to take is whatever one considers is the most loving thing to do.

the objective moral law. God's call is an invitation for humanity to live in a loving relationship with its Creator. Note again, conscience discovers, not creates, the moral law. In finding the moral law, a person discerns his real good.[43]

[Mistakes can and do happen, in that one's conscience at times will be wrong, in error. At these times, if the error is due to the individual's fault (*vincible* ignorance), then he is morally responsible for this, and one's responsibility varies with inverse proportion to the amount of effort taken to inform oneself correctly. Each person is responsible for removing error as far as is possible] For example, a Catholic police officer not making any effort to know the relevant Catholic teaching pertaining to his policing role is highly responsible for any errors in his ethical thinking. In contrast, an officer who makes some effort but not too much, is, still responsible, but less so, for his erroneous conscience. If, on the other hand, the error is not the individual's fault (*invincible* ignorance), then he is not morally responsible. For example, a Catholic police officer may have believed, prior to the publication of the definitive edition of the *Catechism* and based on the teaching within the provisional edition, that it was *not* a lie to utter falsehoods with intent to deceive those who had *no* right to the truth.[44] Such a person may even have had this position endorsed by members of the clergy and Catholic educational institutions too. It would seem that such an officer would have made all reasonable efforts to inform his conscience correctly—even though, based on the teaching within the *Catechism*'s definitive edition, he was mistaken all along.

Interestingly, if it subsequently proves to be that the *Catechism*'s teaching on lying in both its editions, although worded differently, are in harmony when practically applied, then those who lived by the earlier teaching were not in error after all. Ironically, one may also find in the future that those Catholics who nowadays refuse to utter falsehoods with intent to deceive, even when their refusal might in certain situations lead to untold suffering, will similarly be held not responsible (via invincible ignorance) for their upholding of this position. In our discussion of lying

---

[43] Recall what was said about the natural law (see *Appendix 1*), which the Church says 'provides the solid foundation on which man can build the structure of moral rules to guide his choices'. (CCC 1959) Catholics refer to this as the objective moral law: discovered within man but not made by man.

[44] The provisional edition of the *Catechism* taught that speaking a falsehood with intent to deceive is a lie when one's interlocutor *has* a right to the truth, whereas the definitive edition dropped the circumstance of one's interlocutor having a right to the truth from its definition of a lie. This is discussed in detail in Chapter 4.

in Chapter 4, the reader will discover suggested ways in which the two different definitions of lying within the two editions of the *Catechism* may prove to be reconcilable after all.

We are all responsible for educating our consciences properly as far as we can, and Catholic academic theologians and clergy have the means and opportunity to study ethical issues in a far greater degree of depth than what one can expect of Catholic police officers untrained in theological matters.[45] A person must, though, obey his sincerely held (invincible) conscience since, even if it is in error, a theist believes this to be reflective of God's will, and therefore not to act upon it would be a sin for the individual. One must act upon what one genuinely believes to be morally good and avoid what one genuinely believes to be morally bad.

The *Catechism* goes on to speak of conscience as including: 'the perception of the principles of morality (synderesis)'; their application to the various circumstances of life and the subsequent judgement conscience makes about our human acts. (CCC 1780) Furthermore, the *Catechism* reminds us that 'the Word of God is the light for our path'. (CCC 1785) The prudent (wise) person will draw upon various sources to inform his conscience, such as the Bible; the influence of the Holy Spirit; reflecting upon his own experiences; the wisdom and experience of others; *and the authoritative teachings of the Church which, crucially, must play a central role.* The *Catechism* teaches that, within the discerning process of conscience, we must: never do evil to bring about good, apply the Golden Rule of treating others as we wish to be treated, and respect other people and what they hold to be true according to *their* consciences (CCC 1789).

The prudent Catholic will then make good use of the Church's teaching on moral matters. 'The Church in this world is the sacrament of salvation'. (CCC 780) It is the Church's right and duty to teach on moral matters, including moral principles; its authority to do so comes from Christ (CCC 2032 & 2034). The Magisterium is the Church's teaching office, which is made up of all the bishops throughout the world working together, headed by the Bishop of Rome, the Roman Pontiff (Pope). It does not mean that everything the Magisterium teaches is infallible (as indicated previously); indeed, much/most of its teaching is not infallible since infallibility is limited to those aspects of faith and morals necessary

---

[45] Here I think it is right to emphasise once again the pressing need for the Catholic Christian community to make its targeted and significant contribution towards the development of police ethics for the good of Catholic police officers, and ultimately the benefit of the police and society as a whole.

for our salvation (CCC 2035). The *Catechism* also states that the Magisterium's authority also covers 'specific precepts of the *natural law*', the observance of which is deemed necessary for one's salvation. (CCC 2036) What is crucial to acknowledge is that the Church teaches that in seeking to inform and follow their consciences, Catholics must not treat the moral teaching of the Magisterium as just another opinion amongst many. We 'ought carefully to attend to the sacred and certain doctrine of the Church'.[46] The Magisterium's teaching is given to the faithful, for their good to help form their consciences properly, and they are expected to do their utmost to follow it.[47]

The *Catechism* states that:

> [T]he conscience of each person should avoid confining itself to individualistic considerations in its moral judgements of the person's own acts. . . . Personal conscience and reason should not be set in opposition to the moral law or the Magisterium of the Church. (CCC 2039)

In other words, neither our own opinion on a moral matter nor the opinions of others, including moral theologians, should be allowed to undermine the teaching of the Magisterium; instead, we should defer to the Magisterium's authoritative teaching on moral matters when our own opinion and/or the opinion of others happen to differ.[48] Deferring to

---

[46] Paul VI, *Dignitatis humanae*, 14.

[47] Apart from infallible teaching which one is always obliged to follow, for all other teaching what is expected from the faithful is *obsequium religiosum*. This basically means that out of respect for Church teaching and motivated by one's faith, one ought to follow this teaching even when one may not always agree with it and/or see the reasoning behind it on a particular matter. O'Rourke and Boyle summarise the three levels of authority of magisterial teaching and the associated responses expected from the Catholic faithful as: 'infallible or definitive teaching which requires an assent of faith'; 'authoritative teaching, or non-definitive teaching . . . [requiring] religious assent of will and intellect'; and 'pastoral teaching . . . [requiring] habitual "adherence of the faithful"'. (O'Rourke and Boyle, *Medical Ethics*, 23) They also address the question of whether it is acceptable to 'withhold assent of will and intellect from a Church teaching because one thinks the teaching is in error?'. (Ibid., 25) Having acknowledged that there are occasional times when this may occur, they state: 'Some will hold that one ought always to prefer one's own personal conscience to the teaching of the Church. If this were a habitual practice, what role would faith have in informing one's conscience? Can a person consistently put aside the Church's teaching and still remain a Catholic?' (Ibid., 26) To research further in this area, see: CCC 888–892; Paul VI, *Lumen Gentium* 25; Paul VI, *Dignitatis humanae* 14; Curran, *Conscience*, especially Part Two: Church Documents, Commentaries, and Response to Hierarchical Teaching.

[48] See Congregation, *Donum Veritatis*.

magisterial teaching is not, however, meant to be a denial of an individual's vital right to follow one's conscience. Instead, it is that in informing and following one's conscience, the individual should make central the moral teaching of the Church, which is 'at the service of conscience'.[49]

How an individual 'squares' his conscience with various moral teachings of the Magisterium is a sensitive and hotly debated topic in Catholic moral theology. The crux of the matter seems to boil down to whether and when a Catholic can dissent from non-infallible teaching and still be acting in good conscience.

A significant number of Catholic theologians do have serious objections to the claim that it is always wrong to dissent from the Magisterium's non-infallible moral teaching. Hughes, for example, comments that 'it is at least unfortunate that the *Catechism* does not recognise . . . that people might dissent from some non-infallible authoritative teaching *and* be *correct*, having been led to dissent by a love of truth itself. Examples abound'.[50] In other words, Hughes point is that the *Catechism* does not seem to admit that one's sincere and informed search for the truth can at times lead to an authentic judgement in conscience that differs from the non-infallible teaching of the Magisterium.[51] At this point, the reader should recall that our consideration of following one's conscience is about people who are sincerely trying to do the right thing; for theist's, this equates to trying to discern and follow God's will. All sincere persons will be seeking to act prudently (wisely) in making their decisions in conscience.[52]

For the faithful Catholic police officer, it is the case that the Church expects its teaching on the issues highlighted in this book to be followed, namely: lying, perjury, oaths and the cooperation in the evil of another. That does not, all the same, prevent the faithful Catholic from seeking to better understand and interpret these teachings in the most authentic way while remaining faithful to the Magisterium. For the faithful Catholic, one would expect nothing less.

---

[49] John Paul II, *Veritatis Splendor*, 64.

[50] Hughes, 'Our Human Vocation', 349.

[51] See also Hoose, '*Conscience*', 93.

[52] The interested reader may wish to read about the development in the history of the Church between the sixteenth to eighteenth centuries of ways to deal with instances when there are doubts as to the relevance and application of aspects of the moral law to particular situations, aka the moral systems. See, for example, Ashley, *Living the Truth*, 121 and Peschke, *Christian Ethics, Vol. 1*, 177–180.

While remaining faithful to the Magisterium, perhaps a useful check for the individual Catholic police officer, in truth, any police officer, struggling to inform his conscience properly, follow it and hence 'do the right thing,' is to ask himself whether he is prepared to stand before God and defend his decision.[53]

3.6 ADDITIONAL GUIDANCE FOR CONSCIENCE

Catholic moral theology offers additional guidance when dealing with situations where it is not clear to the individual what he or she should do. The specific guidance we shall consider is the principle of double effect, the principle of the lesser of two evils and the principle of *epikeia*. The Church's teaching about when it is and is not acceptable to cooperate in the evil of another is another form of guidance and, given its importance to policing, it is treated separately in a subsequent section.

3.6.1 Double Effect

Sometimes an act can have both good effects and bad effects. Provided the act performed is not in itself morally evil, the principle of double effect (PDE) can help one decide when it is morally acceptable to do something that includes a foreseeable bad effect(s).

Four conditions need to be satisfied:

(i)   The act itself is not intrinsically evil
(ii)   One must only intend the good effect(s), not the bad effect(s)
(iii)   The good effect(s) must not be caused by the evil effect(s)
(iv)   There is a proportionate reason for doing the act

These four conditions uphold the Church's claim that 'one may never do evil so that good may result from it' (CCC 1756), and this also underscores the Church's teaching on the sources of morality in which the object is fundamental to the moral evaluation of the human act. When only the good effect(s) is intended, the bad effect(s) thus becomes an unwanted side effect(s).

---

[53] There is a parallel here with the College of Policing's Code of Ethics' advice regarding ethical decision making that you ask yourself certain questions, including: 'Would I be comfortable explaining this action or decision to my supervisor? [and] Would I be prepared to defend this action or decision in public?'. (College of Policing, *Code of Ethics*, 17, sec. 4.1.7)

Let us consider two examples. First, a police officer 'lies' to a person suspected of working as part of a shoplifting team. The officer falsely claims that closed-circuit television (CCTV) footage will have filmed the perpetrators of the theft and, therefore, it is now in the suspect's best interest to reveal where he is keeping the stolen property. The reality, however, is that the police officer knows the CCTV camera was not working at the time of the theft. The suspect subsequently leads the police to a lock-up garage packed with stolen property. In this scenario, the good effects are the detecting of theft and the recovery of stolen goods, and a bad effect might be that the suspect is less inclined to believe the police in the future due to his having been lied to. PDE cannot be used here because it fails to satisfy condition (i) above since the utterance of the lie (if that is what it is) is deemed to be intrinsically evil and hence never morally acceptable according to Catholic magisterial teaching. If, on the other hand, it can be shown, somehow, that the police officer's utterance is not a lie, but something of the order of a non-lying falsehood, then PDE can apply.[54]

Second example: a police officer (officer X) reports fellow police officers for committing noble-cause corruption. The officers had violated some police procedures in order to gather sufficient evidence, not possible any other way, to bring a known people-smuggling gang to court. As a result, the offending police officers are brought to justice (good effect), but the case is dropped, and the gang continue to smuggle more people into the United Kingdom (UK) (bad effect). The bad consequences were foreseen by officer X. Applying PDE to this scenario it is easy to see how conditions (i) (ii) and (iii) are satisfied, and condition (iv) might be too, although some might argue that in these circumstances there is not a proportionate reason for reporting his colleagues' wrongdoing since one foresees that the reporting will thereby lead to the people-smuggling gang continuing to smuggle vulnerable people.

---

[54] Chapter 4 discusses various ways a statement, such as the one made by this police officer, which, while ostensibly a lie, may not actually fall foul of the norm against lying.

3.6.2 Lesser of Two Evils When one believes oneself to be in an
impossible situation where there appears to be no
The principle of the lesser of two evils is a commonly heard of principle. avoiding
evil
It is not meant to be used to undermine the Pauline principle that one
ought not to do evil so as to achieve good (Rom 3:8). As such,
understandable though it might be, the lesser of two evils principle cannot
be used to justify the use of a lie (an intrinsic evil), no matter the good
consequences achieved and/or evil consequences avoided. The principle
can, nonetheless, be used when an individual's conscience is perplexed
(confused/baffled), where one believes oneself to be in an impossible
situation such that there appears to be no way of avoiding evil.

Suppose police officer A is aware that police officer B has used what
might be construed as excessive force when arresting a violent person.
Officer B is determined to lie about this, not wanting to risk falling foul
of a potential complaint from the arrested person. Notwithstanding a
police officer's duty here in respect of any police code of ethics, and
unable to persuade him to speak the truth, officer A manages to get
officer B to limit his planned deceit to lying but to agree to talk truthfully
if the case ever came to court. Officer A's action is a correct use of
choosing the lesser of two evils: encouraging another to choose to lie
rather than lying and perjury. Use of excessive force and lying are still
wrong, but it is better to persuade officer B to choose the lesser evil (lie)
and avoid the greater evil (perjury). The intention of officer A is
persuasion to prevent perjury, not to conceal what might be construed as
excessive force and then lie about it.

But there may be occasions when a police officer believes, in complete
sincerity, that a lie is necessary in order to avoid the greater evil of failing
in his duty in some way, such as through not protecting the public from
harm (e.g. a lie to prevent a person committing suicide, as in the example
offered in sec. 3.1 Ethics). At these times, the police officer does not sin
by lying (although lying is still wrong). While it remains the fact that he
ought not to lie (i.e. objectively speaking), from the perplexed police
officer's perspective, he acts correctly by lying (i.e. subjectively speaking).
This reasoning appears in accord with Grisez's understanding of the
principle of the lesser of two evils, for he states:

> There is a legitimate sense, recognized by classical moral theology, in which it is right
> to "choose the lesser evil." If someone erroneously supposes that he or she has no
> morally right option (including delaying choosing), his or her conscience is
> perplexed. In reality, there must be a morally right possibility, but if a person sincerely

trying to see what is right and do it cannot discern any way to avoid choosing what seems morally evil, then what seems to be the lesser moral evil should be chosen.[55]

At this point, one should remember that our focus in this book is on police officers who are sincerely trying to do what is right. For Catholic police officers, the principle of the lesser of two evils, while having an essential role for those who find themselves truly perplexed on a particular matter, ought not to be used as a general principle to flout the absolute proscription of acts deemed intrinsically evil by the Magisterium.[56]

3.6.3 Epikeia man made rules

The principle of *epikeia* is applicable when to follow a human law or rule on a particular occasion would lead to a serious injustice and thereby damage the good of persons or the common good. For example, traffic law requires one to observe speed limits. However, if safe to do so, the principle of *epikeia* would justify exceeding the speed limit safely to rush a seriously injured person to the hospital. On such occasions, following the spirit of the law, not the letter of the law, is the just thing to do.

The traditional Catholic understanding of the application of *epikeia* is that while it can, on rare occasions, legitimately apply to man-made law, it does not apply to natural law since the latter is understood to be a manifestation of God's law, of which there are no exceptions. The traditional understanding of the *epikeia* principle could not, therefore, be used to justify so-called noble-cause perjury or any use of lies by the police, since perjury and lying are deemed by the Magisterium to be intrinsically evil acts and hence contrary to the natural law.[57] On the other

---

[55] Grisez, *Way of the Lord Jesus, vol.1*, 166, fn.17.

[56] 'To use it [the lesser of two evils principle] as an ordinary principle of moral solution is to fall into utilitarianism or proportionalism.' (Ashley, *Living the Truth*, 139)

[57] We should at least acknowledge that some nontraditional Catholic theologians do, in contrast, believe that *epikeia* can also apply to the *norms* of natural law as these too are still humanly formulated. Fuchs, for example, in discussing *epikeia*, argues:

[S]ome prefer a "deontological" judgement on some matters (e.g. on perjury, lying, life, sexuality), for such a deontological judgement is the ground of strictly universal norms; others, however, deny such a necessity . . . "the rule must be curved to the stone" and not vice versa; in other words, the norm must be corrected or at least interpreted according to the totality of the concrete reality.

hand, *epikeia* could potentially justify breaking other man-made rules/laws if there is a serious enough reason to do so, e.g. committing a minor violation of police procedure to protect the common good of society in some way. Furthermore, it would seem that the application of *epikeia* is in accord with the Code of Ethics expectation that 'you apply the *intent* of the Code to your decisions'.[58]

3.7 CONSCIENCE WITHIN POLICING

[handwritten: When confronted w/ police corruption]

Sherman states that a police officer has few options in how to react when confronted with police corruption, whether systematic, isolated, noble or otherwise. He identifies four options: (i) go with the flow and do nothing, (ii) get out of the situation, maybe by transferring to another area, (iii) resign, (iv) and the most difficult being to fight back in some way, perhaps through whistle-blowing or some 'behind-the-scenes counterattack'.[59]

The four options identified by Sherman raise four questions: How often do officers go with the flow and do nothing? How easy is it for officers to get away from corruption? Do many officers resign to get away from corruption? How often do officers fight back against corruption? It is not our purpose to seek answers to these questions, but it is evident that some police officers' consciences certainly do lead them to fight back.[60] Also, crucial to the fight against police corruption are the many unsung, unknown acts by police officers following their consciences and protecting important moral values when they become threatened. Of course, in England and Wales, the College of Policing's Code of Ethics of 2014 offers clear guidance and support for officers, helping them to both know how to behave properly and to challenge malpractice and corruption when they come across it.

[handwritten: Someone w/ moral compass + religious beliefs will be in a good place]

(Fuchs, *Personal Responsibility,* 196–197. See also in the same book, ch. 10: *Epikeia* Applied to Natural Law?). For a more detailed coverage of the principle of *epikeia* from the traditional Catholic perspective, see: Aquinas, *STh* II–II, q. 120; Grisez, *Way of the Lord Jesus, vol.2,* 878–879; Peschke, *Christian Ethics, vol.1,* 131–133.

[58] College of Policing, *Code of Ethics,* 17, sec. 4.1.7. Emphasis added.

[59] Sherman, 'Learning Police Ethics', 17–18. Sherman was writing in the 1980s and had a US focus.

[60] See reference to Serpico and Hopson in sec. 2.1.3 Loyalty. Another example would be former Patrick V. Murphy, Commissioner of New York City Police Department (NYPD) in the early 1970s, who made great strides to drive out corruption from within NYPD. See Murphy, *Commissioner: A View.*

Miller states that 'the only force strong enough to resist corruption is the moral sense—the motivating belief in doing what is right and avoiding doing what is wrong'.[61] Miller does not refer to the contribution religion might make to an increased moral sense, but it seems fair to say that Christian police officers and officers from other religious backgrounds should certainly possess this strong moral awareness due to their faith-based moral principles. That is not to deny the existence of a high moral sense within non-religious police officers. It is, though, to make the point that God-fearing (God-loving) police officers *ipso facto* have an added factor to their moral sense which should, hopefully, help them to resist adopting the end justifying the means mentality at the price of sacrificing, what for some, are absolute values.[62] The following extract from James Morton, *Bent Coppers: A Survey of Police Corruption*, seems to support this point:

> From time to time officers did get a rush of conscience, possibly because they had turned to religion, and often with unpleasant consequences to themselves. . . . In May 1988 a policeman of thirteen years' standing and a younger officer admitted making false statements that they had seen a fifteen-year-old youth driving a stolen car and a twenty-two-year-old in the passenger seat. . . . Whilst the youths were awaiting trial the older officer broke down and told one of his seniors that he was a Born Again Christian: 'I have now found religion. I cannot go through with taking a religious oath and lying in the face of God.[63]

All police officers have a conscience, a sense of right and wrong. In addition, all Christian police officers in their pursuit to live morally upright lives will seek to do God's will as perfectly manifested through the life and teachings of Jesus Christ. Aiming to do God's will, it would seem, is an added incentive to do good and avoid evil. It is to the principle of cooperating in the evil of another that we now turn.[64]

---

[61] Miller, 'Integrity Systems', 249. Of course, this begs the questions of what is right/wrong and on what basis?

[62] See sec. 2.2.1 Christians and the National Decision Model (NDM).

[63] Morton, *Bent Coppers,* 266–267.

[64] Note in passing that an area of Catholic teaching closely related to conscience and the morality of human acts is that of the virtues. See Chapter 8.

3.8 COOPERATION IN THE EVIL OF ANOTHER

One's initial response to the title of this section is likely to be: how can it ever be morally acceptable to cooperate in the evil of another? The devil is in the detail—or perhaps, we should say: God is. We live in an imperfect world: imperfect people, imperfect organisations and imperfect societies (all of us are imperfect), and, quite simply, we have to find a way to get along and make the best of things without compromising our moral integrity. Jesus prayed for his followers: 'I am not asking you to take them out of the world, but I ask you to protect them from the evil one.' (Jn 17:15)

The key distinction within the principle of cooperating in the evil of another is between formal cooperation and material cooperation. In a nutshell, formal cooperation is always morally unacceptable because in addition to helping in the evil of another, it also involves approval of the evil. In contrast, material cooperation is where one helps in the evil of another without approving of the evil; in some circumstances, this can be morally acceptable.[65] The principle of cooperating in the evil of another needs careful unpacking and is thwart with difficulties. In this section, the aim is merely to provide a basic overview of the principle and how one *might* apply it to the police. First, let us note the relevance of cooperating in evil to police ethics and the existence of police loyalty.[66]

3.8.1 Misplaced Loyalty

Loyalty within the ranks of the police is obviously both desirable and necessary if the police are to function effectively. Bad police loyalty— misplaced loyalty—also exists, and it occurs when it demands from officers, conduct that is illegal and/or immoral. Miller reports: 'Numerous inquiries into police corruption have noted that police officers typically expect other police officers not to report them, even when they have engaged in criminal acts and notwithstanding the legal requirement that

---

[65] While not wishing to make light of the significance of any level of evil (similarly the significance of venial sin), maybe use of the word 'wrongdoing' rather than 'evil' is better since 'evil' seems to be a more appropriate term for 'serious wrongdoing'. Put simply and arguably, not all wrongdoing is evil in the way many would use the term evil.

[66] Of interest, Health Care Ethics is one area where the principle of cooperating in the evil of another is receiving attention.

they do so.'[67] Indeed, the Mollen Commission, which investigated police misconduct in New York, concluded that:

> [Police perjury is] widely tolerated by corrupt and honest officers alike, as well as their supervisors . . . Officers who report misconduct are ostracized and harassed; become targets of complaints and even physical threats; and are made to fear that they will be left alone on the streets in a time of crisis.[68]

As previously stated, in this book's consideration of policing, there is no intention to enter the frame of attempting to analyse how much police corruption goes on and/or whether it is more prevalent in the United States (US) than the UK (though one suspects it is). Furthermore, we should also keep in mind that there have been significant efforts in the US and the UK in recent years to improve police practice and its associated police culture, so it might not be overly optimistic to be of the opinion that things are better nowadays than what they were hitherto. We will not, therefore, engage in speculation as to how prevalent misplaced loyalty—unjustified cooperation in the evil of others—is within the police. It exists, but one hopes it is not as widespread as some of the evidence suggests. Nevertheless, one notes Koepke's claim that: 'The Blue Wall of Silence and the fear of retaliation by fellow officers are undoubtedly the primary reasons for an officer's reluctance to speak out against a fellow officer.'[69] Note too McConville and Shepherd's claim in respect of British policing that:

> The most important thing that probationary officers learn in their first few months in the police is the need to keep their mouths shut about practices, including those in breach of the rules, which experienced officers deem necessary in discharging policing responsibilities. Secrecy and loyalty are enjoined . . . because the socialization process teaches probationers to subordinate their own views to the needs and demands of the job.[70]

Furthermore, Newburn rejects the explanation of police corruption in terms of a 'few bad apples', adding that 'the history of policing has too many examples of institutionalised corruption for this "explanation" to

---

[67] Miller, 'Integrity Systems', 247.

[68] The Mollen Commission 1994 at 40 and 53, as cited by Chin and Wells (Chin and Wells, 'The "Blue Wall of Silence"', 249 and 254).

[69] Koepke, 'The Failure To Breach', 228–229.

[70] McConville and Shepherd, *Watching Police*, 207. For an analysis of police loyalty, see Richards, 'A Question of Loyalty', and Richards, 'Police Loyalty Redux'.

carry much credence'.[71] But there is another important reason why, says Newburn, the 'few bad apples' theory is inadequate. He says it 'fails to identify all those likely to be implicated in the "wrongdoing" (often failing to hold supervisors or managers to account for example) and also fails to confront the structural problems or issues that tend to underpin the misconduct at the centre of the scandal'.[72] Put another way, the notion of a 'few bad apples' does not acknowledge who and in what ways others cooperate in the evil/wrongdoing (corruption) of some police officers.

Besides, Miller comments that while police integrity systems for the reporting of misconduct rely heavily on fellow officers to report misconduct, '[h]istorically, police officers have been very reluctant to "rat" on their corrupt colleagues'.[73] Hence there exists what Miller terms 'a vicious circle in operation: the "blue wall of silence" undercuts the efficacy of internal investigations which in turn reinforces the "blue wall of silence"'.[74] Furthermore, as previously noted, recent research in the UK by Westmarland and Rowe suggests that the blue wall of silence continues to exercise significant influence within the police.[75]

3.8.2 Material or Formal[76]

To what extent, if any, can Roman Catholic police officers, or any police officer, justifiably cooperate in the unacceptable behaviour of other police officers? One answer lies in the distinction between formal and material cooperation.[77]

Formal cooperation is never morally permissible because it involves the approval of another's evil and hence makes the cooperator as guilty as the perpetrator of the wrongdoing. With formal cooperation, the approval of another's evil is evidenced by how one helps. If one freely and directly partakes in the evil act itself in some way or encourages the

encourages or assists

---

[71] Newburn, *Literature review – Police integrity and corruption*, 7.
[72] Ibid.
[73] Miller, 'Integrity Systems', 246.
[74] Ibid., 254.
[75] Westmarland and Rowe, 'Police ethics and integrity: can a new code'. See also Westmarland, 'Police Ethics and Integrity: Breaking the Blue Code'.
[76] Di Camillo, 'Understanding Cooperation with Evil', has been a helpful point of reference in the writing of this section, 3.8.2 Material or Formal.
[77] For a more detailed discussion of these terms, see Grisez, *Way of the Lord Jesus, vol.1*, 300–304; Grisez, *Way of the Lord Jesus, vol.2*, 440–444; Grisez, *Way of the Lord Jesus, vol.3*, 871–897.

evildoer to commit such an act, then one approves of the evil: this can never be morally justified. A supervising police officer, for example, who advises lower rank officers how to tailor their evidence and hence commit perjury would commit formal cooperation and is as guilty of the act of perjury (morally speaking) as the officers who perjure themselves. This behaviour constitutes *explicit* formal cooperation. Alternatively, consider the case of a supervising officer who does not want his officers to commit so-called noble-cause perjury and does not openly encourage them to do so. Yet, because he also does not want them to suffer the consequences of getting found out, he offers them a confidential place (e.g. his office) to knowingly help them 'get their stories straight' aka the writing up of their false evidence; he then is guilty of *implicit* formal cooperation in their wrongdoing.

The matter of when material cooperation is or is not acceptable is, arguably, where the real debate lies. With material cooperation properly construed, one does not approve of another's wrongdoing when assisting in its occurrence. The assistance given must not involve the committing of an intrinsically evil act. The ideal is not to materially cooperate in any evil. For all that, at times, material cooperation can be an appropriate response in the circumstances one finds oneself in, but it is meant to be an exception to the rule.[78] Common Catholic teaching is that there are various reasons why one needs a stronger reason (proportionate reason) for materially cooperating in the evil of another. The reasons are: the more severe is the evil one cooperates in; the greater is the help one provides; the closer one is to the evil act committed; and the more one's help is necessary for the evil act to occur, rather than one's assistance being of only incidental help. One also needs to consider whether one's material cooperation gives the impression that one is approving of the evil act even though one is not; that is, one ought not to give rise to scandal (discussed in next section).

Ashley and O'Rourke describe the principle of cooperating in the evil of another as follows:

> To achieve a well-formed conscience, one should always judge it unethical to cooperate formally with an immoral act (i.e., directly to intend the evil act itself), or even to cooperate materially (i.e., to provide means necessary to the act) if this cooperation is immediate (i.e., if one acts as an instrumental agent of the principal agent of the evil act). One may sometimes, however, judge it to be morally

---

[78] See Di Camillo, 'Understanding Cooperation with Evil', 2–3, especially 3 re illicit material cooperation.

permissible or even obligatory to cooperate materially and mediately (i.e., before or after the evil act, but not as an instrumental agent of the principal agent of the evil act), depending on the degree of the good to be achieved or evil avoided by the cooperation.[79]

DiCamillo summarises the various elements of the cooperating principle (which he calls the moral principles guiding such cooperation) as:

(i)   Do not directly intend to contribute to evil, even if your goal is good [formal cooperation].
(ii)   Do not contribute to evil indirectly, if you can avoid it [illicit material cooperation].
(iii) Do not contribute to evil indirectly, unless better options are exhausted and the chosen goods outweigh the expected evils [licit material cooperation].
(iv)   Do not cause public confusion about Catholic teaching or identity [scandal].[80]

A few examples will be of help. Suppose several police officers use a small amount of force to extract details from a known terrorist about the whereabouts of a massive bomb he has planted which is soon to detonate in central London. Officer 'A' does not use force himself and tries to stop it. The bomb is defused. The terrorist subsequently makes a complaint about the force used against him; a complaint which might jeopardise the case, as well as leading to what some might consider being draconian disciplinary measures upon the officers concerned. In writing up their accounts of what happened, officer 'A' is pressurised by his supervisory officer and colleagues to lie by stating that no such force was used. Officer 'A' does not want to do this, does not do it, and voices his objection. All the same, not wanting to risk jeopardising the case, he proceeds to write up his evidence without lying yet in a vague way that does not, therefore, contradict the other officers' less than honest accounts of what happened. He hopes that the complaint is dropped, the terrorist is convicted, and the other officers are not overly punished for their understandable, albeit improper interrogation technique. If this is an instance of justifiable (i.e. licit not illicit) material cooperation, debatable though this is, and notwithstanding any contravention of the College of Policing's 2014 Code of Ethics (the intent of which needs to be respected), it will be

---

[79] Ashley and O'Rourke, *Health Care Ethics*, 198–199.
[80] Di Camillo, 'Understanding Cooperation with Evil', 1. Content in brackets comes from Di Camillo's subsequent exposition of these principles (1–3).

because officer A has not formally cooperated and there is a proportionately strong enough reason for 'materially' cooperating.[81]

Sometime later, officer 'A' drives himself and these same police officers to court to give evidence against the terrorist, knowing full well that his colleagues intend to deny using force, they thereby committing perjury. His cooperation at this point is merely driving them to court: it is remote from the potential future act of perjury, not essential to its occurrence, and what he does is not intrinsically evil (i.e. he drives the police car), nor does it give rise to scandal. This element of his cooperation is a much more easily justified case of licit material cooperation.

At court, officer 'A', upon further reflection has a change of heart and decides (to his own satisfaction) that the intended perjured evidence of his fellow officers is justified due to the circumstances of the case. When he gives his evidence, although he does not perjure himself, he is careful not to contradict the perjured testimony of his colleagues. Officer 'A' commits unjustified cooperation because he approves of their perjury (i.e. the evil act) and so what he does seems to amount to at least implicit formal cooperation, if not explicit formal cooperation.[82]

If officer 'A' had not approved of the perjury of the other officers, for his material cooperation to be justifiable (licit), proportionate reasoning would need to take on board the damage police perjury (albeit noble cause in this instance)—detected or not—has on the public trust in the police and the criminal justice system as a whole.

---

[81] Di Camillo's specific point that licit material cooperation also requires the prior fact that 'other options have been exhausted' is relevant too; and one might say this point is subsumed within the over-arching requirement that a proportionate reason exists (Di Camillo, 'Understanding Cooperation with Evil', 3). In respect of cooperating under duress, by way of comparison, Grisez states that, 'people forced against their wills to do something which substantially facilitates a crime (to open a safe, carry out the loot, or the like) only materially cooperate'. (Grisez, *Way of the Lord Jesus, vol.1*, 301, G5) Furthermore, Grisez points out that one can also have a moral responsibility to avoid materially cooperating. He gives the following example: '[I]nstead of cooperating materially in criminal acts, citizens might have a duty to help law enforcement agents, even at some personal risk, by informing on mobsters and seeking the protection of the law'. (Ibid., 301, G6)

[82] This series of examples seem to echo Grisez's observation that one side effect of material cooperation is the subsequent temptation to cooperate formally often due to the relationship that exists/develops between cooperator and wrongdoer. He states: 'For example, whenever friends, relatives, or members of any group or society materially cooperate, solidarity inclines them to hope for the success of the wrongdoing which they are helping.' (Grisez, *Way of the Lord Jesus, vol.2*, 442, F4)

In summary, formal cooperation in police wrongdoing is never morally justifiable; and that which passes as justifiable (licit) material cooperation needs to be decided via the prudential judgement of police officers, and hopefully with the guidance of trusted Catholic theologians and ethicists.[83]

3.8.3 Scandal can be intentional or unintentional

The term 'scandal' comes from the Greek word *skandalon* meaning 'stumbling block'. Scandal, as the *Catechism* describes, 'is an attitude or behaviour which leads another to do evil'. (CCC 2284) We all affect others in various ways: by the way we live, what we say, what we do and what we do not do; the term scandal highlights the bad influence we can have on our neighbour, whether we realise we have such an effect or not. It is a grave (serious) offence when done intentionally (i.e. deliberately leading another into serious sin); and even when not intended, others obviously can still get scandalised. An example of intentional scandal might be where police officers provoke a person who is drunk and *incapable*, thereby leading him to behave in a drunk and *disorderly* manner. An example of unintentional scandal might be where Clint Eastwood's Dirty Harry Film (1971) unwittingly encourages some police officers to take the end justifying the means approach to aspects of their professional role.[84] The *Catechism* speaks of the one causing scandal as 'his neighbour's tempter'. (CCC 2284) The issue of causing scandal links to the issue of cooperating

---

[83] The aforementioned examples are offered only as an attempt to illustrate what, for some, might be deemed instances of the difference between formal and material cooperation. They are merely points for discussion, not to be taken as approval of any of officer 'A's' actions. It is up to the reader to decide what prudential judgement requires in these cases. The topic of justifiably cooperating in the evil of another is evidently a contemporary and controversial issue. Of interest, note the US introduction in 2012 of the Health and Human Services (HHS) Mandate requires employers to pay for health care plans (insurance policies) that include provision for abortion-inducing drugs, sterilisation and contraception. This is seen as a violation of religious liberty by those who do not wish to be associated with the provision of health care plans that include coverage for practices they consider to be unethical. Catholic ethicists differ in their opinions as to whether cooperating with the HHS Mandate can be justified according to the material cooperation. See Miller, 'The HHS Mandate', and Bracken, 'What should be'.

[84] As noted previously, Clint Eastwood played the fictitious police officer Harry Callaghan, who is violent and does not follow correct police procedure, but by use of these methods is hugely successful in his fight against crime.

in the evil of another because, as we have mentioned previously, one of the conditions of justified (licit) material cooperation in the evil of another is that one's cooperation must not give rise to scandal.

More broadly speaking, both scandal and cooperating in the evil of another are part of social sin. 'Sins give rise to social situations and institutions that are contrary to the divine goodness . . . They lead their victims to do evil in their turn. In an analogous sense, they constitute a "social sin".' (CCC 1869) The *Catechism* tells us that scandal is even more serious 'by reason of the authority of those who cause it or the weakness of those who are scandalized'. (CCC 2285) Laws and social structures can also cause scandal, such as when social conditions make it increasingly difficult to live a good Christian life (CCC 2286). In policing terms, if senior officers, for example, turn a blind eye to the wrongdoing of those they have responsibility for, the gravity of the scandal is increased. The seriousness of scandal increases when, for example, new and low-ranking officers are encouraged, cajoled or bullied into taking part in police malpractice by more experienced and/or senior officers. Moreover, as we have already stated, society scandalises its citizens when it encourages, whether directly or indirectly, dishonesty and lies.

Police officers, as acknowledged previously, come from the societies they serve. Does society adequately reflect the values of honesty and lawfulness it wishes to see in its police service? So-called 'white' lies are often used on consequential grounds by many to ease social interactions, to avoid hurting others, or to get oneself off the hook. Then, there are the manipulations of statistical data and facts by organisations which, while not technically untrue, present a less than accurate picture of reality to further their own ends. The point is that society scandalises and bears some of the responsibility for whatever dishonesty and corruption that exists within its police service by the fact that society has contributed, directly and indirectly, to the values or disvalues of its police officers. Police officers are not formed in a moral vacuum.

The scandal caused by social structures is clearly applicable to the unofficial elements within police culture (and outside the police too) that encourage breaking the rules at times in the furtherance of getting the job done. Those who, without further qualification, postulate for others, or adhere themselves to, a philosophy of doing what you have to do to get the job done, are promoting (intended or not) a seedbed for both specific acts of police corruption and the misplaced loyalty that leads to the illicit cooperation in such acts. The judicial system can also be construed as an instrument of scandal. We have noted the prevalence of perjury committed by defendants and defence witnesses, yet prosecutions for the crime of perjury are few and far between. Arguably, this omission to clampdown on perjury causes scandal because it encourages defendants etc. to lie to avoid justice and, sadly, also leads some police officers to counter-lie in what they see as the pursuit of justice.

3.9 SUMMARY

Ethics is about doing what is morally good and avoiding what is morally bad. Ethics is a shared human activity none of us can escape from: even choosing to behave immorally is an ethical choice, but a bad one. All police officers, therefore, engage in ethics. While the ethical decisions of non-religious police officers do not involve reference to God, there are a core set of values that all good police officers will agree to, such as the values of honesty, loyalty and integrity. The interpretation and application of these values can and does differ in response to moral problems. Theist police officers will seek to do God's will. Christian police officers will seek to do God's will as perfectly expressed through the person of Jesus Christ. Catholic police officers are also obliged to inform their consciences with the Church's magisterial moral teaching and make it central to their ethical decision making.

The Church teaches that the object, intention and circumstances collectively determine the morality of a human act—and crucially, the object is the primary source of an act's morality. A morally good act is said to be an act that orders the person to God. Some acts, known as intrinsically evil acts, are deemed, in themselves, incapable of being ordered to God. The Christian ethical theories of situation ethics and proportionalism, as well as Selling's *Reframing of Catholic Theological Ethics*, challenge the traditional Catholic approach to the moral evaluation of human acts.

Our consideration of conscience, the principles of double effect, lesser evil and *epikeia*, as well as the principle of cooperating in the evil of another, all presume a sincere search to know and apply God's will. The prudent Catholic police officer is expected to make good use of Church teaching on moral matters and not to allow this teaching to be undermined by the opinions of others, including his own—but he must always follow his conscience. He or she must be ever vigilant not to do evil himself, and resist pressures to cooperate in the evil acts of others, except licit material cooperation.

Scandal links to the issue of cooperating in the evil of another. It can be caused by individual police officers or social structures such as police culture, the judicial process itself and society in general in the way it influences its citizens for bad rather than good. The *Catechism* teaches that: 'Anyone [including social structures] who uses the power at his disposal in such a way that it leads others to do wrong becomes guilty of scandal and responsible for the evil that he or she has directly or indirectly encouraged.' (CCC 2287) Without condoning police misconduct, it seems, all the same, that critics of the police should ever keep in mind the social sin within which the police operate in the pursuit of the common good. The police should not be treated as scapegoats, whereby society fails to confront the disvalues and sin within itself that has helped shape the police service we now have.

Nevertheless, the moral quandary facing morally aware police officers encountering corruption, when combined with the pull of police loyalty, is clear. As Sherman states: 'For those officers with enough moral consciousness to suffer a moral experience, a failure to "do the right thing" could be quite painful to live with.'[85]

---

[85] Sherman, 'Learning Police Ethics', 18.

From the moment in our lives at which we learn to speak
we are taught that what we say must be true.
What does this mean?
What is meant by 'telling the truth'?
What does it demand from us?
Bonhoeffer[1]

4

LYING: AN ANALYSIS

Recall the tragic events of 11th September 2001 involving the crashing of two planes into the World Trade Centre (Twin Towers) in New York City.[2] Hypothetically speaking, suppose the pilots of these planes could have prevented this catastrophe from happening by uttering a falsehood with intent to deceive ('lie'). Conceivably they might have lied to the hijackers over flight control details, thereby ensuring the planes steered away from and not into the World Trade Centre. The Catholic Church teaches that no lie (falsehood with intent to deceive) can ever be justified; which, in the absence of argumentation to conclude otherwise, would prohibit the lie in our hypothetical scenario surrounding the events of 11th September.[3] Adhering to absolutism against 'lying' presents a problem when it conflicts with the demands of justice. It appears to present a particular problem for policing since, at times, policing requires the use of 'lies' in the pursuance of legitimate policing objectives. Those wishing to respect the value of truthfulness without adhering to an absolute proscription of lying when it violates justice, are, possibly, likely to

---

[1] Bonhoeffer, *Ethics*, 363. Our human bias towards truthfulness and what it requires from us is at the heart of this chapter.

[2] While omissions and revisions have been made, as well as further material added, much of the content in this chapter, with the exception of sec. 4.3.1 Ethical Context, has previously been published in Paul Dixon, 'Police Lies and the Catechism on Lying'. *Irish Theological Quarterly* 78 (2), 162–178. Copyright © [2013] (Copyright Holder). Reprinted by permission of SAGE Publications. Permission also applies to material used in secs. 2.1.1 and 3.3.2.
https://journals.sagepub.com/doi/full/10.1177/0021140012472633.

[3] The Catholic Church's magisterial teaching does not permit the use of falsehoods with intent to deceive ('lie')—even to those who have no right to the truth (as discussed in sec. 4.2 Catechism's Teaching On Lying).

maintain that 'heroes retain responsibility for their decisions; [while] fanatics give it over to rule-following'.[4]

4.1 LYING WITHIN SOCIETY AND THE POLICE

Most people, one supposes, while agreeing with the importance of being honest, upright and truthful will, nevertheless, accept the moral justification of the occasional so-called white lie when used to help not harm. It is reported that about 75% of people admit to telling white lies; white lies make up 80% of all lies told; and that 70% of people say it is okay to lie to protect another, including their feelings.[5] Also, how many of us would not utter a 'white' lie if it was the only way to prevent *severe* harm to another, such as the death of innocent Jews whom one is hiding from the pursuing Gestapo?[6] MacIntyre says of North American culture that there is 'near-universal agreement . . . that any acceptable rule concerning lying and truth telling . . . [is of the form:] "Never tell a lie . . . except when,"' and the favoured 'exception' focuses upon lies to help not harm.[7] In other words, the generally accepted norm is: don't tell lies but 'helpful' exceptions can be made. Interestingly, within Christianity, the probably older, less influential and unofficial tradition on lying supports exceptions to the general rule against lying when done to achieve some good.[8] This unofficial tradition is in contrast to the dominant

---

[4] My thanks to an anonymous reader for this comment.

[5] British Broadcasting Corporation (BBC), 'A Week Without Lying'. This was a social experiment by psychologists to explore the role of deception in human life. Identified psychologists: Professor Paul Taylor (Psychologist), Dr Gordon Wright (Investigative Psychologist) and Dr Sophie van der Zee (Legal Psychologist).

[6] Many lies also get told during wartime, both by allied and enemy forces alike. For example, the lies and deception told surrounding the Second World War Allied D-Day invasion of Normandy. This allied invasion, code-named 'bodyguard' after a speech by Winston Churchill in 1943, would not have been possible without recourse to the strategic deceptions employed by allied forces. Churchill famously stated: 'In wartime, truth is so precious that she should always be attended by a bodyguard of lies.' The same can be said for the lies involved in the work of secret services. The United Kingdom has its Secret Intelligence Service (MI6) and the United States of America has the Criminal Intelligence Agency (CIA). Espionage is one aspect of these intelligence services.

[7] MacIntyre, 'Truthfulness', 318. This material subsequently appeared in MacIntyre, *Ethics and Politics*, 108.

[8] Ramsey, 'Two Traditions', 527 and 531–532.

Augustinian tradition, one that upholds an absolute proscription of lying, and which the Magisterium of the Catholic Church endorses.

MacIntyre cites various statistics concerning lying amongst the population of North America:[9]

- "People tell about two lies a day, or at least that is what they admit to."[10]
- 91 percent of Americans lie regularly, that only 45 percent refrain from lying on occasion because they think it is wrong , and that those who do lie lie most to friends and relatives.[11]

In the United Kingdom (UK), the 2017 Ipsos MORI Veracity Index reveals that when adult members of the British public were asked whether they trust certain professions to tell them the truth, 74% said they trusted the police (the highest trust for the police since records began in 1983), 65% trust the clergy, top of the list were nurses (94%) and doctors (91%). Bottom of the trust pile were politicians generally at 17%. Significantly, since 1983, trust in the police has risen by 13% while trust in the clergy has fallen by 20%.[12]

These figures are not surprising since many in society do not think honesty is *always* the best policy. Psychologist Professor Taylor tells us that 'lying is a fundamental part of being human . . . [and commenting in respect of white lies] lying is not inherently bad. There are times when it has a role in our interactions and relationship with others'.[13] And in response to the issue of living in a world without lying, Taylor comments: 'I'm not sure we could, and I'm certainly sure we wouldn't want to.'[14]

---

[9] MacIntyre, *Ethics and Politics,* 109. All statistics cited in this paragraph are sourced from this page in MacIntyre's text. One is not suggesting that these statistics on lying are all in respect of 'the helpful lie'; some no doubt will be, though presumably some of them are also told merely out of self-interest and others with malice too.

[10] Citing Bella DePaulo, *New York Times,* 12 February 1985, 17. Others report that it has been estimated that everyone lies up to nine times daily (BBC, 'A Week Without Lying'). Note, however, that the BBC2 programme does not define 'lying' and their reference to lying includes not just verbal falsehoods to deceive but also so-called lies of omission. This is an understanding of lying that is broader than what others might take 'lying' to be.

[11] Statistics based on survey research by James Patterson and Peter Kim, *The Day America Told the Truth* (New York: Prentice-Hall, 1991) 45–46.

[12] Full details available on the Ipsos MORI Social Research Institute website (Ipsos MORI, 'Politicians').

[13] Comments made on BBC, 'A Week Without Lying'.

[14] Ibid.

In respect of MacIntyre's work mentioned above, Saul notes that he refers to two broad traditions concerning the morality of lying: first, the permitting of some lies (defined broadly) re motivations and consequences, and second, no lies (defined narrowly) are permitted.[15] Saul comments: 'The second tradition's view is much more puzzling: according to this tradition, one act of deception could be better than another, despite having the very same consequences and motivation. It could be morally superior simply due to the *method* of deception chosen.'[16] Moreover, for those who uphold an absolute proscription of lying, whether it be Kantians or those adhering to the teaching of the Catholic Church, there remains the issue of this *absoluteness* against 'lying' appearing morally untenable to many when confronted with the harsh realities of life.[17]

For those upholding an absolute proscription of lying, clarifying what a lie amounts to is crucial in evaluating such a moral position. This clarification might lead to the realisation that what one thinks is a lie is not a lie after all—so there is no problem. For those who permit the use of lies at times, while still maintaining a concern for the truth, the definition of a lie is not the crucial issue for them since it is the reasons and circumstances for deceiving that matter, not whether a particular type of deception is or is not a lie.[18] The police justify the use of lying at times (e.g. at a minimum within covert activities, though its use is justified at other times too). Police justification of exceptions to the norm against lying show that their perspective on lying is not in the tradition of Kant's absolutism (nor the Catholic Church's absolutism); rather the police are in line with Mill's tradition of permitting lies for good reasons.

Let us be clear: truth matters. A stable society requires truthful relationships. On what basis, however, might one justify upholding an *absolute* stance against all lying (falsehood with intent to deceive)? The recently cited hypothetical scenario based on the tragic events in respect of the World Trade Centre in 2001, highlights the difficulty of upholding an absolute proscription of lying. We shall, in due course, see why the

---

[15] The first tradition is in respect of the utilitarian John Stuart Mill (nineteenth century), while the second tradition is in respect of the deontological approach of Immanuel Kant (eighteenth century).

[16] Saul, *Lying, Misleading*, 69. She refers to MacIntyre's text in its original 1994 format.

[17] Immanuel Kant provides a non-religious, non-consequential justification for an absolute proscription of lying. For Kant, our duty never to lie comes from and out of respect for our rational human nature. See Kant, 'On a Supposed Right to Lie'.

[18] Cf. Saul, *Lying, Misleading*, 69.

Magisterium of the Catholic Church maintains an absolute proscription of lying; but apart from adherents to the Catholic position and followers of Kantian ethics, it is not at all clear on what basis others might subscribe to an absolute stance against lying. A key consideration for us will be whether or not what is *prima facie* a lie (falsehood with intent to deceive) can, at times, be morally justified in a way acceptable to the Catholic Church.[19]

Regarding the use of deception by the police in the performance of their duties, one is neither claiming police officers always need to deceive nor that they never need to. What one is saying is that police deception— which includes the use of 'lies'—is part of the fabric of police work in their effort to protect society from crime. Paradoxically, as Skolnick notes: 'The end of *truth* justifies for the modern detective the means of *lying*. Deception usually occurs in the interest of obtaining truth.'[20] Ends justifying the means is true of how it has been and still is for some United States (US) and UK police officers, though perhaps less so nowadays in the UK following the publication of the 2014 College of Policing's Code of Ethics in England and Wales.[21] That said, as previously noted, nowhere in this Code does it state that lying is prohibited absolutely, the Code not even mentioning the term 'lying'.[22] Can such deceptive police behaviour be morally justified according to Catholic moral theology? If it cannot, Catholic police officers have a problem whether they realise it and/or refuse to acknowledge it. It is a problem, no less, and probably more so, for the Church itself.

It would be useful now to note some straightforward examples of police investigative 'lying' that would, all things considered, meet the approval of both the US and UK legal systems. The reader should also decide his or her position on these matters (i.e. do you approve of the

---

[19] Arguments about the morality/immorality of lying is not a primary concern in this book since our focus is on the interpretation and application of contemporary Catholic teaching on lying. Discussions on the ethics of lying is a path already well-worn over the years, so there is little point in regurgitating the same old arguments. For an excellent discussion of the whole issue of lying see Bok, *Lying*, and Bok, *Secrets*. One recent defence of the absolute proscription of lying is made by the philosopher Christopher Tollefsen in Tollefsen, *Lying and Christian Ethics*.

[20] Skolnick, 'Deception by Police', 51.

[21] 'On the whole, British police have enjoyed a reputation for more stringent ethical standards than American police have, though verifiable data on this topic are lacking.' (Panzarella and Funk, 'Police Deception Tactics', 136)

[22] See sec. 2.2.3 Christianity and Standards of Professional Behaviour.

police action or not) and, more importantly, why you hold the view you do:

(i)   Two police officers work together undercover at a nightclub to carry out surveillance on suspected drug pushers in the area. Part of their cover story is to lie by claiming that they are holiday reps, husband and wife, and are out that evening celebrating their wedding anniversary.

(ii)   To secure entry into a drug-smuggling den, two undercover officers pose as gas servicemen. Once they have lied their way into the property, they conduct a legal drug search and seize large quantities of drugs.

(iii) To infiltrate the criminal activities of suspected football hooligans, a police officer goes undercover to befriend football supporters to identify the hooligans and discover their plans for future violence. To achieve this, the officer lies about many things such as his true identity, background and interests.

(iv) To infiltrate a known paedophile ring, a female police officer poses as a young teenager in an online chat room. Over several months, several paedophiles make contact and seek to establish an online relationship with the bogus young girl. Eventually, the paedophiles arrange to meet up with the young girl. Police officers subsequently arrest the paedophiles concerned.

(v)   Police use various informants to infiltrate the workings of a terrorist organisation. These informants lie to hide their hidden agenda from members of the terrorist organisation. The informants provide vital intelligence, thus saving many lives.[23]

(vi) A police informer has testified against a drugs gang, and consequently, his life is in danger. The police give him a new identity under the witness protection scheme: a false birth certificate and a complete legend (fictitious background) which he has to live by and deceive others with for the rest of his life.[24]

---

[23] In acknowledging the dependence of the use of informants by the police in the control and detection of crime, Maguire and John note that '[a]n increasingly common technique in anti-drug trafficking operations is for a participating informant to be used to introduce an undercover police officer agent as a buyer and for the latter eventually to give evidence in court without revealing the prior involvement of the informer.' (Maguire and John, 'Covert and Deceptive Policing', 330)

[24] Released criminals too can be issued with a false identity by the police. One example of this in the UK would be the false identities given to Jon Venables and Robert Thompson who, at the age of ten, murdered two-year-old James Bulger in 1993.

Skolnick speaks of police work as falling into three stages: investigation (before arrest), interrogation (in police custody) and testimony (in court).[25] Concerning these stages, it is undoubtedly correct to say that, generally speaking, civilised society is more accepting of the police use of deception and lies at the investigative stage than the interrogative stage, and although allowed at times at both of these stages, it is certainly not accepted at the testimony stage. When police use of lies and deception is legally approved, the key concerns are ensuring suspects' rights are neither violated nor the fairness and reliability of evidence compromised.

Barker and Carter state: 'Lying and other deceptive practices are an integral part of the police officer's working environment. . . . Police officers are trained to lie and be deceptive in these law enforcement practices.'[26] They classify police lies into one of three categories: accepted, tolerated and deviant.[27] Accepted police lies are those in furtherance of legitimate policing methods/goals such as undercover work, as well as lies to the media and the public when, essentially, it is necessary for the common good.[28] Tolerated police lies are referred to as necessary evils, and one might say they essentially constitute those lies deemed necessary to fulfil the multifaceted policing role (including lying at the interrogatory stage), while, it would seem, conforming to legal and procedural restraints.[29] 'Deviant police lies are those which violate substantive or procedural law and/or police department rules and regulations.'[30] Barker and Carter subdivide deviant police lies into those in pursuit of 'perceived legitimate goals' and those in pursuit of 'illegitimate goals';[31] what one might equate with the terms referred to previously in this book as: 'bent-for-the-job' and 'bent-for-oneself'.[32] As regards this book's focus on noble-cause corruption (bent-for-the-job/pursuit of goals perceived as legitimate), Barker and Carter's examples include the practice of police fluffing up evidence to obtain a search warrant or to secure a conviction.[33]

In this book, we do not get into a discussion on the amount of lying that goes on, whether done legally or illegally by police officers during

---

[25] Skolnick, 'Deception by Police', 41.

[26] Barker and Carter, *Police Deviance*, 139.

[27] Ibid., 139–149. See also 155–157 .

[28] Ibid., 139–142.

[29] Ibid., 142–145.

[30] Ibid., 146.

[31] Ibid., 147 and 148 respectively.

[32] See secs. 2.1.2 Corruption and 7.3 Bent-For-The-Job Police Perjury.

[33] Barker and Carter, *Police Deviance*, 147.

their police work. It will be useful, all the same, to have some indication of the reality of lying within police work. The following citations offer some insight, though, admittedly, the amount of deception and lying by the police will probably differ from country to country.[34]

Peter Villiers asks in respect of policing, 'In what other trade, occupation or profession are people trained and encouraged to lie, not only to those whom they are entitled to deceive, as it were, but to their colleagues, friends and family.'[35] Similarly, Alpert and Noble state that:

> Police officers often tell lies; they act in ways that are deceptive, they [manipulate] people and situations, they coerce citizens, and are dishonest. They are taught, encouraged, and often rewarded for their deceptive practices. . . . Although they are allowed to be dishonest in certain circumstances, they are also required to be trustworthy, honest, and maintain the highest level of integrity. . . . To perform their job effectively, police officers lie.[36]

Furthermore, in the US, Jewish Police Chaplain, the late Professor Rabbi Stephen Passamaneck commented:

> Deception often provides the only means to get enough good information on a criminal enterprise to foil it or to catch a criminal in the performance of some crime. The development of a rather large and sophisticated array of deceptive practices in law enforcement has become more and more necessary of course in an age of electronic technology.[37]

Moreover, following eighteen months of fieldwork in a large US urban police force, including twelve weeks participation in recruit classes in a police academy, Hunt (of Hunt and Manning) reports:

> In the police academy, instructors encouraged recruits to lie in some situations, while strongly discouraging it in others. Officers are told it is "good police work," and encouraged to lie, to substitute guile for force, in situations of crisis intervention, investigation and interrogation, and especially with the mentally ill (Harris 1973). During classes on law and court testimony, on the other hand, students were taught

---

[34] In addition, recall the evidence of lying cited in Chapter 2, and note also *Appendix 5*.

[35] Villiers, *Better Police Ethics,* 75. Villiers is the editor of *The Journal of Ethics in Policing* and a former lecturer at Police Staff College, Bramshill.

[36] Alpert and Noble, 'Lies, True Lies', 237. Geoffrey P. Alpert is professor of criminology and criminal justice at the University of South Carolina. Jeffrey J. Noble Esq. is a commander with the Irvine Police Department in Southern Carolina. See also Moore, 'Ten (10) Ways Police Can Legally Lie To You'. Moore is a US San Diego criminal defence lawyer.

[37] Passamaneck, *Police Ethics and the Jewish Tradition*, 114.

that the use of deception in court was illegal, morally wrong and, unacceptable and would subject the officer to legal and departmental sanctions.[38]

In the US again, Professor Alpert and Commander Noble's research highlights a troubling challenge facing police officers. They state:

> [M[any recruits who enter police work wanting to be honest learn to lie in the academy, observe their training officers make changes in reports, reduce the seriousness of crime statistics in certain areas, and augment the information of warrants (Hunt & Manning, 1991). . . . After a while, it becomes a learned behavior and one of the common tools of the job.[39]

Scripture lying is something that isn't favored

4.2 CATECHISM'S TEACHING ON LYING

At paragraph CCC2 2482, the definitive edition of the *Catechism* cites Augustine's definition of a lie: 'A *lie* consists in speaking a falsehood with the intention of deceiving.'[40] It goes on to state:

> To lie is to speak or act against the truth in order to lead someone into error. (CCC2 2483)

> Lying consists in saying what is false with the intention of deceiving one's neighbour. (CCC2 2508)

We can see from this that the two essential elements of a lie are: (i) a falsehood, and (ii) intent to deceive. We previously noted that the *Catechism* also teaches that no lie can ever be justified because they are all deemed to be intrinsically evil: 'By its very nature, lying is to be condemned.' (CCC 2485) It is this definition of a lie combined with the absolute proscription of lying that causes problems for many when the obligation not to lie conflicts with other demands such as justice, compassion and maybe common sense.[41]

purpose: use speech for deception is a rejection of the gift of speech bc it fails to use speech for its appointed ends

[38] Hunt and Manning, 'The Social Context', 54. Reference to Harris is to Harris, R. *The Police Academy* (New York: Wiley, 1973). Footnote from original text (removed) explained how lies help deal with persons suffering from psychotic delusion by purporting to share in their delusions.

[39] Albert and Noble, 'Lies, True Lies', 249.

[40] The *Catechism* references this to St Augustine, *De mendacio*, 4, 5: Migne, *Patrologia latina* 40, 491.

[41] Note that Saul uses the 'murderer at the door' scenario (e.g. Gestapo in search of Jews) in her effort to show why it is wrong to think misleading is always preferable to lying.

Our particular focus is on the fact that the above teaching (as it stands) would mean that a police officer is never permitted to use any falsehood with intent to deceive ('lie') during police work. It is crucial to acknowledge this, lest some erroneously believe that such is not the case. The reader should note that this book is not challenging the absolute proscription of lying—though many would, no doubt, wish to do so. Rather, one is searching for the conceptual space needed to resolve the apparent tension that exists when an absolute proscription of lying conflicts with the demands of justice.[42]

The reasons why the Magisterium upholds an absolute proscription of lying needs to be carefully studied since it does not uphold this position out of a desire to make life difficult for people; rather, the Magisterium believes it is in our best interests to live by the absolute proscription of lying. First, their position is rooted in the eighth commandment: 'You shall not bear false witness against your neighbor.' (Ex 20:16) The *Catechism* teaches that the obligation not to lie flows from a prior obligation to bear witness to God who is the truth, and our human dignity requires and morally obliges us to follow the truth (CCC 2465–2467). In addition, the duty of Christians to witness to the Gospel 'is a transmission of the faith in words and deeds'. (CCC 2472) Furthermore: '*Martyrdom* is the supreme witness given to the truth of the faith: it means bearing witness even unto death.' (CCC 2473) Also, the *Catechism* teaches that lying lacks justice and charity, and damages trust, social relationships and hence society (CCC 2485 & 2486). Since the human act of telling a lie is deemed to be intrinsically evil (CCC 2485), like all intrinsically evil acts, these acts of lying which are evil in and of themselves are not pleasing to God 'because they radically contradict the good of the person made in his

---

After acknowledging that Kant thought it would be wrong to *lie* but okay to *mislead* the murderer instead, she says that most of us, in contrast, would 'do whatever is most likely to succeed in the goal of preventing murder—and that there is absolutely no moral difficulty with lying to the murderer'. (Saul, *Lying, Misleading*, 73)

[42] It is worth acknowledging that different degrees of seriousness (badness) are, understandably, attributed to lying. Wishing to spare the reader all the technicalities of this, we can simply note that the helpful lie (officious lie) is treated as the least evil of lies. Furthermore, to use Catholic speak about types of sin (mortal sin is serious sin, while venial sin is light sin but still sin all the same), the utterance of a helpful lie in itself would be a venial sin, though would become mortal if it damaged the virtues of justice and charity (see CCC 2484). Ring-fencing any lies uttered under oath in a court of law for the moment (i.e. perjury), the context of our consideration of the police use of lies is only in respect of the helpful lie. One is not, of course, ignoring the fact that some police officers will also lie maliciously too, though hopefully this is rare.

image'.[43] The fundamental teaching derived from the Apostle Paul (Rom 3:8) that it is not licit to do evil that good may come of it, therefore applies to all lies—even the so-called helpful lie.

What is one to do with the Catholic teaching on lying—besides, of course, adhering to it? The *Catechism*'s provisional edition (written several years before the publication of the definitive edition) also cites Augustine's definition of a lie (CCC1 2482). However, at paragraphs CCC1 2483 and CCC1 2508, Augustine's definition of a lie is developed by adding to the definition of lying the circumstance that the one spoken to 'has the right to know the truth' and 'the right to the truth' respectively. The precise texts read:

> To lie is to speak or act against the truth in order to lead into error someone who has the right to know the truth. (CCC1 2483)
>
> Lying consists in saying what is false with the intention of deceiving the neighbour who has the right to the truth. (CCC1 2508)

With this definition of lying, the absolute proscription against lying does not seem to be a problem since the act of uttering a falsehood with intent to deceive another who has *no right to the truth* does not amount to a lie. This would be the case, for example, with the so-called 'lie' to the Gestapo and the World Trade Centre scenario since in both situations one's interlocutor intends to use the truth for an evil reason—and because of this they have no right to the truth, hence no lie. Hence, when police officers use falsehood with intent to deceive those who have no right to the truth, by applying the above definition of lying, these utterances too would not constitute lying either. The faithful Catholic, however, is expected to adhere to the treatment of lying in the *Catechism*'s definitive edition, not its prior provisional version (which was subject to various amendments prior to the publication of the definitive text).[44]

By changing the definition of a lie, one changes the criterion for determining the object of the act of lying. Unless other factors can come into play in the process of identifying an act of lying, the definition of a lie one works with (in our case, the definition in the *Catechism*'s definitive edition), is *the* criterion for identifying acts of lying.

---

[43] John Paul, *Veritatis Splendor*, 80.
[44] For an analysis of why the *Catechism*'s definition of lying changed between its provisional and definitive editions, see Dixon, 'Police Lies', 168–171.

Where does one go from here? The faithful Catholic police officer reading the *Catechism*'s teaching on lying for guidance is, arguably, not given enough help. The *Catechism* offers this advice: 'No one is bound to reveal the truth to someone who does not have the right to know it.' (CCC 2489) At these times one should be 'silent' or use 'discreet language'.[45] (CCC 2489) The distinction made is that while there is an absolute rule not to lie, the rule about revealing the truth is conditional upon whether another has the right to the truth. While we all know what silence means, one may very well ask, what does discreet language mean? We explore this in detail in Chapter 6. For now, one can say that discreet language refers to speaking discreetly and ambiguously such that the truth is— hopefully—not revealed by the words spoken, while at the same time managing to avoid uttering a lie.

A common example would be when the vicar's wife tells a parishioner at the presbytery door that her husband is away on a course; the truthful meaning being a golf course, though the false meaning present in the ambiguous statement is that the vicar is on a clerical course. This sort of logic gets trickier, and arguably more dubious, as we shall soon see. Be that as it may, let us come back to the serious point: if neither silence nor discreet language protects a truth another has no right to, then many would argue that common sense demands the use of falsehood with intent to deceive—especially when revealing the truth is likely to cause serious harm.

It is reported that Catholic theologian, Janet Smith, suggests that if asked by the Vatican to debate the issue, many theologians nowadays would justify the act of speaking falsehoods against the perpetrators of evil who threaten innocent life. However, they are reluctant, at present, to defend this position because they do not wish to appear challenging Church teaching or encouraging such behaviour.[46] Furthermore, Smith is reported to have stated: 'The formulation of the first edition (of the Catechism) has not been officially repudiated, and I believe it is not necessarily incompatible with the formulation of the second.'[47]

There is, one believes, much truth in Smith's reasoning above. Elsewhere, Smith also states that the removal of the circumstance of 'to

---

[45] Commenting on this part of the *Catechism*, Selling states: 'It will be no surprise if the reader feels trapped at this point' (Selling, 'You Shall Love Your Neighbour', 286).

[46] As reported by EWTN News, 'Live Action'. The report includes comments made by Smith and others.

[47] Ibid.

one who has the right to the truth' from the definition of lying in the *Catechism*'s definitive edition does not necessarily mean the previous definition was wrong.[48] Rather, the change of wording did not manifest any doctrinal change but was an attempt to express better the unchanged deposit of the Catholic faith.[49] Smith's interpretation of the *Catechism*'s treatment of lying is relevant to our purposes because, in the next section, one argues that both definitions of lying in the *Catechism* can be shown to be equal to each other in their practical application.

4.3 INTERPRETING THE CATECHISM

Our purpose here is to consider whether one can legitimately interpret the definitive edition of the *Catechism*'s teaching on lying in a less restrictive way, such that the use of falsehood with intent to deceive is not ruled out entirely. One is seeking 'in a particular way an ever deeper understanding of the word of God found in the inspired Scriptures and handed on by the living Tradition of the Church'.[50] This seeking to interpret the *Catechism* in a less restrictive way is not an exercise in loophole theology to find ways of dodging the ramifications of the teaching of the Catholic Church on the issue of lying. Instead, in harmony with the Magisterium, it is a search to understand better and interpret the moral teaching of the Catholic Church in the light of shared human experience. One is, therefore, upholding Church teaching in this area of moral concern, while also finding the conceptual space to accommodate an intellectual approach that permits the utterance of falsehood with intent to deceive in a way that removes the tension between the absolute proscription of lying and the demands of justice.

The Church, via its definition of lying and absolute proscription thereof in the *Catechism*'s definitive edition, on the surface at least, seems to have backed itself into a morally untenable corner. The point is that,

---

[48] Smith, 'Fig Leaves and Falsehoods', 46. Smith notes that Pope John Paul II's Apostolic Letter *Laetemur Magnopere*, which accompanied the *Catechism*'s definitive edition, did not claim the provisional edition was erroneous; it is more the case that the definitive edition better expresses the deposit of the Catholic faith without there being any doctrinal change. Smith, I believe, is correct on this point. See John Paul II, *Laetamur Magnopere*.
[49] Smith, 'Fig Leaves and Falsehoods', 46.
[50] John Paul, *Veritatis Splendor*, 109. Pope John Paul II made use of these words in reference to the role of the Catholic theologian at the service of the Church. They originate from: Congregation for the Doctrine of the Faith, *Donum Veritatis*.

prima facie, Church teaching would, for example, neither permit one to utter a falsehood with intent to deceive (lie) the Gestapo to protect Jews whom one is hiding nor to the plane hijackers in our hypothetical scenario based on the events of 9/11. Also, it seems to prohibit the police use of falsehood with intent to deceive (lie) in the pursuance of lawful and legitimate policing objectives. Admittedly, some Catholics would, in contrast, maintain that what is morally untenable is the utterance of falsehood with intent to deceive (lie), always and everywhere, whether it be to the Gestapo, hijackers, or via its lawful use by the police.[51]

4.3.1 Ethical Context

An approach to the ethics of falsehood and lying made by Benedict Guevin, suggests that by appealing to the ethical context within which one speaks, one can utter falsehood with intent to deceive without it amounting to a lie.[52] Using the example of 'lying' to the Gestapo to protect innocent Jews, he argues that speaking a falsehood with intent to deceive is not a lie in this case because 'the commandment against lying does not even begin to operate in situations where there is not in existence "the mutual trust needed to live together in society"'.[53] Guevin states: 'The ethical context in which she willingly deceived the Gestapo is part of the morally objective dimension of her action, objectified by the practical reason.'[54] Essentially, Guevin is claiming that, in harmony with Aquinas' treatment of lying in the *Summa Theologiae* (*STh*), no lie has been uttered in this scenario because the virtue of truthfulness has not been violated.[55]

---

[51] In 2006, I wrote to the offices of Cardinal Schönborn, Archbishop of Vienna, seeking clarification about the change to the definition of lying at CCC 2483 and CCC 2508 between the *Catechism*'s provisional and definitive editions (Cardinal Schönborn was editing secretary for the drafting of the *Catechism*). In a letter of reply from an official within Cardinal Schönborn's offices, it was stated that CCC1 2483 and CCC1 2508 had erroneously included a circumstance (i.e. a right to the truth) within the definition of lying. As such, it was taken out. Furthermore, the letter stated that lying is always prohibited whether or not one has a right to the truth.

[52] Guevin, 'When a Lie Is Not a Lie'. Guevin's article is discussed briefly in Dixon, 'Principle of Objectified Circumstances', 576–577, and is referred to in Dixon, 'Police Lies'.

[53] Dixon, 'Principle of Objectified Circumstances', 576, citing Guevin, 'When a Lie Is Not a Lie', 273.

[54] Guevin, 'When a Lie Is Not a Lie', 273.

[55] Ibid., 267, 273–274, as noted in Dixon, 'Principle of Objectified Circumstances', 576. See Aquinas, *STh* II–II, q.q. 109–113.

Guevin's interpretation is an interesting one and highlights what is known as the social character of lying (i.e. an offence against justice).[56]

In like manner, Molinski states:

> Truthfulness is only right and rational insofar as it serves the purpose of communication between the speakers. But if it is exploited by one of the speakers to injure the other, human communication is actually impeded, on the level in keeping with human dignity. If the exploitation of the speaker by the questioner can only be avoided by the former's using a false form of words, this seems a necessary means for impeding misuse of speech.[57]

Similarly, Bonhoeffer states:

> An individual utterance is always part of a total reality which seeks expression in this utterance. If my utterance is to be truthful it must in each case be different according to whom I am addressing, who is questioning me, and what I am speaking about. The truthful word is not in itself constant; it is as much alive as life itself.[58]

For Guevin's approach concerning ethical context to be in harmony with the *Catechism*'s definitive edition, it requires that CCC2's definition of a lie is only meant to apply in situations where the context is one in which being truthful 'fosters the mutual trust needed to live together in society'.[59] The *Catechism* does not discuss this, it merely defines a lie (without the circumstance that one's interlocutor has a right to the truth), and classifies lying as intrinsically evil and is, hence, always prohibited. Moreover, in respect of police ethics, it would also need to be ascertained and agreed upon as to when police use of falsehood with intent to deceive does operate in situations which are lacking what one might call the necessary social trust. A situation of this type, one suggests, is when the police are dealing with those who are guilty of (or are suspected of) committing a crime.[60]

---

[56] See Molinski, 'Truthfulness', 1779–1780. In comparison, the internal character of lying refers to its offence against the truth.

[57] Molinski, 'Truthfulness', 1781–1782.

[58] Bonhoeffer, *Ethics*, 365.

[59] Guevin, 'When a Lie Is Not a Lie', 273. Noted in Dixon, 'Principle of Objectified Circumstances', 576.

[60] The next section deals with the application of speech acts and assertions within police work, and it has relevance to Guevin's focus on ethical context. Also, note in passing that a recent article by Christopher Nathan discusses undercover policing and argues that 'those who engage in wrongdoing make themselves morally liable to preventive

In light of Guevin's important point concerning the significance of ethical context to lying, one wonders whether the Church might consider introducing a principle to accommodate a distinction between those situations where the utterance of falsehood with intent to deceive is beneficial for society, from those situations when it is damaging to society. Such a principle would then legitimise the use of falsehood with intent to deceive to protect society, without it violating the absolute norm prohibiting lying. No such principle would, of course, be necessary if one used CCC1's definition of a lie since the reality of one's interlocutor not having a right to the truth (which would surely be when the interlocutor intends to harm society/others) means that a lie is not uttered according to CCC1's definition of a lie. Be that as it may, the faithful Catholic is required to adhere to CCC2's definition of a lie.

4.3.2 Speech Acts and Assertions

In seeking to resolve the issue of the absolute proscription of lying appearing too restrictive, Kemp and Sullivan state: 'We would like to suggest that there are cases, overlooked by the rigorists, in which saying what is false with the intent to deceive is not lying and thus does not fall under the scope of the absolute prohibition.'[61]

Key to their approach is the claim: 'A lie is an assertion *contra mentem*.'[62] In other words, an assertion is the claiming to another of what one believes to be true; and hence a lie is asserting what one does not believe to be true (i.e. a false assertion).[63] In responding to possible objections, Kemp and Sullivan point out that it is because speech acts are used for more purposes in addition to making assertions, does it make sense not to interpret the absolute prohibition of lying as being against all speech acts *contra mentem*.[64] Rather, what makes sense is to do what they have suggested and interpret the absolute prohibition of lying as applying only to assertions *contra mentem*. Their position on this point appears correct since, as they point out, it would be ludicrous to brandish as lying such

---

activities' which he says include the police use of deceptive and manipulative methods (Nathan, 'Liability to Deception and Manipulation', 370).
[61] Kemp and Sullivan, 'Speaking Falsely and Telling Lies', 159.
[62] Ibid. Emphasis belongs to Kemp and Sullivan.
[63] 'Properly defined, an assertion is rather the use of a linguistic form which by convention is used in the circumstances of utterance to represent what the speaker believes to be true.' (Ibid., 160)
[64] Ibid., 165–167.

things as 'drama, disputation, and narrative fiction' which is what would happen if one erroneously understood the nature of a lie to be 'a speech act *contra mentem*' rather than being 'an assertion *contra mentem*'.[65]

Kemp and Sullivan make the logical step of stating that 'one cannot make assertions *contra mentem* in situations in which one cannot make assertions at all. So, there are some situations in which nothing that one says could be a lie'.[66] The argument progresses thus by not seeking to ascertain all the sufficient conditions necessary to make assertions even possible, but to identify a necessary condition that is lacking.[67] The key point established is that a necessary condition for assertion-making to be even possible is that there is 'a reasonable expectation that the speaker is using speech to communicate his thoughts to us'.[68] There are many examples of when there would be no expectation that assertions are being made—and even if desired, it would be most difficult to make such an assertion in these contexts.[69] The examples offered include a prior explicit statement by the speaker informing the hearer to not treat what one will say as an assertion; speech acts in conventions such as plays, ritual speech, bluffing games; and conventions such as the magician, comedian and diplomacy.[70]

Kemp and Sullivan consider so-called lies used during wartime and the keeping of secrets in general. First, they claim that when one country declares war (which means they are likely to come under violent attack), there is also implicit in the message a warning to the enemy of an intent to deceive.[71] This implicit intent to deceive is evident by the fact that certain signs such as the Red Cross and the waving of a white flag are universally agreed to be off-limits even during wartime as being methods by which one could legitimately deceive the enemy.[72] Hence, so-called

---

[65] Ibid., 165.

[66] Ibid., 160.

[67] Ibid.

[68] Ibid., 161. In comparison, one notes the philosopher Saul's endorsement of Carson's use of the term 'warranting' to signify a truth statement: 'If one warrants the truth of a statement, then one promises or guarantees, either explicitly or implicitly, that what one says is true. ([Carson, 'The Definition of Lying'] 2006: 294)'. (Saul, Lying, Misleading, 10) The point is also made that, as Carson acknowledges, in the absence of reasons to think otherwise, the 'presumption of warrant' is the norm (Ibid.). This 'warranting context' seems to be equal to our 'assertion-making context'.

[69] Ibid., 160–161.

[70] Ibid.

[71] Ibid., 162–163.

[72] Ibid., 162.

wartime lies are not lies at all since one cannot make assertions in this context. In other words, during wartime it is not reasonable to expect the enemy to be making assertions via its speech acts—hence, it is not possible to lie in this context.[73] It would seem this argument is plausible as applied to wartime lies, provided the hearer in any particular interlocution has a reasonable belief that his interlocutor is, in fact, the enemy. However, if the hearer has no reason to believe his interlocutor is the enemy, then, all things considered, he would have a reasonable expectation that the speaker is making assertions—and hence it is possible to lie. Second, in applying their above reasoning to the problem of keeping secrets in general, the nub of their position is that, whether it is a busybody or an aggressor seeking knowledge of a secret, it is not reasonable in these situations for the busybody or aggressor to expect their interlocutor to be using speech to communicate one's thoughts. Therefore, in situations of this type, Kemp and Sullivan state: 'The very act of asking the questions undermines the conditions necessary for making assertions.'[74] Such is the case, they claim, in the Gestapo/Jew type scenario and indeed 'all cases of legitimate secrecy in which pressure is placed on the secret-keeper, but no further'.[75]

Kemp and Sullivan refer to Grotius' definition of a lie as an example of what they call 'revisionism'; that is to say those critics of the rigorist/traditionalist approach who seek to revise the definition of a lie.[76] They reject 'revisionism' as 'a satisfactory solution to the liar-betrayer dilemma'.[77] Despite their desire to distance their position from Grotius' definition of a lie, which they consider to be too lax, it is not clear, why, logically, Kemp and Sullivan's position differs—in practice—from the application of Grotius' definition of a lie. This is because if one's interlocutor does not have a right to the truth, then it does seem that any

---

[73] They extend their logic to spies, stating: 'The enemy is not in a very good position to recognize all the agents of the nation with whom [one] is at war. So, they believe the spy who says he's a businessman from a neutral country. They shouldn't; again, they've been warned.' (Ibid., 162–163) A problem with this, it seems, is that since a spy's identity is not known, one could argue that one should not, therefore, believe anyone at all during wartime since, for all one knows, anyone could be a spy. That said, one could argue that it is, self-evidently, reasonable to believe one's interlocutor is *not* a spy until one has reason to suspect otherwise.

[74] Ibid., 163.

[75] Ibid., 164.

[76] Ibid., 158. Grotius' definition of a lie is explained in sec. 5.1.3 Grotius and Newman. It is the same as the definition of a lie in the *Catechism*'s provisional edition.

[77] Ibid., 159.

question asked amounts to an inquiry (by a busybody) into a legitimate secret and thus it is unreasonable for the inquisitor (busybody) to expect the speaker to be communicating his thoughts. Hence a necessary condition for making assertions is lacking, viz. a reasonable expectation that the speaker is communicating his thoughts.[78] It is a shame that Kemp and Sullivan, writing in 1993 and thus before the *Catechism*'s 1997 Latin definitive edition, neither refer to the definition of a lie in the *Catechism*'s 1992 French provisional edition nor acknowledge that it too, some might argue, conforms to this so-called 'revisionism' since it 're-defined' the lie.

Our concern is with the application of the *Catechism* 2000 English definitive edition's teaching on lying and definition of a lie. It states: 'By its very nature, lying is to be condemned. It is a profanation of speech, whereas the purpose of speech is to communicate known truth to others.' (CCC 2485) The default setting of assertive speech is, it seems, that one is expected to assert the truth.[79] Common sense surely dictates that the *Catechism* does not mean that speech is *only* to be used 'to communicate known truth to others'. Self-evidently there is more than one purpose of speech: while the *main* purpose is to communicate truth to others (make assertions), this is *not* the *only* purpose. Speech is used, for example, in fiction, jokes and the issuing of commands. When the *Catechism* states lying 'is a profanation of speech,' it is reasonable, therefore, to interpret this as referring only to assertions and not speech acts in general.

Furthermore, one suggests that the CCC2 definition of a lie should *not*, somewhat surprisingly, apply to instances when one is speaking to one who does not have a right to the truth. On these occasions, what is said would not appear to amount to an assertion because the inquirer would not hold a reasonable expectation that the speaker is communicating his thoughts.[80] Kemp and Sullivan seem logically obliged to agree since they state: 'Can anyone reasonably expect to be told the truth about matters that are, objectively speaking properly secret?'[81] As previously noted, Kemp and Sullivan's article was published after the 1992 French provisional edition and before the 1997 Latin definitive edition. Ironically, their approach, unwittingly, appears to be capable of resolving the

---

[78] Ibid., 163–164.
[79] On this point, MacIntyre refers to 'the rule prescribing truth telling . . . That rule governs speech-acts of assertion. To assert is always and inescapably to assert as true, and learning that truth is required from us in assertions is therefore inseparable from learning what it is to assert'. (MacIntyre, *Ethics and Politics*, 103)
[80] Same point made previously in respect of Grotius.
[81] Kemp and Sullivan, 'Speaking Falsely and Telling Lies', 163.

problem of the definitive edition of the *Catechism*'s definition of lying being too restrictive. It does this, albeit, at the expense of the practical application of the definition of lying in the *Catechism*'s definitive edition being tantamount to the practical application of the definition of lying in the *Catechism*'s provisional edition.

A new analogy can be drawn between the different definitions of lying in the *Catechism*'s two editions and the Church's teaching on the two essential elements of the marital act (aka sexual intercourse). In respect of the marital act, the Church speaks of 'the inseparable connection, established by God, which man on his own initiative may not break, between the unitive significance and the procreative significance which are both inherent to the marriage act'.[82] It does not take much imagination to view the procreative significance as the internal character and the unitive significance as the social character of the marriage act, both elements being *inherent* to the marital act.

Deliberations over the ethicality of lying have, as noted previously, had recourse to the terms internal character and social character of a lie: internal character referring to the truth-asserting aspect of speech, and the social character referring to the requirement to communicate justly with others. Both the internal and social aspects are, it seems, inherent in the correct use of communicative speech (aka assertions). The definition of a lie in the *Catechism*'s definitive edition, when taken in isolation from any context of its use, has, by its removal of the unitive (social) aspect of speech, done to communicative speech what artificial birth control, by its removal of the procreative (internal) aspect of sex, has done to the marital act. Therefore, similar to the way the Church teaches that man cannot break the inseparable bond between the two significances of the marital act, it would seem that man cannot break the two significances of communicative speech (assertions): its internal character and social character when applying the definition of a lie to the context of life

The definition of a lie in the *Catechism*'s provisional edition contains both these elements of communicative speech, whereas the definition of a lie in the *Catechism*'s definitive edition does not. But crucially, the *application* of CCC2's definition does contain both elements (internal and social) when its application is understood to be relevant only to assertion-making contexts. That is, in contexts where one's interlocutor necessarily has a reasonable expectation that one is speaking the truth, such as in situations when one has a right to the truth. Furthermore, it seems correct

---

[82] Paul VI, *Humanae Vitae*, 12.

to say that this otherwise inseparable bond is *naturally* broken by the circumstances when one does not have an assertion-making context.[83] The issue for us now is to explore when it is or is not reasonable to expect the police to be making assertions, and hence lying is or is not possible.

4.4 POLICING AND ASSERTION-MAKING CONTEXTS

Are there situations where it is not reasonable to expect a police officer to be making an assertion? If so, based on the distinction between speech acts *contra mentem* and assertions *contra mentem*, in these situations a police officer's utterance of falsehood with intent to deceive would not be a lie.

Kemp and Sullivan briefly apply their approach to the police. As previously noted, they claim that the unreasonableness of expecting to be told the truth concerning secrets—which thereby destroys the conditions necessary to make assertions and hence makes lying impossible—applies 'to all cases of legitimate secrecy in which pressure is placed on the secret-keeper, but no further'.[84] They also state that 'victims of unjust persecution may legitimately keep their identities secret and use a false identity in its place. Spies attempting to uncover the secrets of aggressors and *policemen fighting crime may do the same*'.[85] Furthermore, according to their approach, while the police can protect their identities by use of falsehood with intent to deceive without committing a lie, Kemp and Sullivan make the specific point that it is still possible to make assertions to suspects in criminal cases.[86] They give the following examples of police deceit which would be illicit if done by lying: 'leading a suspect to believe that an accomplice has confessed, exaggerating the seriousness of the offense, falsely saying that the victim has died (or has recovered), claiming that evidence has been found, and disguising police officers'.[87] Kemp and

---

[83] One could also relate this *natural* break in the two inherent significances of communicative speech to the natural break in the two inherent significances of the marital act when the woman's cycle makes her *naturally* infertile.

[84] Ibid., 164.

[85] Ibid. Emphasis added. They do not think their principle can extend much beyond the cases already cited. They assert rather than argue for this position, and they see this limitation as a strength on the basis that their principle would not become guilty of the charge of being too lax as regards the justification of the use of falsehood with intent to deceive.

[86] Ibid.

[87] Ibid.

Sullivan's approach, *as presented and understood by them*, does not, therefore, provide a solution to the problem of police lying.

It is necessary to cite in full the only detailed specific police example Kemp and Sullivan offer, in order to distinguish it from this book's application and development of their approach to police practice. Referring to a 1983 Iowa murder case (*State v. Oliver*), Kemp and Sullivan comment:

> Leeper [a polygraph operator] asked Oliver [a suspect], in five separate questions, which of five objects had been used to tie the victim. In contrast to the "truthful" reaction he received on mentioning the other four objects, he obtained an "inconclusive" reaction when the telephone cord (which he knew had been used) was mentioned.
>
> Leeper then went around the desk, beside Oliver, and talked to her. . . . Leeper claims he said that "there are problems with the test". . . . Oliver claims he told her that the machine "went haywire" and that he knew she had lied. In any event, Oliver broke down, cried, and then confessed.[88]

Kemp and Sullivan conclude that it was possible for the police officer Leeper to make assertions to the suspect Oliver. Hence, they reject the moral permissibility of the police use of falsehood with intent to deceive in this situation (i.e. 'the machine "went haywire"') because they conclude it amounts to a lie since it is possible to make assertions. In contrast, my following broader application and development of the distinction between speech acts and assertions will include argument to show that in a situation such as Leeper and Oliver's, it is not reasonable for a suspect to expect a police officer to be making assertions—and hence police use falsehood with intent to deceive is not a lie.

Use is now made of Skolnick's threefold typology of police work.[89] First, the testimonial stage of police work is, it would seem, clearly illustrative of a situation in which it is most certainly reasonable to expect the speaker (i.e. the person giving evidence) to be using speech to communicate his thoughts to the court (i.e. to be making assertions). The fact that before giving evidence, a witness is required to take the oath or affirmation to confirm his intention to speak 'the truth, the whole truth and nothing but the truth' makes clear that in the context of the courtroom one is dealing with assertions. It is the case that the court has a legal right to the truth, and one assumes a moral right to the truth too,

---

[88] Ibid., 164–165.
[89] Skolnick, 'Deception by Police', 41.

so the court has a reasonable expectation of being told the truth from those giving evidence. Hence it is an assertion making context, lying is possible, and therefore the use of falsehood with intent to deceive is morally illicit.[90]

At the interrogatory stage, the stage within which the Leeper and Oliver case occurred, one asks: is it reasonable for the arrested person to expect the interrogating police officer to be using speech to make assertions? To help answer this question, we can draw a comparison with wartime lies. We saw previously that Kemp and Sullivan suggested that *implicit* in the declaration of war is the warning to the enemy of an intention to deceive—hence they should not expect the enemy during wartime to be using speech to communicate their thoughts. Similarly, one could argue that *implicit* in the arresting of a person (whether that person is guilty or not of the crime for which he is under suspicion) is the warning of an intent to deceive during the subsequent interrogatory stage.[91] The arrested person should not, it seems, at least not all the time, expect the interrogating police officer to be using speech to communicate his thoughts to him during the interrogatory process. Put another way, the arrested person should expect a certain amount of deception by the police in their efforts to get at the truth, and as such, it is *not* reasonable to expect a police officer to be making assertions during the interrogatory process.

The suggestion that there is an *implicit* intent to deceive in the process of being arrested seems to hold some sway, especially if one further compares this situation again to the case of wartime lies. Kemp and Sullivan noted that particular signs during wartime, such as the Red Cross and the waving of the white flag, are universally agreed to be off-limits as a means of deceiving the enemy—thereby enforcing the claim that other

---

[90] We shall return to the issue of testimonial deception in secs. 6.4 Mental Reservation in Court and 7.3 Bent-for-the-Job Police Perjury.

[91] It is acknowledged, however, that neither the United States' practice of a Miranda warning nor the United Kingdom's use of a police caution following arrest make any *explicit* suggestion that police deception may be used during the subsequent interrogatory stage. Perhaps an updating of the Miranda warning and the police caution could make *explicit* the possibility that the police may use deceptive methods during the subsequent interrogatory stage. For an explanation of the Miranda warning, see Montaldo, 'Miranda Warning'. For details of the police caution, see Home Office, *Policy Paper PACE*, sec. 3.5. Kleinig points out that the Miranda warning 'does not automatically rule out all deception, and some interrogatory deception has been thought permissible. . . . Obviously there are limits to the deception in which interrogating officers may engage'. (Kleinig, *Ethics of Policing*, 140)

methods of deception are not off-limits.[92] Similarly, at the interrogatory stage of police work, to deny an arrested person his legal rights, whether by lying or some other way, is also universally agreed to be off-limits—thereby endorsing indirectly the claim that 'lies' used at the interrogatory stage which do *not* deny the arrested person his legal rights are not off-limits.[93] Therefore, an interpretation of the absolute proscription of lying as applying only to assertions *contra mentem* and not speech acts *contra mentem*, can offer a way of making morally licit the police use of falsehood with intent to deceive at the interrogatory stage of police work, provided there is no denial of the legal rights of the arrested person.

At the investigative stage of police work, the use of lies by the police is far more pervasive and more readily accepted and endorsed by society. Is it reasonable for the public (both criminal and law-abiding) to expect police officers at the investigative stage to be using speech to communicate their thoughts (i.e. to be making assertions)? To help answer this question, we can once again draw a comparison with wartime lies. We saw that one could construe the enemy during wartime as having received an implicit warning to be prepared to be deceived. Similarly, one could argue that those elements of society who are engaging in criminal activity have, by their very engagement in such action, given *their* implicit acknowledgement that they expect the police to intend to deceive them when trying to detect their criminal activity. 'Criminals can hardly express surprise if they are investigated by deceptive means.'[94] Hence, one could argue that the very act of engaging in criminal activity undermines the conditions necessary for police officers to make assertions when speaking to these criminals during the process of carrying out their *lawful* investigations. If investigating police officers use illegal methods, such as torture, the planting of evidence or the use of blackmail, even the criminal fraternity would protest against what is a violation of their human rights. It is unreasonable, therefore, for criminals to expect police officers to be using speech to communicate their thoughts to them (i.e. making assertions) when lawfully investigating. Consequently, under these conditions, the use of falsehood with intent to deceive by the police against criminals would not amount to a lie.

---

[92] Cf. Kemp and Sullivan, 'Speaking Falsely and Telling Lies', 162.

[93] By saying universally agreed, one means this is the norm by which society expects its police to conduct themselves. As might be expected, there will always be individuals who wish to flout these socially approved norms.

[94] Kleinig, *Ethics of Policing*, 133.

During their investigative work, police officers will also dialogue with law-abiding citizens and may need to use falsehood with intent to deceive them as part of the process of catching criminals. The question is: do law-abiding citizens have a reasonable expectation that police officers are using speech to communicate their thoughts to them (i.e. are making assertions)? The answer requires two perspectives. First, *at the time of being spoken to* by a police officer, it is reasonable to say a law-abiding citizen would expect a police officer to be making assertions.[95] Second, if the investigative context of the police speech became known to the law-abiding citizen *retrospectively*, it is reasonable to conclude that the law-abiding citizen would give consent to being so deceived in this way on the basis that the police officer was lawfully doing his job.[96] As such, law-abiding citizens would not expect, with hindsight, police officers to have been making assertions to them when they were engaged in lawful investigative work.[97] If the analysis so far is correct, it seems reasonable to suggest the following. Law-abiding citizens, by being law-abiding citizens, *implicitly* give their consent to be subjected to falsehoods with intent to deceive by the police when the police are acting in the lawful execution of their investigative duties. With this tacit consent, investigating police officers' use of falsehoods with intent to deceive law-abiding citizens, when lawfully performing their policing duties, does not amount to a lie.

The notion of public consent, implicit or otherwise, seems to be in harmony with the Home Office's document discussing the definition of 'policing by consent' in which it states:

> It should be noted that it [policing by consent] refers to the power of the police coming from the common consent of the public, as opposed to the power of the

---

[95] This applies whether or not the police officer's police status was known to the law-abiding citizen.

[96] It is acknowledged that this approach reflects one of Grotius' cited cases in which there is no right to the truth and hence falsehood with intent to deceive does not amount to a lie. That is, where a false statement benefits the deceived who will later approve of being so deceived, as in an untrue statement to benefit a sick friend (Grotius, *On the Law*, bk. 3, ch. 1, XIV).

[97] One notes that having conducted a preliminary survey and study of American and British police, police superiors and civilians on the acceptability of police deceptive tactics, Panzarella and Funk state: 'Only minor differences were found between these different groups in terms of their approval of deception tactics. All groups showed a generally high level of approval.' (Panzarella and Funk, 'Police Deception Tactics', 133)

state. It does not mean the consent of an individual. No individual can chose to withdraw his or her consent from the police, or from a law.[98]

Note also, that since this common consent comes from the public, not an individual, and that no individual can withdraw his consent from the police, it further supports the claim that at the investigative and interrogatory stages of police work, when the public approves of the police deceiving and lying when lawfully carrying out their duties, then any protestations by individuals against these socially approved police practices do not negate this common public consent.

In summary, by applying the speech act/assertion distinction to police work, when one has a moral right to the truth from the police, it is reasonable to expect the police to be making assertions, and hence lying is possible. All the same, if and when one does not have a moral right to the truth from the police then it is not reasonable to expect the police to be making assertions, and hence lying is not possible. While Kemp and Sullivan do not and probably would not extend their approach to lying in the way I have done, the argument offered in this analysis logically follows. The approach taken provides a solution to the problem of institutionalised police lying for Roman Catholic police officers, and, possibly, the Roman Catholic problem of lying in general. Even if one does not entertain the suggestion that Kemp and Sullivan's approach equates to the practical application of Grotius' definition of a lie, their method can still be used to morally justify the use of falsehood with intent to deceive by the police. This is so if there is a social expectation for the lawful use of falsehood with intent to deceive at the investigative and interrogatory stages of police work.[99]

4.5 SUMMARY

In this chapter, we acknowledged the pervasive presence of lying within society, society's general disapproval of lying, as well as the not uncommon belief that exceptions to the norm against lying can be morally justified. We also noted that police work can be divided up into three stages: testimonial, interrogatory and investigative, and that lying might

[98] Home Office, *Definition of policing by consent.*
[99] Recall Kemp and Sullivan's claim that conventions (social expectations), such as those relating to plays, ritual speech, wartime, games, jokes, etc., can determine that speech acts in these and such like context are not to be taken as assertions.

occur at any of these stages. Police lying is certainly not acceptable at the testimonial stage (at least most people would agree with this), but its legitimate use at the two other stages of police work is accepted, though by how much and in what circumstances are a matter of debate, and opinions do differ between societies. We also considered the *Catechism*'s treatment of lying and noted the change to the way it defines a lie. We explored different ways to interpret the *Catechism*'s teaching on lying, in order to soften the impact of its current definition of lying when combined with lying's absolute proscription; namely, the ethical context within which one speaks, and the distinction between speech acts and assertions. We have sought a way to uphold and interpret Church teaching on lying, while also removing the tension that exists between this teaching and the demands of justice. This logic was applied to policing.

You shall not bear false witness against your neighbour.
—The eighth commandment (Ex 20:16)

5

LYING: AND TRADITION

This chapter makes a selective and chronological overview of the treatment of lying within the Christian tradition, to see what light it might shed on the use of lies within police work. After that, we consider what help the Christian just war tradition and the associated pacifist stance can offer to our consideration of the use of lies by the police.

5.1 CHRISTIAN TRADITION AND LYING

We begin with Scripture, some of the Early Church Fathers, fourth-century Augustine of Hippo and then to Thomas Aquinas in the thirteenth century. After this, we move to the seventeenth century to consider the significant contribution of Hugo Grotius, the nineteenth-century ideas of John Henry Newman, arriving then at the twentieth century to review the thoughts of Alasdair MacIntyre. We also consider how, from the second half of the twentieth century, the issue of lying links into the challenge the ethical theory of proportionalism has brought to the Magisterium's teaching on the evaluation of human acts. Our selective historical journey brings us to our destination: the significant change in the *Catechism*'s definition of lying between its provisional and definitive editions, to which we previously referred.

5.1.1. Scripture and Early Church Fathers

Texts such as the eighth commandment of the Decalogue, 'You shall not bear false witness against your neighbor' (Ex 20:16), 'You destroy those who speak lies' (Ps 5:6) and 'a lying mouth destroys the soul' (Ws 1:11), suggest to some an absolute prohibition of lying. Other parts of the Bible, for example, Rahab's lie (Jos 2:1–14) and the Hebrew midwives' lies (Ex 1:15–21), suggest to others that some lies can be morally permissible if, in a particular set of circumstances, it is the just and loving thing to do.[1] The eighth commandment, in itself, will not settle the issue of lying, any more than the sixth commandment (thou shall not kill) will resolve the matter of when killing is permissible.[2]

Julius A. Dorszynski argues that prior to the teachings of Augustine of Hippo (354–430), most Christian writers upheld the absolute prohibition of lying.[3] Others, says Dorszynski, argued for the moral justification of exceptions to this prohibition of lying.[4] Scholars from both positions claim to have found biblical evidence to support their respective views. Boniface Ramsey acknowledges two such approaches to lying in the early Church and notes that the allowing of exceptions to the rule against lying seems to be the older of the two traditions, though because it is older does not, in itself, make it correct.[5] Over the centuries, the scenario of the pursuing murderer in respect of whom the need to lie appears necessary to protect a potential victim from harm has been a frequent test case used to assess the rigorous prohibition of lying for its moral credibility.[6] It would be instructive now to refer to Rahab's lie in the story about the hiding of Joshua's spies (Jos 2:1–14) and the Hebrew midwives' lies (Ex 1:15–21).

Rahab lied to protect two Israelite spies she was hiding in her house from soldiers of the king of Jericho. The Hebrew midwives Shiphrah and Puah lied to the king of Egypt about why they had not obeyed the king's instruction to kill any newborn males they had helped deliver. However, concerning God's treatment of Rahab and the Hebrew midwives,

---

[1] Rahab's lie and the Hebrew midwives' lies, discussed shortly, are examples of the helpful lie.

[2] My thanks to an anonymous reader for this point. It is unjustified killing (murder) that is absolutely prohibited, not killing per se. Using the same logic, some might argue that it is unjustified lying which is at the heart of the eighth commandment. A possible link between the justification of violence and the justification of deception is developed in sec. 5.2 Just War Tradition (JWT), Pacifism and Police Lies, with an exploratory application of the just war tradition and pacifism to the police use of lies.

[3] Dorszynski cites the following who upheld an absolute proscription of lying: St. Clement of Rome, St. Basil, St. Prosper, Eusebius of Caesarea, and St. Jerome (Dorszynski, *Catholic Teaching*, 16, fn. 7).

[4] Dorszynski cites the following who permitted exceptions to the norm against lying: Clement of Alexandria, Origen, St. Chrysostom, J. Cassian, St. Hilary of Poitiers, and John Climacus (Dorszynski, *Catholic Teaching*, 17, fn. 8).

[5] Ramsey, 'Two Traditions', 532.

[6] Augustine considered this situation himself. See Augustine, *De mendacio*, 23 and Augustine, *Contra mendacium*, 32–34.

Augustine comments that what 'was rewarded in them was, not their deceit, but their benevolence; benignity of mind, not iniquity of lying'.[7] Aquinas endorses Augustine's teaching on this point, stating that they 'were rewarded, not for their lie, but for their fear of God, and for their good-will, which latter [sic] led them to tell a lie'.[8] This interpretation of the Hebrew midwives' lies is also endorsed by Grisez who makes the point that their self-defence lie (which cannot be justified) was a subsequent act independent of the previous act of fear of God (for which they were praised).[9] Then, in respect of Rahab's lie, others, such as Barnes, justify it. He states:

> Anger is normally regarded as wrong (e.g. Pr 29:22; Eph 4:31), but in a fallen world, anger is a part of a godly response to sin (cf. Mk 3:5; Eph 4:26–27). So too with lying . . . Rahab had the right – indeed, the obligation – to deceive the men of Jericho. She would have been guilty in an unfallen world, but in a fallen world, it seems that God has justified Rahab's words (Jm 2:25).[10]

In other words, only in an imperfect world is there a perceived need at times to utter helpful 'lies' to one who does not have a right to the truth; in a perfect world, there is no need since there is no evil present for these 'lies' to combat. And, so it is with policing: heaven, as it were, does not need the police.[11]

5.1.2 Augustine and Aquinas

Augustine: Augustine upheld an absolute prohibition on lying. Ramsey informs us that '[i]t was this absolute prohibition, stamped with all the weight of Augustine's considerable authority, that formed the tradition on lying that was embraced by the Western Church'.[12] It is in his works, *De mendacio*, *Contra mendacium* and *The Enchiridion on Faith, Hope and Love*,

---

[7] Augustine, *Contra mendacium,* 32.
[8] Aquinas, *STh* II–II, q. 110, a. 3, ad. 2.
[9] Grisez, *Way of the Lord Jesus, vol. 2,* 407, fn. 34. Had Grisez applied the definition of lying in the 1994 provisional edition of the *Catechism* (also available in the original1992 French edition, a year prior to his 1993 publication) to these and similar cases, he may have drawn a different conclusion.
[10] Barnes, 'Was Rahab's Lie a Sin?', 8.
[11] Not so in Vatican City. In addition to the Swiss Guard, it has its own police force: the Gendarmerie Corps of Vatican City State. Apparently, one has to be a practising Catholic in order to join.
[12] Ramsey, 'Two Traditions', 514.

that Augustine set out his position on lying.[13] He claimed that a lie consists in asserting something one does not believe to be true with the intention of deceiving the hearer into erroneously believing that the speaker thinks the assertion to be true.[14] Augustine concisely stated the essential element of his teaching on lying as follows:

> But every liar says the opposite of what he thinks in his heart, with purpose to deceive. Now it is evident that speech was given to man, not that men might therewith deceive one another, but that one man might make known his thoughts to another. To use speech, then, for the purpose of deception, and not for its appointed end, is a sin. Nor are we to suppose that there is any lie that is not a sin, because it is sometimes possible, by telling a lie, to do service to another.[15]

In explaining Augustine's position, Paul Griffiths says that Augustine is teaching that when we lie, we incoherently reject the gift of speech (speech being the gift that makes lying possible); similarly to commit suicide is to incoherently reject the gift of life (life being the gift that makes suicide possible).[16] In other words, speech is God's gift to us so that we may speak truthfully; to lie is to fail to treat speech as a gift from God. Augustine, one notes, also classified lying into degrees of greater or lesser seriousness, while still maintaining that all lies are sinful and therefore never to be permitted. Augustine did though acknowledge the difficulty in upholding this absolute prohibition, especially as regards the officious lie, the lie to help. Even so, as Ramsey informs us, Augustine's powerful influence and legacy in the Church ensured that his definition of lying (a false statement with intent to deceive) and the absolute prohibition thereof was the dominant position within the Western Church.[17]

Aquinas: In the thirteenth century, Thomas Aquinas, in his *Summa Theologiae*, endorsed the Augustinian absolute prohibition of lying. Aquinas categorised lies according to their degree of sinfulness, the mischievous lie (harmful lie), jocose lie (joke) and officious lie (helpful lie) and linked these into Augustine's degrees of lying.[18] Aquinas added the qualification that intent to deceive was not part of the essence of a lie; it

---

[13] Augustine, *The Enchiridion*.

[14] Augustine, *De mendacio*, 4, 5.

[15] Augustine, *The Enchiridion*, 22. The issue of the purpose of speech, to which Augustine refers, is considered within our discussion of Aquinas.

[16] Griffiths, 'The Gift and the Lie', 13–22.

[17] Ramsey, 'Two Traditions', 514 and 531.

[18] Aquinas, *STh* II–II, q. 110.2c.

merely completed it.[19] In short, for Aquinas, if one makes a false statement, one lies regardless of whether any intention to deceive is present in the speaker.[20] For all that, like Augustine before him, Aquinas upheld the absolute prohibition of lying: "'Be not willing to make any manner of lie.'"[21]

John Finnis, commenting on Aquinas' teaching on lying, states:

> [The basis for Aquinas' upholding of the absolute proscription of lying] is not, as many have hastily supposed, that lying is contrary to the natural function of tongue or speech. There are several reasons why that could not be a ground for Aquinas' position; most obviously, it is incompatible with his acceptance that much speech has nothing to do with truth or falsity; and it jars with his thesis that one can lie with a nod, a wink, a movement of one's finger.[22]

Finnis adds that for Aquinas, the fundamental wrongness of lying derives from the fact that when one communicates one asserts what one believes to be true and that '[a]ssertion is an act of self-disclosure (and veracity is a matter of personal authenticity).'[23] Furthermore, upon reflection of

---

[19] Ibid., q. 110.1c & ad. 3.

[20] For our purposes, what is important is the absolute proscription of lying; whether intent to deceive is (Augustine) or is not (Aquinas) part of the essence of a lie is not a concern for us. Note in passing, the philosopher Saul's comment that 'contrary to what almost everyone who has discussed the subject thinks—an intention to deceive is not required for an utterance to count as a lie' (Saul, *Lying, Misleading*, 10). It is surprising that Saul makes no reference to Aquinas on this matter. Furthermore, MacIntyre also points out that for Aquinas: 'Even without an intention to deceive, the intentional assertion of what is false is wrong ([*STh*] q. 110, 1 resp. and 3 ad. 6)' (MacIntyre, *Ethics and Politics*, 106).

Saul does provide an interesting example in support of the view that intent to deceive is not necessary for a lie to be uttered. She uses a scenario of Carson's (2006) involving courtroom testimony where a witness, fearing for his life if he admits he witnessed a murder, denies he has so witnessed it, even though CCTV camera evidence used in court has already proven he did so witness the event; hence the witness knows he won't deceive anyone, and is therefore not intending to deceive anyone by his false denial. Saul says that it remains obvious to us that this person has still lied when giving evidence— even though he is not trying to deceive anyone (Saul, *Lying, Misleading*, 8–10). What makes the above courtroom scenario interesting is that it is similar to the claim, by Seabrook, that police officers do, at times, falsely claim when giving evidence that they gave the caution after arrest, knowing that those in court do not believe the caution was actually given (Seabrook, *Coppers*, 60. Seabrook's comment is cited in *Appendix 5*).

[21] Aquinas, *STh* II–II, q. 110, a. 3sc, citing Si 7:14.

[22] Finnis, *Aquinas*, 155. Footnote references from Finnis' text have been removed for ease of citing.

[23] Ibid., 157.

Aquinas' treatment of lying, Finnis states that 'one lies if and only if one asserts a proposition as true, believing it to be false'.[24] Key to note here for our purposes re speech acts and assertions, is that lying is again seen to be concerned with assertions, not just any type of speech act.[25]

5.1.3 Grotius and Newman

Hugo Grotius: In the seventeenth century, Hugo Grotius suggested an understanding of lying that differed from the Augustinian definition. 'The character of falsehood, in so far as it is unpermissible, consists in its conflict with the right of another [to the truth] . . .'[26] Essentially, what Grotius has done to the definition of a lie is add the circumstance that, for a lie to be a lie, one must be speaking to one who has a right to the truth. Grotius' understanding of a lie amounts to the claim that to lie is to say what is false with an intention to deceive another who has a right to the truth. Hence, if one has a legitimate secret to protect, one can use a false form of words without lying since the questioner in these situations does not have the right to the truth. With the Grotius definition of lying, the wrongness of falsehood comes not from violating one's obligation to truthful speech; instead, the wrongness comes from it conflicting with another's right to the truth. In other words, the social not internal character of lying is what fundamentally determines the moral worth of the act. Debates concerning the morality of lying have continued right up to the present day. It is Grotius' understanding of a lie that featured in the earlier provisional version of the *Catechism* at CCC1 2483 and CCC1 2508 but, as we have seen, was subsequently amended to reflect Augustine's definition in the *Catechism*'s definitive edition at CCC2 2483 and CCC2 2508.

By using Grotius' definition of a lie, when police officers utter falsehoods with intent to deceive in the lawful performance of their duties, they are not lying because on these occasions they are (as previously argued) speaking to persons who do *not* have a right to the truth. One needs, of course, to establish who does or does not have a right to the truth, as noted when discussing the distinction between

---

[24] Ibid.
[25] See secs. 4.3.2 Speech Acts and Assertions and 4.4 Policing And Assertion-Making Contexts.
[26] Grotius, *On the Law*, bk. 3, ch. 1, para. 1. In Bok, *Lying*, 263.

speech acts and assertions.[27] Grotius' approach would seem to be a relatively straightforward way to resolve the tension that exists between the Church's absolute proscription of lying when the demands of police work require the use of falsehood with intent to deceive those who have no right to the truth. This strategy would, it seems, still classify as lies, all falsehoods uttered with intent to deceive in a court of law (testimonial deception), as well as the same type of utterances to the public whether in custody or not if it involves violating their rights in some way or the fairness and reliability of evidence is compromised.[28]

John Henry Newman: In the nineteenth century, Newman first states that he is 'very unwilling to say a word here on the subject of Lying and Equivocation. But I consider myself bound to speak; and therefore, in this strait, I can do nothing better, even for my own relief, than submit myself, and what I shall say, to the judgement of the Church'.[29] He then proceeds to consider the various possible options available in situations when there are rare cases when there is a just cause to deceive or mislead another, such as to defend life and protect a secret. Having considered the options in these situations of remaining silent, using evasion, equivocation and using falsehood, Newman concludes that using falsehood with intent to deceive is acceptable. He states:

> First, I have no difficulty whatever in recognising as allowable the method of *silence*. Secondly, But, if I allow of *silence*, why not of the method of *material lying*, since half of a truth *is* often a lie? And again, if all killing be not murder, nor all taking from another stealing, why must all untruths be lies? . . . If I had my own way, I would oblige society, that is, its great men, its lawyers, its divines, its literature, publicly to acknowledge as such, those instances of untruth which are not lies, as for instance untruths in war. . . . I think I should have a right to say an untruth, or that, under such circumstances [finding it difficult to protect a secret in any other legitimate way], a lie would be *material* . . . [30]

Clearly, Newman bases his argument for justifying what amounts to be the helpful 'lie' on a distinction he makes between the materiality of lying and lying in its formal sense. In other words, Newman is claiming that the utterance of falsehood with intent to deceive when there is a just cause to do so is not an act of lying in the moral (formal) sense, despite being a lie in the natural (material) sense. This distinction between lying in the

---

[27] See sec. 4.4 Policing And Assertion-Making Contexts.
[28] See Ibid.
[29] Newman, *Apologia*, 355.
[30] Ibid., 358–359, 361.

material and formal senses is similar to the approach taken by proportionalists towards lying, which we shall consider later.[31]

Interestingly, John Henry Newman (1801–1890) was a contemporary of Sir Robert Peel (1788–1850), though one does not know whether Newman and Peel exchanged views in respect of Peel's formation of the Metropolitan police force in 1829. If they had, Newman's distinction between material and formal lying would have been (and still is) relevant to the police use of deception and lies; not that Peel's nine policing principles make any explicit reference to the use of deception and lies by the police. Nevertheless, Peel's sixth principle that deals with the use of force could very easily act as a template for a similar approach to the police use of deception and lies.[32] Within Peel's sixth principle it states that the police should 'use only the minimum degree of physical force which is necessary on any particular occasion for achieving a police objective'.[33] That is to say, substitute 'deception' for 'physical force' in the wording of the above principle.

5.1.4 MacIntyre

In the twentieth century, Alasdair MacIntyre sought what he calls a 'rationally justifiable framework' concerning lying that integrated the different concerns about lying found within the traditions of the eighteenth-century German philosopher Immanuel Kant and the nineteenth-century British philosopher John Stuart Mill.[34] Put simply, Kant upheld an absolute proscription of lying, whereas Mill upheld a general rule against lying but allowed exceptions. Two key concerns were: (i) from Kant, that lying offends against truth as it misuses assertive speech acts, (ii) from Mill, that lying offends against trust and credibility and hence is destructive of relationships.[35] In other words, one might say that the 'rationally justifiable framework' MacIntyre sought to establish needs to address the wrongness stemming from the internal character of

---

[31] See sec. 5.1.5 Proportionalism and the Catechism.
[32] This type of approach is developed in sec. 5.2 Just War Tradition (JWT), Pacifism And Police Lies, and was initially suggested in sec. 2.2.3 Christianity and Standards of Professional Behaviour.
[33] Peel, *Principles of Law Enforcement*.
[34] MacIntyre, *Ethics and Politics*, 108.
[35] Ibid., 107.

lying (offends against truth) and the social character of lying (offends against trust and credibility).[36]

MacIntyre says that Mill takes a rule utilitarian approach to lying, which accepts very few exceptions to the prohibition of lying.[37] He notes that Mill bases the rule against lying and rare exceptions to thereof, on consequentialist considerations.[38] Kant, on the other hand, bases the absolute prohibition of lying in the 'rational nature of human beings'.[39] MacIntyre considers that there is good reason to reject the absolute proscription of lying, though he adds that whatever principle is found to justify rare exceptions to the norm against lying, it must not lead to a logical contradiction with the norm against lying.[40]

MacIntyre arrives at a rule to govern one's approach to lying; one that seeks to respect one's rationality as a person in a relationship of truth with others and in respect of whom one has duties. MacIntyre's rule (norm) to regulate lying is:

> Uphold truthfulness in all your actions by being unqualifiedly truthful in all your relationships and by lying to aggressors only in order to protect those truthful relationships against aggressors, and even then only when lying is the least harm that can afford an effective defense against aggression.[41]

MacIntyre believes this rule (norm) governing the use of lying has taken the best from Kant and Mill's approaches. First, the rule respects the rationality of persons who as rational qua rational persons need to live in truth—though as rational persons in a relationship with others in truth. Second, it acknowledges concern for the consequences of lying and not lying in terms of how they affect the necessary trust needed for the good of society.[42]

Macintyre's rule seems to be in harmony with the Code of Ethics' Standard 1: Honesty and Integrity. It would, for example, be difficult to

---

[36] One believes offending against all three: truth, credibility and trust is, practically speaking, synonymous with offending against the nature of speech and justice.

[37] Ibid., 115.

[38] Ibid., 122.

[39] Ibid.

[40] Ibid., 133. Although MacIntyre reaches this point upon his reflection of Kant's position, it also applies to the absolute proscription of lying per se, whether it be that held by Augustine, Aquinas or indeed as that taught within the *Catechism of the Catholic Church*.

[41] Ibid., 139.

[42] Ibid., 139–141.

comprehend on what basis the public would have any legitimate grounds to complain against a police officer who followed MacIntyre's rule concerning lying. In addition, MacIntyre's rule is very close to the practical application of Grotius' definition of a lie (i.e. the definition of lying within the *Catechism*'s provisional edition), with the qualification that the use of falsehood with intent to deceive must only be when it is the least damaging way to thwart an aggressor effectively.[43]

5.1.5 Proportionalism and the Catechism

The Catholic Church's teaching concerning the definition of a lie, its intrinsic evil nature and absolute proscription thereof, links into a much bigger issue within Catholicism, namely the challenge posed to magisterial teaching by proponents of the ethical theory of proportionalism.[44]

Proportionalism: As noted in Chapter 3, the Magisterium teaches that the object, intention and circumstances constitute the sources of morality in the evaluation of human acts and that the object (what you do) is the fundamental element in this evaluation. Also, as we previously noted, Richard McCormick captures the essence of the proportionalist challenge to magisterial teaching on the sources of morality.[45] For proportionalists, the morally relevant circumstances can morally justify a so-called lie. This approach is evident in the work of Catholic proportionalist theologian Louis Janssens, as discussed below.[46]

Contrary to magisterial teaching that classifies lying as an intrinsic evil, the proportionalist Catholic theologian Louis Janssens introduced the term *ontic* evil to make a distinction between moral evil and what he considers to be non-moral evil. He states: 'We call ontic evil any lack of a perfection at which we aim, any lack of fulfilment which frustrates our natural urges and makes us suffer. It is essentially the natural consequence of our limitation.'[47] Ontic evil is that which prevents us from reaching fulfilment as human beings.[48] For example, Janssens teaches that falsehood is deemed an ontic evil because it frustrates man's natural urge (inclination) towards truthfulness.[49] There may, at times (according to

---

[43] Aggressor is being used here to equate to a person with no right to the truth.
[44] See John Paul II, *Veritatis Splendor*, 79.
[45] See sec. 3.3.2 Human Act: Proportionalist Approach.
[46] See Janssens, 'Ontic Evil and Moral Evil', 73–74.
[47] Ibid., 60. The notion of 'ontic evil' is akin to the notion of 'physical evil'.
[48] Ibid., 67.
[49] See Ibid., 73–78 for Janssens' discussion of falsehood.

Janssens), be a valid reason to use falsehood, but falsehood, in itself, remains contrary to man's natural urge to truthfulness and is thus always an ontic evil. In contrast, an ontic good is consonant with man's natural inclinations, and hence, it helps man reach fulfilment. For example, speaking the truth is an ontic good because it contributes towards man's natural urge to relate in truthfulness to his fellow man (not that it is always appropriate to speak the truth, such as when one has a good reason to hide a secret).

Ontic good and ontic evil are considered distinct from but inherently linked to moral good and moral evil.[50] Janssens' perception is that, given our limitations, ontic evil is an unavoidable aspect of human action. Janssens' general principle to guide human action is that one should always aim to minimise ontic evil and maximise ontic good. What Janssens consequently seeks to ascertain is '[w]hen and to what extent are we justified in causing or allowing ontic evil?'[51] Essentially, what Janssens concludes is that one is justified in causing or allowing ontic evil if there is a proportionately good reason to do so (which Janssens deals with in terms of the goal of one's intention in acting, what one is trying to achieve). If there is such a good reason, no moral evil is committed when ontic evil is caused or allowed when one acts.[52]

With this approach, specific acts and specific types of behaviour, e.g. lying, are only ontic evil, not moral evil. Hence, moral norms relating to specific acts and specific types of behaviour, such as lying, cannot be absolutely prohibitive.[53] Janssens gave the example of the use of falsehood with intent to deceive to protect a secret. He said that this is not a moral lie (*mendacium*), but it is a non-moral lie (*falsiloquium*).[54] Hence in using a *falsiloquium* as a necessary means to hide a secret, Janssens specifically states that the 'meaning of the entire act is secrecy'.[55] Such an approach is contrary to the Magisterium's teaching.

How might the proportionalist approach apply to the use of lies by the police? This question is answered by reference back to section 5.1.3 above where one linked the proportionalist approach to lying with Newman's distinction between material and formal lying. The position of

---

[50] Moral good and moral evil are used here to denote moral value. In contrast, the terms ontic good and ontic evil do not signify moral value.

[51] Ibid., 67.

[52] Ibid., 78.

[53] Ibid., 84–86.

[54] Ibid., 73–74.

[55] Ibid., 74.

proportionalism would be that falsehood with intent to deceive within police work is only deemed a moral lie (*mendacium*) when a proportionate reason does *not* exist to justify its use. However, when a proportionate reason exists, these types of utterances are deemed a non-moral lie (*falsiloquium*). In short, when the police have a proportionate reason to utter falsehood with intent to deceive, they commit ontic evil (pre-moral evil) not moral evil, which thus morally justifies these acts. Whatever various grounds might exist for a proportionalist to claim a proportionate reason exists to justify the ontic evil of using a falsehood with intent to deceive, one such ground Janssens cites is when the speaker's interlocutor tries to ascertain a professional secret for which he has no right.[56]

Deciding when one has the right to the truth from the police at the various stages of their work, has already been discussed in respect of ethical context and the speech act/assertion distinction. The next chapter also considers the issue of a right to the truth in respect of the use of discreet language. Points made at these other places as regards the right/no right to the truth apply to the proportionalist approach to lying as well.

Catechism: We arrive now at the publication of the *Catechism of the Catholic Church* at the end of the twentieth century. The *Catechism*'s 1992 French provisional edition (English version 1994), as we have already seen, used a definition of a lie at paragraphs CCC1 2483 and CCC1 2508 that echoed Hugo Grotius' definition in which the circumstance 'to someone who has the right to know the truth' was part of the definition.[57] It is worth making the point again that with such a definition, many/most of the problems surrounding the demands of truth-telling disappear in the sense that an utterance of a falsehood with intent to deceive someone who has no right to the truth is not classified as a lie and hence not prohibited. Still, the *Catechism*'s 1997 Latin definitive edition (English version 2000), as we have already seen, used at paragraphs CCC2 2483 and CCC2 2508 the definition of a lie put forward by Augustine—in which the right of the hearer to the truth is *not* part of the definition.[58] With this Augustinian definition, one cannot use falsehood with intent to deceive anyone since such an utterance amounts to a lie—regardless of whether the hearer has/has not a right to the truth. Consequently, as we have previously noted, the definition of lying in the *Catechism*'s definitive

---

[56] Janssens, 'Teleology and Proportionality', 111.
[57] John Paul II, *Catéchisme De L' Église Catholique*. Cf. CCC1 (English translation).
[58] John Paul II, *Catechismus Catholicae Ecclesiae*. Cf. CCC2 (English translation).

edition faces the criticism, by some, of being too restrictive in situations where the utterance of falsehood with intent to deceive seems necessary to prevent injustices.

The difficulty with understanding and applying to the realities of life the definition of lying in the *Catechism*'s definitive edition when coupled with its absolute prohibition thereof continues to be an unresolved/ongoing issue within Catholic moral teaching. This book's discussion of the problem of lying in respect of police practice is part of this ongoing debate. One wonders whether the difficulty of this nuanced topic might encourage the police to be more transparent about what they consider lying to be and when they consider lying and other forms of deception to be proper methods to use in the police arsenal against those who would harm society. One notes that while both religious and non-religious police officers might embrace consequential reasons to justify the helpful lie, purely religious reasons for upholding an absolute proscription of lying are not, of course, open to the non-religious. Also, apart from the few who would subscribe to the Kantian justification for never lying, it seems fair to claim that most non-religious ethical views on lying seem to permit of helpful lies, especially in exceptional circumstances.

5.2 JUST WAR TRADITION (JWT), PACIFISM AND POLICE LIES

Societal approval of the use of force by the police varies, dependent upon location; an obvious example being the norm of armed police in the United States (US) but not in the United Kingdom (UK). Also, the general reduction in the police use of force has seen the corollary rise in the increased use of deceptive police tactics. While the police use of force is not an issue specifically discussed in this book, we shall, nonetheless, consider what light the Christian just war tradition and the associated pacifist stance might shine on the use of lies (deception) by the police.

Although Catholic Christian academic literature on police ethics is scant, there are a couple of articles relevant to our present concerns. First, Tobias Winright, writing in 1995, applies the just war tradition to policing to offer a rationale for the justified use of force by the police.[59] Second,

---

[59] Winright, 'Perpetrator as Person'. Winright acknowledges that he is building on the work of others who have also made the analogy between the use of force in war and its

Darrell Cole, writing in 2008, applies Christian ethics to some of the moral problems associated with spying; a spy's use of lies in word and deed being one such issue.[60] He likens spying to a soldier's use of force and justifies a spy's use of lies along the lines of just war criteria.

In the same way that no sensible person wants war, most people want the truth, not lies, to prevail in society; the real issue is whether war and/or lies can ever be justified. In the Early Church, the Christian position was essentially one of pacifism, but this began to change in the fourth century after Emperor Constantine made Christianity the official religion of the Roman Empire. Christians had to work out when it might be acceptable to fight for the empire, and it was these circumstances that triggered the just war tradition within Christianity. Use of JWT criteria is the method by which many Christians (and others) judge whether a war can be waged in a morally upright way and hence justified. Pacifism, nevertheless, still exists within the Christian tradition. Although the JWT is the leading Christian position towards war, dependent upon one's Christian denomination, one can either be a pacifist or an advocate of the doctrine of the JWT. For example, whereas Catholicism advocates the doctrine of a just war, the Religious Society of Friends (Quakers) is a well-known pacifist Christian denomination, while Anglicanism teaches that both pacifism and JWT doctrine are acceptable positions to hold.[61]

5.2.1 JWT and Police Lying

JWT criteria are usually grouped into two categories: *jus ad bellum* (when to fight) and *jus in bello* (how to fight).[62] *Jus ad bellum* requires that there must be a: (i) just authority: a legitimate authority is needed to declare war; (ii) just cause: to protect human life and/or human rights; (iii) just intention: one must be genuinely seeking good and not evil; (iv) comparative justice: consider your opponent's point of view, not only your own; (v) last resort: all reasonable alternatives to war must be tried first; (vi) chance of success: to avoid unnecessary harm, don't go to war

---

use by law enforcement officers, such as Edward A. Mallroy, James Turner Johnson, Charles P. Lutz, Paul Ramsey and Michael Walzer.

[60] Cole, 'Whether Spies Too Can Be Saved'.

[61] Catholicism, of course, also acknowledges the right of everyone to follow their conscience, which might for some require the upholding of a pacifist position (Pacifism is not deemed intrinsically evil).

[62] Sometimes a third group is referred to: *jus post bellum* (conduct after the fighting ends), though this third group is not relevant to our discussion of the police use of lies.

if unlikely to win; and (vii) proportionality: harm caused by the war must be in proportion to the evil being fought. Once fighting in a just war, *jus in bello* requires: (a) proportionality: amount of force used must be proportionate to the just cause; (b) minimum force: only use reasonable force necessary to achieve goals; and (c) discrimination: take all reasonable steps to avoid harming civilians. Similar to the distinction between *jus ad bellum* and *jus in bello*, when the police have the right to engage in deceptive tactics, it is still imperative that individual officers continue to act justly in the use of deceptive practices; similar to how a soldier fighting in a just war is also required to fight justly.

In Cole's justification of spying (which involves lies and deception) using elements of just war criteria, he highlights the importance of there being a just authority, just cause, just intention, proportionality and discrimination.[63] In our adaption and application of the JWT to the police use of lies, the same criteria as well as minimum force and last resort, are the elements we will use.[64]

Saul makes an interesting analogy between justified violence and justified deception, whereby even though there is a common acceptance that violence is wrong, there are also times when it is justified, e.g. self-defence. She adds:

> But we differentiate the morally acceptable violence from the morally unacceptable violence not by focusing on method of violence (knife, gun, fist, kick, etc.) but instead on the occasion for violence (e.g. self-defence or without provocation [or was it reasonable violence/force]). This would be by far the more natural way to deal with the situation concerning deception: differentiate between permissible and impermissible deceptions according to their purpose—rather than according to their method. (Differentiating between them on the basis of method seems analogous to the view that, say, punching is better than kicking.) A norm focused on *method* of deception is utterly mysterious.[65]

The objection to this for Kantians and Catholics is that the former considers the absolute proscription of lying necessary due to our rational

---

[63] Cole, 'Whether Spies Too Can Be Saved'.
[64] For previous suggestions in this book on how to improve Standard 1 of the College of Policing's Code of Ethics in England and Wales (which deals with honesty and integrity), see sec. 2.2.3 Christianity and Standards of Professional Behaviour.
[65] Saul, *Lying, Misleading*, 85. A footnote in Saul's text (fn. 20) adds that while differentiation is made between use of say a gun or a fist, this it seems is because the results flowing from these different methods is significantly different, unlike with lying and misleading.

nature, while the latter deems it necessary because of the intrinsic evil nature of lying.

The adaptation and application of the JWT to the police use of lies now follows. First, it is for society itself (which is the *just authority* via its legislation, policies and codes of practice) to decide which deceptive police tactics are acceptable and when to use them. It is then incumbent on police officers to follow these socially approved norms. These norms, of course, exist now. Deception at the testimonial stage, for example, is prohibited absolutely by UK and US law, whereas the conditional approved use of deception exists at the investigative and interrogatory stages of police work. Police use of deception has a *just* cause when it furthers legitimate policing aims, such as fighting crime, preserving the peace and protecting society from those who would do it harm. The criterion of *just* intention flags up the importance of pursuing good and avoiding evil in the police use of deception; in other words, one must sincerely be motivated by the pursuit of legitimate policing aims when using deception. The police should not, for example, use deception in a spirit of revenge, hatred or the acquisition of self-seeking goals. When police officers use deception in compliance with these three criteria (just authority, just cause, just intent), they are acting in conformity with their policing role and responsibilities, and hence honouring the Code's requirement to act with honesty and integrity.

In respect of the criterion of last resort, given the natural bias society has towards truthfulness over deceit, it seems preferable for the police to achieve their legitimate policing aims without recourse to deception whenever possible. Furthermore, the potential damage caused by the police use of deception (including lying) on the public's trust in the integrity and honesty of the police, may also suggest that non-deceptive tactics are the preferred default setting. Be that as it may, when, however, the efficacy of legitimate police work is seriously hampered by not deceiving and 'lying', then some/many would probably say it is not unreasonable to invoke these deceptive tactics as a matter of priority, and even to encourage their use.

[The criterion of proportionality regarding police deception means that the context of challenging evil/wrongdoing must justify the potential and actual damage caused by using any such deception. For example, at the interrogatory stage, 'lying' to a terrorist to reveal the location of a ticking time bomb would, for many, certainly meet the criterion of proportionality; in contrast, 'lying' to a juvenile to reveal the location of a stolen stash of sweets probably would not] The criterion of proportionality is particularly pertinent to the evaluation of the use of deception at the different stages of police work. For example, the courts are more accepting of the use of police deception at the investigative stage, but less so at the interrogatory stage, and not at all at the testimonial stage where the potential damage caused to the judicial system and broader society is immense.

Closely linked to proportionality is the criterion of minimum force or in our case 'minimum deception'. In other words, the degree to which the police use deceptive tactics should be governed by what is necessary to get the job done in an ethically upright way; in other words, the deception used must be reasonable in the circumstances. Such an approach echoes the Code of Ethic's reference in Standard 10 to the use of force that is 'reasonable . . . in all the circumstances'. By analogy, like how a soldier on the battlefield must keep the mantra—minimum force—in his mind, so too a police officer in the lawful execution of his duty ought to keep the mantra—minimum deception—ever-present in his mind. For example, at times, deceiving using a vague answer or by not answering at all may be sufficient, whereas, at other times, some would argue, a bold as brass barefaced 'lie' might be the order of the day. Being too prescriptive in what constitutes minimum deception is probably not the best approach to take since police officers will need to use their discretion to decide what constitutes an appropriate level of deception for any given set of circumstances. That said, reflection on the past use of police deception will inform and hone one's present and future ability to discern with greater accuracy what is the required minimum necessary amount of deception.

The criterion of discrimination is also useful to help govern the police use of deception. As far as possible, the police should, no doubt, limit their deceiving to those under investigation. However, whereas in a war context one could not justify using force against non-combatants, in a policing context the use of deception can be justly targeted against non-criminals too (law-abiding citizens) if it is reasonable as part of the wider pursuit of protecting society from those who seek to do it harm. As we saw previously in respect of assertion-making contexts, it is not unreasonable to expect law-abiding citizens to retrospectively approve of being so deceived when this deception is in the furtherance of legitimate policing aims, and so is in accord with the public's implicit consent.[66]

---

[66] See sec. 4.4 Policing And Assertion-Making Contexts.

5.2.2 Pacifism and Police Lying

A pacifist believes that violence, such as the violence of war, is wrong. There are different types of pacifism, such as absolute, contingent and nuclear. One can usefully apply these differences to the use of 'lies' by the police. An *absolute* pacifist maintains that all violence is wrong no matter what the circumstances; this position would not even allow the use of violence in self-defence, whether used by an individual being attacked or used by a nation under attack from enemy forces. This absolute prohibition of violence is comparable to the Augustinian tradition that maintains that the utterance of a falsehood with intent to deceive ('lie') can never be justified regardless of the circumstances; which is also the teaching on lying within the *Catechism*'s definitive edition.[67] Absolutism, as regards the use of 'lies' and deception, is not the position the police maintain, as we have seen.[68]

A *contingent* pacifist believes that while violence/war is wrong, it can sometimes be justifiable on the grounds of it being the lesser of two evils. Similarly, when the police and members of the public sometimes justify the use of 'lies' while also maintaining their fundamental belief in the value of truthfulness, they are, in effect, acting as contingent pacifists about the use of lies. This analogy is a useful one, if for no other reason than it helps to demonstrate why some would be of the view that the integrity of the individual is not compromised by moving from an absolutist to a contingent position, whether it is in respect of violence or 'lies'.[69] One recalls the life of the German Lutheran pastor Dietrich Bonhoeffer who, after witnessing the atrocities Hitler was inflicting upon the Jews in the Second World War, changed his position from that of an absolute pacifist to that of a contingent pacifist. Furthermore, as regards the issue of lying, Bonhoeffer maintained that lies could sometimes be justified when a higher value is at stake, and for that reason, he 'lied' and engaged in deception against the Nazi Regime.[70]

A *nuclear* pacifist maintains an absolute prohibition on the use of nuclear weapons though not on conventional methods of warfare. Within the context of police deception, the nuclear bomb of deceit is testimonial

---

[69] Obviously, from the Magisterium's perspective, the act of lying is still wrong, objectively speaking, though others see it as objectively right due to the circumstances.
[70] Bonhoeffer, *Ethics*.

deception (police perjury). The absolute prohibition of testimonial deception in our courts means that society (at least the legal system) is, metaphorically speaking, a nuclear pacifist towards perjury. The nuclear analogy is useful since it highlights the enormous damage police perjury can cause to our judicial system and within wider society. Yet, in another sense the nuclear analogy is not enough since, while there are reasoned though hotly contested arguments in the public domain for the justified use of nuclear weapons in the most extreme circumstances of war, there are not, to my knowledge, any arguments in the public domain put forward for the justified use of police perjury. That said, as we have previously noted, there does exist within the police the phenomenon of noble-cause corruption (bent-for-the-job), and this does at times lead some officers to drop a nuclear bomb, aka commit police perjury. For those police officers who do not accept the absolute prohibition of perjury, the analogy of the damaging effects of police perjury to that of a nuclear bomb's aftermath will, hopefully, discourage them from embarking on such behaviour. At the very least, it should prompt them to give serious consideration to the circumstances within which they commit perjury and the likely consequences of such conduct.

5.3 SUMMARY

We have made a selective, historical and analytical review of the Catholic Christian tradition concerning the morality of lying, from biblical times right up to the present. Comparisons have been made between lying, the JWT and pacifism. Neither within society generally, nor within the ecclesiastical community, are the finer points surrounding the ethics of lying and deception a settled issue. This book and the reader's considerations on the matter are part of this ongoing debate.[71] In various ways, it has been shown, both in this and the previous chapter, that the circumstance of whether or not one's interlocutor has a right to the truth is of central importance to discussions concerning the ethics of lying. The right or no right to the truth is also of fundamental significance to the concept of discreet language: an alternative to lying found within the Catholic tradition. Our next chapter explores the concept of discreet language in detail, and to this, we now turn.

---

[71] By way of comparison, see *Appendix 4* for a brief account of a Jewish approach to lying and how it relates to the police use of lies.

The golden rule helps one discern, in concrete situations, whether or not it would be appropriate to reveal the truth to someone who asks for it.
—*Catechism of the Catholic Church*[1]

6

DISCREET LANGUAGE

The approach that advocates preference for non-lying methods of deception as an alternative to lying, contains within it the belief that the former is morally preferable to the latter. For the Magisterium of the Catholic Church this is the case, given the intrinsic evil status it attaches to all lies and, therefore, its absolute prohibition of their use, including those lies uttered to help and protect. Non-lying deceptions, on the other hand, are not considered intrinsically evil, though the use of them may still be wrong due to the intention and/or circumstances surrounding their use. For society in general, it is probably fair to say that there is a natural default setting towards the avoidance of lying, though not absolutely since exceptions are approved. Also, society, presumably, prefers non-lying deceptions to lies whenever possible. For all that, if, as some argue, there is no moral difference between the use of non-lying deception and lying, all things being equal, it seems to matter not which method is used.[2] The distinction between lying and non-lying deception is, nevertheless, hugely significant in the courtroom setting because, as Saul notes, the offence of perjury requires the uttering of a lie; non-lying deception (misleading) is not enough.[3]

---

[1] CCC 2510. Discerning when one should reveal the truth is closely related to Bonhoeffer's question as to what the truth demands from us. See Chapter 4's epigraph.
[2] Saul argues 'that it is simply false to claim that misleading is always preferable to lying' (Saul, *Lying, Misleading*, 70). See also sec. 5.2.1 JWT and Police Lying for Saul's use of the analogy between justified violence and justified deception to argue that it is the *purpose* of a deception, not its *method*, that is important. In contrast, Green argues that, all things being equal, 'merely misleading is less wrongful than lying because what I call the principle of *caveat auditor,* or "listener beware," applies to merely misleading but does not apply to lying' (Green, 'Lying, Misleading, and Falsely Denying', 165). By *caveat auditor*, Green means that the listener (your interlocutor) has a responsibility to check the veracity of your statement before believing it.
[3] Saul, *Lying, Misleading*, 41 and 95.

6.1 DISCREET LANGUAGE (MENTAL RESERVATION)[4]

The *Catechism*'s suggestion of 'making use of a discreet language' as an alternative to lying when one needs to protect a secret from those who have no right to the truth (CCC 2489), looks very much like an allusion to the doctrine of *wide/broad* mental reservation (WMR). Even if the *Catechism*'s reference to discreet language is not an allusion to WMR, it still warrants our careful consideration. Indeed, the *New Catholic Encyclopedia* (NCE) states that WMR is a legitimate approach to take if it is appropriate to hide a secret.[5] There are two kinds of mental reservation: wide (broad) and strict. WMR is essentially the use of equivocation, where the words used have ambiguous meaning, the truth being potentially discernible to the hearer. Strict mental reservation (SMR) is different because the truth is not potentially discernible to the hearer because the speaker qualifies the meaning of the words uttered by some addition only in his mind.

Jonsen and Toulmin inform us that in the sixteenth century, driven by the need to hide priests from the Queen's forces, Catholic gentry in England made use of mental reservation in efforts to use so-called non-lying methods to protect priests whom they were sheltering.[6] Under the reign of Queen Elizabeth, one hundred and eighty-three Catholics were executed, including one hundred and twenty-three priests.[7] The need to deal with unjust questioning about their beliefs and practices became a problem, especially when so questioned before a magistrate.[8]

Before we discuss WMR, it is profitable to make a brief comment on SMR which came about in the sixteenth century as an attempt to refine the much earlier use of wide mental reservation. SMR claims that it is not a lie to assert to another what is false if one qualifies the falsehood in one's mind by some thought that, taken in conjunction with the assertion, makes it a truthful utterance. For example, a defendant's alibi is asked, "Were you with the defendant at the time when the crime was

---

[4] In addition to the particular references and citations used, the following texts have been of help in writing this chapter: Slater, 'Mental Reservation'; Hughes, 'Mental Reservation'; Slater, *A Manual of Moral Theology*, bk. 6, pt. 8, ch. 4 'On Lying'; Härring, *The Law of Christ, vol.3*, 572–576.

[5] Hughes, 'Mental Reservation', 662.

[6] Jonsen and Toulmin, *The Abuse of Casuistry*, 203.

[7] Ibid.

[8] Ibid., 204.

committed?" and he replies, "Yes" and then qualifies this in his mind with the thought, "I was with him in spirit but not physically".

Bok informs us that the use of SMR was particularly prevalent in the history of the Church in respect of court proceedings because since the oath in court was sworn in God's name, to commit perjury, it was feared, would bring down the wrath of God upon the perjurer.[9] However, in 1679, Pope Innocent XI condemned SMR because it was deemed to amount to lying. After this condemnation, Catholic theologians have not subsequently advocated the use of SMR.

In contrast, the Church has not condemned the doctrine of WMR. St. Raymund of Pennafort in his *Summa* of 1235 appears to be one of the first to postulate WMR.[10] There is the often-cited case of fourth-century St Athanasius who, when rowing past his enemies, they asked him where Athanasius was, to which he (Athanasius) replied, "Not far away", as he rowed on by, his identity thus protected.

With WMR, one utters more than one meaning, within which the meaning intended by the speaker is hidden (though not absent) in the ambiguity present. If the hearer is deceived, it comes from his interpretation of the words spoken and/or context. The truthful meaning is available to the hearer, albeit alongside the false sense, and hence it is held that this ensures no falsehood is asserted—thus no lie. At least, that is the logic of WMR—discreet language—the alternative the Church offers to the uttering of a lie, alongside, of course, the option to remain silent as a means to protect a legitimate secret.

The Catholic Church's teaching on the practice of mental reservation is summarised succinctly and thoroughly by Slater in his manual of moral theology:

> Mental reservations are either strictly or widely so called. The former is the restriction of one's meaning in making an assertion to the proposition as modified by some addition made to it within the mind of the speaker. . . . In wide mental reservations the words used are capable of being understood in different senses, either because they are ambiguous in themselves, or because they have a special sense derived from the circumstances of time, place, or person in which they are spoken. . . . Although strict mental reservations are lies, and therefore sinful, yet wide mental reservations are in common use; they are necessary, and they are not lies. . . . They are not lies

---

[9] Bok, *Lying*, 36.

[10] Grisez points out that Aquinas at *STh* II–II, q. 110.3, ad. 4, appears to allude towards the use of mental reservation, but does not elaborate on it, for he (Aquinas) says that it is licit to prudently hide the truth through concealment (Grisez, *Way of the Lord Jesus, vol.2*, 408, fn. 37).

because . . . words take their meaning not only from their grammatical signification, but from the circumstances in which they are used.[11]

Compare the Church's approach to the practice of mental reservation with its approach to contraception and responsible parenthood. In encouraging the end/goal of responsible parenting (i.e. not having more children than you can provide for), the Church promotes the use of Natural Family Planning (NFP) methods but not contraception. Put simply, the reason for this is that NFP is open to the possibility of a new life via the conjugal act whereas contraception is not; even though both sets of users can have the same intention of avoiding pregnancy when used as part of responsible parenting. Relating this to the practice of mental reservation, we can see that the users of both SMR and WMR to protect a secret have the same intention to hide the truth. The Church's acceptance of WMR is because the communication is open to the truth being potentially discerned (cf. open to life), whereas its condemnation of SMR is because the communication is not open to the truth being discerned (cf. not open to life).

6.2 POLICE USE OF WIDE MENTAL RESERVATION (WMR)

Is it possible—practically speaking—for police officers to use WMR as an alternative to the use of lies and still meet the operational demands of their work?[12] It seems reasonable to say that the police, like anyone else, can, as an alternative to lying, use WMR to try to protect a legitimate secret. Even so, like anyone else, this will depend on the quick-wittedness of the individual to apply ambiguity. One can easily imagine police officers in situations when it is just not practicable to adequately protect a secret in this way. For example, if an undercover police officer who has infiltrated a criminal gang was asked searching questions about his background, identity and job, it seems ludicrous to even think that the officer could—even should—attempt to protect his true identity via a virtuosic display of repeated mental reservations. The police officer in this and similar types of situation will inevitably need to have recourse to the

---

[11] Slater, *A Manual of Moral Theology*, 292–293.
[12] To desire that this comes about, implies the belief that non-lying methods are preferable to lying methods.

use of falsehood with intent to deceive ('lie') to maintain his legend (false identity).

Furthermore, not only do police officers need to protect secrets reactively from those who have no right to the information they seek; during the investigation of crime, police officers will also need to be proactive in deceiving others. For example, to even initiate one's infiltration into the criminal fraternity, an undercover police officer would no doubt proactively use falsehoods (in words or deeds) with the intention of deceiving criminals that he is someone other than a police officer. The point is that while WMR may very well have its uses, both for civilians and police officers alike, it is reasonable to say that, at times, only the utterance of falsehood with intent to deceive ('lie') will enable the police to meet the operational demands of their work effectively.[13]

6.3 MASK OF TRUTH

There is, though, arguably, even a problem with the use of discreet language (WMR), as this too may possibly be tantamount to lying. If this is the case it raises a serious challenge to the Catholic teaching on how to protect a legitimate secret without lying; and thereby, causes further problems for the faithful Catholic police officer wishing to uphold the Magisterium's absolute proscription of lies.

Consider the following. In commenting on how some Irish prelates illegitimately used the concept of mental reservation in the form of equivocation to justify misleading people about the clergy sexual abuse scandal in Dublin, Cathleen Kaveny commented that: 'it is never right to lie . . . [but] it is sometimes permissible to give an ambiguous answer— not a falsehood—in the hope that the questioner will take it the "wrong" way and act accordingly'.[14] Evidently, from these words, Kaveny appears to understand WMR as possessing an intent to deceive yet without it constituting a lie. An intent to deceive does seem to be present in the use of WMR to protect a secret since the speaker wants the questioner to interpret the meaning of the words in the wrong way. Still, what Kaveny

---

[13] The same is true with espionage. The claim that a spy could effectively meet the secretive operational demands of this work solely via the use of WMR is simply not credible, indeed ludicrous.

[14] Kaveny, 'Truth or Consequences', 6. It is important to note here that the erroneous use in this case refers to the fact that the hearers had a right to the truth sought and hence there was no proportionate reason for invoking the use of the mental reservation.

and many others would describe as an ambiguous answer may be, unwittingly, the assertion of falsehood—and hence, on this basis, even WMR amounts to being nothing other than a lie. Before we analyse whether this is the case, we need to focus upon the two essential elements of a lie as evident in CCC2's definition of a lie: viz. falsehood and intent to deceive.[15]

6.3.1 Intent to Deceive WMR is used to protect a secert

In one of its uses, WMR does *not* seem to possess an intent to deceive. Grisez states:

> In one sense, it [mental reservation] refers to expressions which can obscure the truth even if no one is deceived, and so can be effective without expressing an assertion believed to be false. The use of such expressions is not lying. Quick-witted individuals use ambiguity in this way. . . . [M]any statements are generally recognized as ambiguous: "Mr. Jones is not available just now," "Mrs. Jones is not at home," and even, in certain contexts, "I don't know."[16]

WMR used in this way suggests that the speaker is only intending to put uncertainty into the mind of the hearer as to what amounts to the truth, not deceiving as such. In other words, one could say that it is in effect claiming that the hearer on these occasions knowingly accepts the ambiguity, is not deceived by the ambiguity, and is somehow content not to pursue the speaker for further clarity to remove the ambiguity. It is akin to a hearer knowingly receiving an evasive answer, or no answer at all and the hearer accepts that he has not been given the truth, but a brush-off. While language is, for sure, used in this way, it is hardly the reality experienced by one who is seeking to protect a secret from an unjust and persistent questioner since all the questioner needs to do, and will do, is question further.[17]

---

[15] There is no need for us to analyse Aquinas' view that intent to deceive was not part of the essence of a lie but merely completed it. See sec. 5.1.2 Augustine and Aquinas. And, as previously discussed in sec. 4.2 Catechism's Teaching On Lying, despite the differences between the provisional and definitive editions of the *Catechism*'s text at CCC 2483 and CCC 2508, both cite Augustine's definition of a lie at CCC 2482.

[16] Grisez, *Way of the Lord Jesus, vol. 2,* 408. A footnote in the original text has been removed in this citation.

[17] An interesting and humorous use of ambiguous statements is given by Robert J. Thornton. In discussing the challenge of writing references (recommendations) that are honestly negative in a way that avoids potential litigation, he makes use of double

As we have argued above, when WMR is used to protect a secret, intent to deceive is present.[18] Grisez states:

> In another sense, however, *mental reservation* refers to studied ambiguities which cannot effectively obscure the truth without deceiving, and so cannot be used without intent to deceive. Such a mental reservation depends for its success entirely upon the false sense of the expression, whose true sense remains irrelevant to the communication. Thus, it both expresses something at odds with what one has in mind and carries out the intent to deceive, and so is a lie.[19]

Hoose similarly seems to suggest that when use is made of WMR to deceive, one speaks a lie.[20] He comments: 'Where broad mental restriction [WMR] is concerned, however, is there not an additional problem which arises from one's awareness that one is probably misleading another person, and that it is with such misleading in mind that one is resorting to this device of mental restriction?'[21] In other words, what is going on is that the speaker intends to deceive by communicating a falsehood to the hearer, the truthful meaning present within the ambiguity is something of a red herring.[22]

Does the use of WMR with intent to deceive constitute a lie? Using CCC2's definition of lying as our point of reference, the two essential

---

meanings whereby the intended negative meaning exists alongside the potential for a positive (and false) interpretation to be made of the form of words used. For example: 'I am pleased to say that he is a former colleague of mine; I assure you that no person would be better for the job; you'll be lucky if you can get this person to work for you' (Thornton, *Lexicon Of Intentionally Ambiguous Recommendations (L.I.A.R.),* front and back covers).

[18] Grisez refers to the broad (wide) mental reservation with intent to deceive famously used by St. Athanasius (Grisez, *Way of the Lord Jesus, vol. 2,* 409, fn. 38). One accepts, though, that it is not impossible for one to attempt to protect a secret using WMR without possessing an intent to deceive. Even so, in reality it is unlikely that *intending* to merely cause uncertainty in the hearer, *causing* such uncertainty, and the hearer being *content to accept* such uncertainty, captures the reality of these sorts of situations when the truth needs to be protected.

[19] Ibid., 408–409.

[20] Hoose questions: 'Is it the case, then, that broad mental restriction does not fit into Augustine's definition of a lie (regardless of what Augustine himself and Aquinas may have said about dissimulation)?' (Hoose, 'Towards the Truth', 71).

[21] Ibid.

[22] Similarly, Saul comments that 'in the cleverest cases of mere misleading the speaker does not *mean* the true proposition that is said, since their plan is that the audience will not grasp and reflect on it, instead leaping straight to a false proposition' (Saul, *Lying, Misleading*, 68).

elements of a lie are intent to deceive and falsehood. We have argued that the user of WMR to hide a secret intends the hearer to be deceived and hence *not* take up the true meaning of the words uttered. Only because the hearer unwittingly takes up a false sense via his self-deception is the true meaning protected.[23] The bone of contention now is whether using WMR with an intent to deceive is tantamount to the asserting of falsehood. To say the same thing slightly differently: when WMR is used to deceive, is the truthful element irrelevant to the communication uttered?

6.3.2 Falsehood

If falsehood is not used, no lie is spoken.[24] Of course, the whole point about WMR, as distinct from SMR, is that the truth is present and accessible to the hearer via the words spoken, albeit somewhat hidden within the ambiguity. The claim that WMR amounts to a lie (falsehood with intent to deceive) could be argued for if one adopted Alexander Pruss' concept of speaking your interlocutor's language. Pruss states that 'a basic principle of human language is that one speak in ways that one expects the interlocutor to understand'.[25] Consequently, it is a lie to make 'an assertion which you believe to be false when understood in your interlocutor's language (i.e., the language in which your interlocutor will take your assertion to have been made), with intent to deceive'.[26]

With the principle of speaking your interlocutor's language, falsehood is understood from the *hearer's* perspective of what the speaker means, not from the *speaker's* perspective. If this is correct, any true meaning from the standpoint of the speaker is not allowed to qualify the falsehood from the hearer's perspective. The hearer's false meaning is primary; the speaker's true meaning is secondary.[27] Pruss himself states: 'The principle of speaking your interlocutor's language does appear to rule out equivocation, though the matter is perhaps not completely certain, since

---

[23] While the deception comes from the hearer, not the speaker, the speaker still has an intent to deceive.

[24] By falsehood, one means that what is said or done does not reflect what the speaker believes to be true, whether or not what he believes is actually objectively true.

[25] Pruss, 'Interlocutor's Language', 441. See also sec. 4.3.2 Speech Acts and Assertions.

[26] Ibid., 443.

[27] I treat the speaker's truth as the secondary meaning and the hearer's falsehood as the primary meaning because the whole point of using WMR to protect a secret is for the hearer to take up the false meaning.

the equivocation might be within one's interlocutor's language.'[28] The whole point of using equivocation to protect a secret is that one's interlocutor takes up the wrong meaning, and hence the speaker wills his interlocutor takes up the wrong meaning. The language of the interlocutor amounts to being precisely whatever meaning the interlocutor takes from the words uttered—regardless of whether the equivocation is in the interlocutor's language or not. As such, what is spoken with the intent to deceive, according to Pruss' principle, is the—hoped-for—false taken-up meaning by the interlocutor—hence WMR on this basis certainly does seem to amount to lying.

Furthermore, the Catholic Church's rejection of SMR way back in the seventeenth century can also be seen to support Pruss' concept of speaking one's interlocutor's language. Condemnation of SMR was based on the observation that it consists of a false assertion despite the claim that the false assertion is allegedly made truthful when combined with a mental restriction privy only to the speaker. The point is that SMR asserts the false meaning available to the hearer of the communication. It is this false meaning the speaker wants the hearer to take up, not the meaning the speaker holds (which is true) and is privy only to him and in respect of which the speaker does not want the hearer to take up. Where the truth is available to the hearer via an ambiguity in the case of WMR, it still seems logical to continue to maintain that the assertion is the hoped-for false meaning the hearer takes from the communication. The assertion is not the truthful sense which, this time, while not locked away in the speaker's mind, is merely within the ambiguity of the communication. The truthful meaning is not what the speaker wants the hearer to take up and so it is not in any meaningful sense that which the speaker asserts. It is disingenuous to claim one is asserting the disguised truth one is trying to keep secret.

6.3.3 Is WMR to Protect a Secret a Lie?

Our analysis of intent to deceive and falsehood (the two essential elements of a lie), leads to the logical conclusion that WMR used to protect a secret is a lie. Be that as it may, for a different reason, an argument is now proffered as to why one should still not class WMR to protect a secret as a lie; though one acknowledges that this argument will

---

[28] Ibid., 451, fn. 9.

pose a challenge to the Catholic Church's centuries-old teaching on the practice of mental reservation.

We need to pay careful attention to the distinction, noted previously in Chapter 4, between speech acts and assertions. There it was established that lying could not take place in a context within which it is not possible to make assertions since a lie is an assertion *contra mentem*.[29] If one applies this logic to the concept of mental reservation, an interesting conclusion follows. Given the fact that it is licit to invoke WMR to protect a secret from those who have no right to the truth, ironically, the circumstance of one's interlocutor not having a right to the truth is the very condition necessary to make assertion making impossible, and hence lying (assertion *contra mentem*) is impossible too. The point is that it is not reasonable for a busybody or aggressor to expect the speaker to be making assertions as they do not have a right to the truth. Even though there is both a false meaning and a true meaning within an ambiguous speech act (WMR), there is no assertion of falsehood because no assertions are possible (false or true) because it is not an assertion-making context. Hence, there is no lie.

Therefore, if the distinction between speech acts and assertions is correct, the Church's centuries-old acceptance of WMR when used to protect a secret is unnecessary, and its condemnation of SMR needs a qualification to avoid being in error. About WMR, its use seems superfluous as a non-lying way to protect a secret because, as we have argued, no lie takes place without an assertion, which is the case when it is licit to use WMR to hide a secret. Moreover, the teaching that SMR amounts to a lie becomes erroneous on those occasions when SMR was employed to protect a secret from an inquisitor who has no right to the truth—again because the necessary condition for assertion making to take place does not exist here either. Hence SMR used to protect a legitimate secret does not amount to a lie. Nevertheless, when SMR was in common use in the history of the Church in respect of court proceedings in an attempt to avoid committing perjury, its use there would amount to a lie, provided it was a just court, and it had a right to the truth. On the other hand, at other times, when one's interlocutor does not have a right to the truth, SMR is not lying, based on the argument put forward above.

Having placed one's hand inside the mouth of the famous fourth-century stone mask lie detector, *Bocca della Verità* ('Mouth of Truth'), it gets bitten off if one is a liar. By trying to find ways to protect secrets

---

[29] See sec. 4.3.2 Speech Acts and Assertions.

without lying in order to be faithful to the Augustinian definition of a lie (falsehood with intent to deceive) and absolute proscription thereof, the advocates of the Catholic teaching on the practice of mental reservation may very well find their hands are bitten off too. To escape this fate, it would seem they also need to make use of the speech act/assertion distinction when one's interlocutor has no right to the truth.

6.4 MENTAL RESERVATION IN COURT[30]

We noted in the introduction to this chapter that the distinction between lying and non-lying ways to hide the truth has relevance to the courtroom setting because the offence of perjury requires the utterance of a lie; non-lying deception (misleading) is not enough.[31] Can WMR ever be justifiably used at the testimonial stage, whether by the police or any other person?[32] A court of law is the home of reason where truth is key to the achievement of judicial justice. As such, even if there is a legitimate place for WMR in a court of law, one ought to treat any deviation from openness and transparency with extreme caution.

Ashley comments that there are situations when it is wrong to hide the truth, one such case being 'when questioned by a *judge*, superior, confessor or *others who have the right to do so*'.[33] This view is echoed in the NCE, though one notes that it says there that WMR is not acceptable 'to a judge asking *legitimate questions*'.[34] Moreover, the earlier version of the Catholic Encyclopedia states: 'When mental reservation is permissible it is lawful to corroborate one's utterance by an oath, if there be an adequate cause.'[35] In respect of the use of WMR under oath for a grave reason, Peschke states that: 'Very many moralists reply in the affirmative, since in itself the

---

[30] Content in this section is related to content in secs. 4.4 Policing And Assertion-Making Contexts and 7.3 Bent-For-The-Job Police Perjury.

[31] Saul, *Lying, Misleading*, 41 and 95. One is not claiming here to have any expertise in matters of criminal law; one is merely acknowledging the logical inference based on the constituent elements of the definition of perjury as commonly understood.

[32] We shall not discuss SMR because it was condemned by Pope Innocent XI in 1679. Furthermore, in this section we work on the assumption that WMR is a credible alternative to lying.

[33] Ashley, *Living the Truth*, 412. Emphasis added. We can infer that this includes a court of law.

[34] Hughes, 'Mental Reservation', 663. Emphasis added.

[35] Delany, 'Perjury'.

reservation is permissible.'[36] He cites the example of unjust questioning, in response to which the reply may legitimately be "'I know nothing about it,'" meaning that one knows nothing about it "'which I could be rightly interrogated about'".[37] Such a reply is understood by Peschke to be an instance of WMR (not strict) because the truth (what the speaker means) is, arguably, discernible by a perceptive person intuiting the unjustness of the questioning (i.e. via the context).

The Catholic Church's teaching concerning WMR in a court of law, if valid, applies to police officers just like anyone else. Accepting the inherent dangers of the use of WMR in a court of law, we have at least to entertain the possibility that a witness, police or otherwise, when giving evidence in a court of law may be subject to unjust questioning. As such, this may provide sufficient cause (morally speaking) to hide the truth about something. While the court has the *legal* right to the truth, what we are contemplating here is whether it always has the *moral* right to the truth. It is not unreasonable, for example, to imagine a police officer being privy to information that, if revealed, may lead to severe and unjustified harm, which he, therefore, wishes to keep secret. Maybe on these occasions, WMR is appropriate.[38] Interestingly and by way of comparison, Saul refers to the work of Solan and observes that the rules governing lawyers requires them not to lie during legal proceedings, yet they are permitted to mislead and are often taught that to do so may sometimes be their professional obligation.[39]

The importance of the truth in a court of law for just judicial outcomes is, though, self-evident. The lawyer's role of drawing out the truth from witnesses reflects this. Saul comments:

> In a courtroom, a witness is required to answer the questions that a lawyer puts to them. If either of the lawyers in an adversarial system is not satisfied with their answers, it is the lawyer's job to pursue the questions further . . . It is very much the lawyer's job to notice that a witness is not answering the question asked, and to force them to answer the right question . . . whose job it is to get clear and unequivocal statements out of those testifying.[40]

---

[36] Peschke, *Christian Ethics, vol. 2*, 590.

[37] Ibid.

[38] Note that sec. 7.3: Bent-For-The-Job Police Perjury, albeit in relation to police perjury, explores a little further the possibility of a court lacking the *moral* right to the truth.

[39] Saul, *Lying, Misleading*, 97, fn. 28. Reference to Solan is to: Lawrence Solan, 'Lawyers as Insincere (But Truthful) Actors', ms, presented at Trust and Lying Workshop, Sheffield, UK, 2010.

[40] Ibid., 95–96.

One hopes that when lawyers do question in this way, they are not acting 'as gladiators seeking victory rather than as advocates for justice'.[41] In the search for truth and the desire to hide the truth from those who have no right to it, both lawyers and police officers might gain something from the following words of Dietrich Bonhoeffer:

> [A] teacher asks a child in front of the class whether it is true that his father often comes home drunk. It is true, but the child denies it. The teacher's question has placed him in a situation for which he is not yet prepared. He feels only that what is taking place is an unjustified interference in the order of the family and that he must oppose it. What goes on in the family is not for the ears of the class in school. The family has its own secret and must preserve it. The teacher has failed to respect the reality of this institution.[42]

The devil may very well be the father of lies, but: 'There is a truth which is of Satan.'[43]

6.5 SUMMARY

This chapter has shown that according to the Catholic moral tradition, it is licit to use WMR to protect a secret (private truth), but it is illicit to use SMR. Acknowledgement has been made of the legitimate use of WMR by the police, should it be of use within policing. Concerning the definitive *Catechism*'s definition of a lie, we have also considered the argument suggesting that discreet language (WMR) amounts to a lie when it is used with intent to deceive since what is happening in such behaviour is the asserting of the false meaning not the truthful sense of the ambiguous statement. However, an argument was provided to suggest that by invoking the distinction between speech acts and assertions, mental reservation, both WMR and SMR, with or without an intent to deceive, need not be construed as lying when their use is not in an assertion-making context. Still, by doing so, we also saw that there is, conceivably, no longer any need to use mental reservation to hide a secret at all because when there is no right to the truth sought (which, of course,

---

[41] This is how some police officers think lawyers behave at times (Kleinig, 'Ethical Questions', 221).
[42] Bonhoeffer, *Ethics*, 367.
[43] Ibid., 366.

is when WMR can legitimately be used) there is no assertion-making context, and so it is not possible to make assertions *contra mentem*—lie. As might be expected, including the right to the truth within the definition of a lie would, similarly, remove the need for WMR when one's interlocutor does not have a right to the truth.[44] The ethics of using mental reservation within a court of law, to avoid lying, has also been considered. It is in the next chapter we tackle the issue of lying in a court of law: in other words, perjury.

---

[44] This has relevance to Grotius' definition of a lie, the definition of a lie in the *Catechism*'s provisional edition, Guevin's notion of ethical context, and proportionalism's treatment of lying.

*I swear by Almighty God that the evidence I shall give
shall be the truth, the whole truth and nothing but the truth.*
—The Oath[1]

7

PERJURY AND OATHS

We have considered the issue of lying generally, the Catholic Church's teaching about it, and the use of lying at the investigative and interrogatory stages of police work. We now take a similar approach to perjury: lying at the testimonial stage.

Catholic Christian police officers will encounter perjury, whether committed by defendants, witnesses, other police officers or perhaps even themselves. Where police corruption exists, at times it can and does use loyalty amongst fellow police officers to cover up this harmful practice. Corruption, as we have noted, can occur for private gain (bent-for-oneself) or the perceived benefit of society (bent-for-the-job), the latter also known as noble-cause corruption. Police perjury is one type of police corruption. Also, any police misconduct or corruption committed prior to the testimonial stage has the potential to lead to police perjury. United Kingdom (UK) and United States (US) police will serve as our exemplars, though what we find there will have an application, in varying degrees, to policing worldwide.

7.1 PERJURY PHENOMENON

r¹ type of corpurtion

What is perjury? The Perjury Act of 1911 in England and Wales states:

> If any person lawfully sworn as a witness or as an interpreter in a judicial proceeding wilfully makes a statement material in that proceeding, which he knows to be false or does not believe to be true, he shall be guilty of perjury . . .[2]

---

[1] This is the typical form of the oath. The precise wording of the oath varies from country to country, but the essential elements are similar.

[2] The National Archives, 'Perjury Act 1911', ch. 6, sec. 1(1).

In addition, the Church describes perjury as a public statement contrary to the truth that is made under oath (CCC 2476). According to both criminal law and ecclesiastical law, even when an utterance is objectively true, perjury can be committed when a person speaks what he or she believes to be false.

In recent years, the UK has suffered from some high-profile cases of corrupt police practice. Keith Vaz MP, former Chair of the House of Commons Home Affairs Committee was not alone in calling for a Royal Commission into policing; in part, due to the public loss of confidence in the police service.[3] We have witnessed the Plebgate scandal concerning an altercation between Andrew Mitchell MP former Chief Whip and several police officers.[4] David Davis MP, Shadow Home Secretary (2003–2008), had this to say about policing in the UK:

> There are suggestions of a culture of cover-up, and a worrying trend of police smearing innocent people to cover their own mistakes. . . . Britain needs root-and-branch reform of policing culture . . . Regrettably it appears that the Mitchell case is merely a high-profile example, not an isolated one. The decline in public trust in the police is a serious threat to the ability of the vast majority of decent officers to do the job they signed up for, catching villains and protecting the public.[5]

Also, the inquiry into the Hillsborough Disaster of 1989 has revealed the alteration of statements and accusations of a police cover-up.[6] There are other high-profile UK police corruption scandals too, involving miscarriages of justice, such as the cases of the Bridgewater Four (1978), Guildford Four (1989) and Birmingham Six (1992).

The US also has suffered from corrupt police practice. The New York City Police Department (NYPD) in particular has endured a variety of police malpractices as identified, for example, in the Knapp Commission and the Mollen Commission.[7] And, as noted previously,[8] Slobogin states: 'Few knowledgeable persons are willing to say that police perjury about investigative matters is sporadic or rare, except perhaps the police, and . . . even many of them believe it is common enough to merit a label all its

---

[3] Ross, 'Keith Vaz calls for Royal Commission into policing'. For the full report see House of Commons Home Affairs Committee, *Independent Police Complaints Commission*.

[4] See, Eleftheriou-Smith, 'Plebgate'.

[5] Davis, 'Police culture needs root and branch reform'.

[6] Hillsborough Independent Panel, *Hillsborough: The Report*.

[7] City of New York, *The Knapp Commission Report*, and City of New York, *Commission Report*.

[8] See sec. 2.1.4 Perjury.

own [testilying].'⁹ See also the previously referred to 2018 series of three articles in *The New York Times* concerning the perceived prevalence of police perjury within the NYPD.[10]

While the legal systems of the UK and the US do not approve of police perjury, nor indeed one supposes does any civilised society—it seems that, at times, some police officers, unofficially, support its use.[11] In this book, we do not get into a debate as to how prevalent perjury is within society, police or otherwise; for our purposes, what is important is the fact that it exists. It is essential, all the same, to offer some indication of the extent of perjury within police ranks and broader society, lest some might *dishonestly* claim perjury/police perjury never happens, or when it does its existence is so rare that it is not worth discussing. That would be a tragedy and one which is likely to entrench perjury even further into the fabric of our society.

In 2000, Foley published the results of his doctoral study into police perjury, which involved a survey of 508 New York City police officers, using questionnaires, interviews and focus groups. NYPD granted permission for the research, and the US National Institute for Justice funded it. In his conclusion, he states that 'it appears that the use of perjury is widespread in policing'.[12] Foley acknowledges the sensitive nature of police perjury, and alerts us to the difficulties he had when conducting his research:

> Several times during the course of this research police officers threatened me with physical violence, asked if I was sure I really wanted to open "this can of worms", told that nothing good could come from this (research) and stated I was going to get cops fired from their jobs.[13]

The reader may wish to refer to *Appendix 5*, which consists of a collection of material further highlighting something of the reality of perjury in the UK and US judicial systems.

---

⁹ Slobogin, 'Testilying: Police Perjury', 1042. 'Testilying' is a euphemism for lying under oath (perjury).
[10] See Chapter 1, p. 3, fn. 8.
[11] Although coverage of perjury in this section includes police perjury committed for any reason, our primary focus is on perjury motivated by the so-called noble-cause ethic.
[12] Foley, 'Police Perjury: A Factorial Survey', 137.
[13] Ibid., 132.

7.2 CHURCH TEACHING ON PERJURY

Everything said so far in respect of the Magisterium's teaching on lying also applies to perjury, since perjury is a form of lying. However, perjury is a particularly serious form of lying. 'When it is made publicly, a statement contrary to the truth takes on a particular gravity. In court it becomes false witness. When it is under oath, it is perjury.'(CCC 2476)

The Church teaches that perjury is a serious disrespect to God and is contrary to His Holy name (CCC 2152). After having established that the Lord's name is holy (CCC 2142–2149), the *Catechism* states: 'The second commandment *forbids false oaths*. Taking an oath or swearing is to take God as a witness to what one affirms. It is to invoke the divine truthfulness as a pledge of one's own truthfulness.' (CCC 2150)[14] This means that a false oath (i.e. invoking God as a witness to untruthfulness) is forbidden since it calls on God to witness a lie (CCC 2151).

Furthermore, the *Catechism* teaches that perjury 'contribute[s] to condemnation of the innocent, exoneration of the guilty or the increased punishment of the accused . . . [and that perjury and false witness] gravely compromise the exercise of justice and the fairness of judicial decisions'. (CCC 2476) Perjury is thus classified as an intrinsically evil act and hence 'always gravely illicit' and cannot, therefore, ever be justified (CCC 1756). Perjury is also the subject matter of mortal sin (CCC 1856). The Church teaches that mortal sin if not redeemed through repentance and God's forgiveness, leads to eternal damnation (CCC 1861). The *Catechism* somewhat tempers this radical consequence of the commission of mortal sin with the additional statement that 'although we can judge that an act is in itself a grave offence, we must entrust judgement of persons to the justice and mercy of God'.[15] (CCC 1861) For those who take this Catholic teaching seriously, it provides a significant incentive not to commit

---

[14] The second commandment states: 'You shall not make wrongful use of the name of the Lord your God, for the Lord will not acquit anyone who misuses his name' (Ex 20:7).

[15] For a sin to be mortal three conditions collectively are required: the object of the act must be of grave matter (serious matter), it is committed with full knowledge and with deliberate consent (See CCC 1857–1859). For any Catholic who has a concern about this in respect of perjury, their best option must surely be to seek the counsel of a Catholic priest. One should, however, search to find a priest who can offer authentic Catholic teaching and guidance on this issue, coupled with an informed understanding, appreciation and sensitivity of the matter at hand.

perjury, in addition to what already is, hopefully, one's aversion to dishonesty in the first place.[16]

It is abundantly obvious that the Catholic tradition is opposed to perjury. In terms of the sources of morality,[17] perjury is intrinsically wrong, not only because it involves lying, but also due to its irreverence of invoking God's truthfulness as a witness to the untruthfulness of one's lie (object). The consequences of perjury regarding the innocent condemned, guilty exonerated, increased punishment (circumstances) are further reasons counting against such a practice. There can be no doubt that false witness and perjury (both punishable as perjury) can and do contribute towards the distortion of justice and fairness of judicial decisions. For example, a miscarriage of justice can occur when a factually *guilty* defendant perjures himself to evade conviction, or through the prosecution of a factually *innocent* defendant on the strength of false evidence. One acknowledges, for all that, that the *intention* behind noble-cause police perjury is *not* the conviction of innocent defendants. However, in respect of the consequences of perjury (circumstances), it is without doubt that it has the potential to cause untold damage to the judicial system. That said, one also acknowledges that when noble-cause police perjury is successful in helping to secure the conviction of defendants, the perjury will have remained hidden and hence whatever damage perjury does to the criminal justice system is not so apparent—at least in the short term.

This book is certainly *not* justifying noble-cause police perjury, but it does seek to understand better the rationale of this behaviour. Further analysis of noble-cause police perjury (bent-for-the-job) now follows.

7.3 BENT-FOR-THE-JOB POLICE PERJURY

While accepting the fact that there will be instances, hopefully very rare, of police officers committing perjury for their own benefit, aka bent-for-oneself, one takes the view that most cases of police perjury, whatever their frequency, occur for a so-called noble cause: the intention of

---

[16] From the perception of those who do not believe in the existence of God, talk of perjury as offending God's Holy name and leading to the prospect of an unsavoury post-mortem existence is at best irrelevant, at worst utter nonsense.

[17] See sec. 3.3.1 Human Act: Traditionalist Approach (Magisterium's Approach).

prosecuting factually guilty defendants for the good of society.[18] Skolnick argues that the end justifying the means mentality is used within police culture to justify courtroom lying, similar to how courts permit lying at the investigative stage.[19] While there will be less noble reasons for committing perjury, this does not thereby make so-called noble-cause perjury morally acceptable. Nonetheless, in light of the lawful use of the end justifying the means mentality within police work, for those who do not subscribe to an absolute proscription of lying, courtroom lying is, for some at least, open to the potential for moral justification along consequential lines.[20]

It is essential for many, perhaps most, that the due process of the law is upheld absolutely—even if the price to pay for this, at times, is the acquittal of factually guilty defendants and the conviction of factually innocent defendants. Grisez captures the essence of the due process model of crime control in the following way:

> The purpose of a trial . . . is to reach a just verdict grounded in the truth. . . . [A] guilty verdict [of an actual guilty defendant] will be just only if the admissible evidence supports it and the relevant law is correctly applied. And the relevant law is both substantive and procedural, so that if there is any procedural fault in the authorities' handling of [the defendants] case, [the defence counsel] should seek on that basis an order or verdict freeing him.[21]

The public may very well prefer procedural correctness to a just outcome.[22] Arguably, all the same, some people might find it impossible

---

[18] We should also remember that many cases do not result in police officers giving evidence in a court of law, such as when there is a prior guilty plea, a plea deal or when charges are dismissed or dropped. Common sense leads one to the view that in a certain percentage of these cases there will, no doubt, be some false police evidence too within the relevant written police statements. Again, it is not the intention of this book to enter the debate as to *how prevalent* deception, lying and perjury is within policing; that it certainly exists is all that matters for our purposes.

[19] Skolnick, 'Deception by Police', 42.

[20] The Catholic Church, as we have seen, upholds an absolute proscription of lying. On that point, arguably, it has the moral high ground. Yet MacIntyre informs us that those who uphold an absolute proscription in respect of lying and/or the use of force are likely to be moral free-riders. 'The social and civic orders within which the vast majority of human beings live out their lives are sustained by systematic uses of coercion and lying that Kantians, pacifists, and others may disown and condemn, but the benefits of which they cannot escape.' (MacIntyre, *Ethics and Politics*, 134)

[21] Grisez, *Way of the Lord Jesus, vol.3*, 768.

[22] Ashworth informs us that experiments by psychologists such as T.R. Tyler, *Why People Obey the* Law (New Haven, Yale University,1990), 'suggest that procedural fairness is

to live by this principle if personally facing the consequences of acting upon this rationale. For example, how many would prefer due process if the price to pay was the erroneous conviction of an innocent loved one for murder when perhaps a false alibi that does not incriminate anyone else might have prevented the unjust conviction? For those engaging in noble-cause corruption, maybe the absolute adherence to due process is viewed as the making of a false god out of this due process.[23]

In trying to understand better the mindset of police officers who justify—to themselves and amongst themselves—breaking the law via the corruption of noble-cause perjury, one can say that there is a sincerity by which some of these guardians of the law violate the law in this way. Without justifying this behaviour it does, nevertheless, seem only fair to say that noble-cause-perjurious police officers are not, ipso facto, bad people. Misled, yes; bad, not necessarily so. Some might argue that in risking being prosecuted themselves for committing perjury to help ensure the conviction of the factually guilty—especially in cases of protecting society from serious harm—they are, paradoxically, displaying respect for society and its legislature.

Moving on, are there occasions, one wonders, when an otherwise just court of law might lack a *moral* right to the truth? If so, on those occasions, instances of what are ostensible acts of perjury might not be acts of perjury at all if it is not possible to utter a lie (assertion *contra mentem*) because an assertion-making context is lacking. Recall the logic that one

---

valued more highly by many citizens than the outcome of the procedure' (Ashworth, 'Ethics and Criminal Justice', 167).

[23] Having acknowledged the obvious illegality of police perjury, from a legal perspective an analogous link could possibly be made between noble-cause police perjury and the defence of duress within criminal law. Green points out that a defence to a crime is that the act was committed under duress out of fear to avoid immediate death or serious bodily injury (Green, 'Lying, Misleading and Falsely Denying', 170, fn. 44). Green adds that this defence is difficult but not impossible to successfully invoke when a defendant (he is not talking about the police here) is under trial for the crime of perjury, since in the courtroom where perjury is most likely to have been committed it is a relatively safe environment (Ibid.). Be that as it may, if and when a police officer giving evidence in a court of law finds himself in an 'impossible situation', some might wish to argue that there is room for a legal defence to noble-cause perjury in extreme situations (controversial though this is). For example, a police officer being overwhelmingly coerced by the police culture within which he works to commit noble cause perjury, perhaps so as to protect society from serious harm. These reflections seek to sensitively and reflectively ponder aspects of noble-cause police perjury, *not* to endorse its use.

cannot make an assertion *contra mentem* (lie) if one is not first making an assertion.[24] If there is no lie, then neither is there any perjury.

A court of law has the *legal* right to the truth; but does it always have a *moral* right to the truth? At the time court testimony is given, under normal circumstances most would surely accept that the court has a moral right to the truth and hence expects witnesses to be making assertions. If a severe miscarriage of justice is only avoidable, ironically, by a witness (police or otherwise) deceiving the court, could members of the court on these occasions licitly be construed as having given up their moral right to the truth? There might be a retrospective consenting to the deception—once members of the court (if they) became aware of the full reality of the situation.[25] If so, members of the court, albeit unknowingly to them at the time, would not have a reasonable expectation that police officers are making assertions when engaged in noble-cause perjury, and hence, what is ostensibly an act of perjury may not be an act of perjury.

The above suggestion is controversial, and one would have thought *prima facie* counter-intuitive to most. Even if the logic is sound, presumably its relevance to everyday policing is minimal since we are dealing here with the avoidance of extreme miscarriages of justice which, one assumes, are few and far between. But, given the fact that some police officers sincerely believe noble-cause perjury is justifiable at times, the issue of whether a court might be construed as giving up its *moral* right to the truth through a retrospective consenting to the deception, deserves some further analysis.

---

[24] This is Kemp and Sullivan's fundamental observation (Kemp and Sullivan, 'Speaking Falsely and Telling Lies', 160), though they do not apply it to the testimonial stage, as discussed in secs. 4.3.2 Speech Acts and Assertions and 4.4. Policing And Assertion-Making Contexts. Note that in sec. 6.4 Mental Reservation In Court, concerning the use of WMR, we also touched upon (tentatively) the issue of whether a just court of law can ever be legitimately construed as not having a *moral* right to the truth while retaining its *legal* right.

[25] The suggestion that members of a court of law can be construed as giving up their right to the truth via a retrospective consenting to having been deceived is, perhaps, more persuasive in exculpatory cases where an innocent defendant commits perjury in order to avoid being wrongly convicted of a *serious* crime—especially if a death sentence loomed. In contrast, the police desire to avoid a serious miscarriage of justice is inculpatory. This *retrospective* approval approach is similar to that used in sec. 4.4 Policing And Assertion-Making Contexts, to justify the use of falsehood with intent to deceive on law-abiding members of the public by police officers lawfully investigating crime. It also shares similarities with one of Hugo Grotius' stated cases where a false statement benefits the person deceived, this person subsequently approving of being so deceived (Grotius, *On the* Law, 3.1.14).

Consider the following example: Police officers are led by the flimsiest of evidence to believe they have identified a suspected terrorist. When the suspect is not at home, police officers climb through an open window of his house in search of evidence. Upon entering, the police discover various items which, together, strongly suggests that the suspect makes bombs at these premises. In the preparation of the evidence for court, the police are advised that their entry into the house *may* have been illegal, and as such, the evidence gathered is inadmissible in court. This will result in the prosecution case collapsing, the defendant being acquitted, with the knowledge that the suspected terrorist will continue to pose a grave and imminent threat to society. The police officers commit perjury by claiming that before entry they could see what looked like bomb-making equipment through the window of the suspect's house, and for that reason, they entered the premises—and hence had *legal* grounds for so doing.[26] Might it be construed that, in these circumstances, the court gives up its *moral* right to the truth?[27]

It is, undoubtedly, a matter of debate as to whether the distinction between speech acts *contra mentem* and assertions *contra mentem* can extend to court testimony. But if the above analysis is correct, it might be construed that a just court of law gives up its *moral* right to the truth through a retrospective consenting to avoid a *serious* miscarriage of justice. Of course, members of a court may very well not so consent.[28] Even so, *if* this implicit consent is present at the time of the court hearing, these ostensible acts of perjury might not constitute acts of perjury.[29]

---

[26] This is the reworking of a similar type of example used by Kleinig (Kleinig, 'Ethical Questions', 212).

[27] By analogy, some might argue that, despite the obvious serious wrongness of misleading Parliament through deception and/or lies, extremely rare exceptions are ethical if and when national security is at stake. The seriousness of the consequences at stake and the rarity of the exception are paramount. For others, no such exceptions could ever be ethical.

[28] Deliberation on whether or not to consent would include a consideration of whether procedural correctness can/should be sacrificed in *serious* cases to ensure the conviction of the factually guilty or acquittal of the factually innocent. Positing a loved one as the factually innocent defendant (exculpatory) or future victim of a factually guilty defendant (inculpatory) in such cases might assist the deliberation process.

[29] This line of reasoning is offered as an exploratory extension, not an endorsement, of the application of the distinction between speech acts *contra mentem* and assertions *contra mentem* to the testimonial stage of police work. It is only meant to apply to what would otherwise be *serious* miscarriages of justice. What amounts to a *serious* miscarriage of justice is a matter of debate.

It is crucial to note that the above analysis does *not* mean acts of ostensible perjury are, therefore, ethically upright. Recall the three sources of morality: object, intention, and circumstances.[30] Even if the intention and object of an act are good, the circumstances can be so bad that the act as a whole is still wrong. The damage (potential and actual) caused by testimonial deception on the judicial system and to the public trust in the integrity of the police service is, for some/many, too high a price to pay for ensuring the avoidance of serious individual miscarriages of justice. People's views on this, naturally, will differ. The above analysis seems to have removed ostensible acts of perjury from being ruled out a priori,[31] thus leaving the discussion of the ethics of such an action mainly at the level of a consideration of the consequences. This conclusion requires qualification. The point is that ostensible acts of perjury committed under oath still involve perversely invoking God's truthfulness as a witness to one's falsehood, albeit a non-lying falsehood. On the other hand, that would not occur when evidence is given under affirmation.[32] As might be expected, a consideration of the consequences (good or bad) is the basis upon which most people assess the justifiability of making exceptions to the norm against lying, and for that matter, the justifiability of acts in general.

Kleinig highlights the moral dilemma public servants (e.g. politicians) can sometimes encounter when concern for the common good seems to require from them—and often in response to an evil done by others—actions that jar with the norms of our everyday moral sensitivities.[33] He considers whether police officers too can face these same types of dilemma.[34] He refers to Max Weber's 'Politics as a Vocation' in which Weber distinguishes an 'ethic of ultimate ends' (doing what is right and/or following a rule regardless of the consequences) from an 'ethic of responsibility' (where one's sense of public responsibility justifies doing what is morally dubious out of concern for avoiding bad consequences to the public).[35] Furthermore, Kleinig notes that while Weber favoured an

---

[30] See sec. 3.3.1 Human Act: Traditionalist Approach (Magisterium's Approach).
[31] A priori is used here to mean without consideration of, prior to, the particular circumstances of the reality one is dealing with.
[32] See secs. 7.4.2 Meaningless Oaths and 7.4.3 Affirmation.
[33] Kleinig, 'Rethinking noble cause corruption', 296.
[34] Ibid., 297.
[35] Kleinig, 'Rethinking noble cause corruption', 297. Max Webber, German Sociologist (1864–1920). In addition, note Weber's exact words:

'ethic of responsibility', he acknowledged limits as to the morally dubious methods one's conscience can permit.[36] From our perspective, this would mean that even those police officers who are prepared to engage in noble-cause corruption, via perjury or otherwise, will have their limits too as to how far they will stray from the straight and narrow. Perhaps we should remind ourselves that while misguided moral reasoning is not always synonymous with bad people, sincere moral reasoning, erroneous or not, is always synonymous with good people.

7.3.1 Noble-cause Corruption?

In analysing noble-cause corruption, Kleinig reviews two arguments for its justification: the rationale of ends justifying the means and the concept of dirty hands which holds that sometimes one is in an impossible

---

We must be clear about the fact that all ethically oriented conduct may be guided by one of two fundamentally differing and irreconcilably opposed maxims: conduct can be oriented to an 'ethic of ultimate ends' or to an 'ethic of responsibility.' This is not to say that an ethic of ultimate ends is identical with irresponsibility, or that an ethic of responsibility is identical with unprincipled opportunism. Naturally nobody says that. However, there is an abysmal contrast between conduct that follows the maxim of an ethic of ultimate ends—that is, in religious terms, 'The Christian does rightly and leaves the results with the Lord'—and conduct that follows the maxim of an ethic of responsibility, in which case one has to give an account of the foreseeable results of one's action.

(Weber, 'Politics as a Vocation', 41, online pagination).

[36] Kleinig, 'Rethinking noble cause corruption', 297. In addition, note Weber's exact words:

However, it is immensely moving when a mature man—no matter whether old or young in years—is aware of a responsibility for the consequences of his conduct and really feels such responsibility with heart and soul. He then acts by following an ethic of responsibility and somewhere he reaches the point where he says: 'Here I stand; I can do no other' [citing the alleged words of Martin Luther, Diet of Worms, 18 April 1521]. That is something genuinely human and moving. And every one of us who is not spiritually dead must realize the possibility of finding himself at some time in that position. In so far as this is true, an ethic of ultimate ends and an ethic of responsibility are not absolute contrasts but rather supplements, which only in unison constitute a genuine man—a man who can have the 'calling for politics.'

(Weber, 'Politics as a Vocation', 47, online pagination).

situation and hence evil has to be done to bring about a greater good.[37] He argues that both approaches offer little justification,[38] and proceeds to discuss what he calls the 'murky middle'.[39]

Kleinig describes the murky middle as a grey area not covered by the means and ends and dirty hands discussions. He offers some examples of the murky middle where police officers technically break the law under the banner of what he calls 'noble cause decision-making' as different from but close to noble cause corruption.[40] He states: 'All I want to suggest is that in at least some cases of these kinds, what might be formally characterised as "noble cause corruption" is an understandable response to the complexity of the world and our inability to develop rules that are adequate to every exigency.'[41] Cases of the murky middle are perhaps another type of situation where good, sincere police officers might be tempted to commit perjury, as well as those situations where they are under pressure to secure a conviction for one reason or another.

Kleinig provides five examples of the murky middle, of which we shall consider two. In the first case:

> Officer *B* observes a drug deal taking place, and takes off after one of those involved. The chase takes him round two or three corners before he catches up with the suspect. Retracing his steps, he finds several vials of crack, presumably off-loaded as the suspect rounded one of the corners. A couple of identical vials of crack are subsequently found in one of the suspect's pockets. In court, he testifies to keeping the suspect in sight and observing him drop the vials.[42] [Note: the officer commits perjury]

---

[37] Kleinig, 'Rethinking noble cause corruption', 292–298. While perjury for a noble cause is part of the concept of noble-cause corruption, such corruption need not necessarily involve perjury since 'noble-corrupt activities' may not always lead to court testimony.
[38] Ibid., 292.
[39] Ibid., 298–301.
[40] Ibid., 298–299. The examples concern technical breaches of the law involving 'attempts to ensure that unreasonable doubts are not sown in the minds of the fact finder . . . [and also where] certain working economies take place' (Ibid., 299). I shall treat all such activity as noble-cause *corruption*. For *our* purposes, the difference in labels (noble-cause decision-making and noble-cause corruption) is of no real significance.
[41] Ibid., 301.
[42] Ibid., 299. Kleinig acknowledges that his examples are contracted versions of Jim Fyfe and Brandon del Pozo's more detailed versions of these cases. Four of the five examples Kleinig cites explicitly involve the use of police perjury, and one example implicitly implies such use.

In the second case, two police officers (E and F) arrest a suspected thief in the sector area of two other police officers (C and D), whereby officers C and D subsequently arrive at the scene. The police officers agree that it is better if C and D go down in the report as the arresting officers. They also testify to this untruth in court.[43] Note, the officers commit perjury.

In cases such as these, Kleinig suggests that, arguably, discretion is extended but not necessarily abused when general rules are logically applied in making situational judgements in complex situations.[44] The first case involving officer *B* is an example of what Kleinig refers to as an attempt to avoid unreasonable doubts being placed 'in the minds of the fact finder'.[45] That is, the link between the person's drug dealing and the finding of the drugs is not broken on the 'technicality' that the dropping of the drugs was out of sight from the police officer. The second case, involving officers *C, D, E & F*, is an example of what Kleinig refers to as 'certain working economies taking place' in which police sector boundaries are being observed.[46]

Without denying the place of formal rules in the moral life, Kleinig states that blindly following formal rules is not part of morally responsible decision-making. 'The rules may not be sufficiently nuanced or entirely compatible. Judgement is required.'[47] This logic in respect of perjury is not acceptable from the traditional Catholic perspective: acts deemed intrinsically evil (such as perjury) always contravene God's moral law and cannot, therefore, admit of exceptions.[48]

Kleinig acknowledges the reasonableness of the counterargument that it is perhaps better for police officers to be scrupulous in following 'procedural requirements and the truth' lest they fall down the slippery

---

[43] Ibid.

[44] Ibid., 300. Kleinig states that he does *not necessarily* defend the police officers' decisions in these cases (Ibid., 301).

[45] Ibid., 299.

[46] Ibid., 299–300.

[47] Ibid., 298.

[48] For completeness, one notes again, there are also voices within Catholic Christianity, such as proportionalists, who dissent from magisterial teaching and reject the notion of intrinsically evil acts as understood by the Magisterium. The proportionalist way of thinking seems to be more in tune with Kleinig's approach. See, for example, Josef Fuchs, *Personal Responsibility*, ch. 10: *Epikeia* Applied to Natural Law? As we noted previously in sec. 3.6.3 *Epikeia*, Fuchs states that while some take a deontological approach to norms such as those against lying and perjury, others do not (Fuchs, *Personal Responsibility*, 196).

slope to worse forms of corruption.[49] In response, he adds that nevertheless:

> [I]t is probably better for professionalism and professional development in policing to teach police to ski on slippery slopes than to institute rules that, if rigidly adhered to, would by their very nature fail to address the full complexity of the situations in which they have to be applied.[50]

Kleinig is essentially saying that morality requires more than the mechanical application of rules when confronted with the particularity of situational circumstances.[51] In discussing his notion of the murky middle, Kleinig states: 'It is important that, in the effort to root out the weeds of noble cause corruption, we do not also destroy the potential for wise judgment.'[52] This logic appears consonant with those who argue that the police officer who unswervingly upholds the moral absolute against perjury is no moral hero; instead, he is a moral fanatic if he thus becomes situationally insensitive.[53] Many others would disagree.

7.4 OATH AND AFFIRMATION

Most law-abiding citizens will never set foot in a courtroom, so for them, the issue of oath-taking is not high on their list of concerns. Also, the prevalence of perjury in the criminal justice system suggests that for some defendants and witnesses, oath-taking is a mere formality and is not much of a concern for them either. Still, for police officers, oath-taking is/should be an issue high on their agenda of concerns, if for no other reason than they are required to give evidence in a court of law probably more than any other section of society. On top of that, oath-taking will have an added poignancy for religious police officers since they will be swearing on what they believe to be a sacred text. In this chapter, we will discuss whether it is acceptable for Christians to swear on the Bible when giving evidence in a court of law and then consider the practice of affirming as an alternative to oath-taking.

---

[49] Kleinig, 'Rethinking noble cause corruption', 300.
[50] Ibid.
[51] Ibid., 301. There is a similarity here both to proportionalism and situation ethics.
[52] Ibid.
[53] My thanks to an anonymous reader for making this suggestion about moral absolutes in general.

7.4.1 *Validity of Oaths*

A typical example of an oath used in a court of law is: 'I swear by.......(according to religious belief [e.g. Almighty God]) that the evidence I shall give shall be the truth the whole truth and nothing but the truth.'[54] The precise wording of the oath differs from country to country, but a common element within them, as is also the case with its affirmation counterpart (discussed later), is that there is a commitment to speak 'the truth, the whole truth and nothing but the truth'.

First, there is an issue with the notion of speaking the 'whole truth'. What is the whole truth, and is it possible to speak it?[55] Not lying is one thing, but speaking the whole truth is something else. Ashworth points out: 'Telling the whole truth precludes silence on a key matter, although it remains possible that the questions asked by the advocate will, sometimes deliberately,[56] fail to afford an opportunity for the witness to give a full explanation.'[57] If the judicial system does not always give witnesses an opportunity to speak the whole truth, is there not a problem taking the oath or affirmation when witnesses cannot do what they have sworn to do?

Perhaps a helpful analogy can be drawn here between a witness answering the constraining questioning by an advocate and the completing of an application form of some sort. The honest applicant answers truthfully within the constraint of the form's requirements, while the honest witness answers truthfully within the limitation imposed by the advocate's strategic questioning. However, while the one completing an application form pledges to answer truthfully, a witness is required to do more since he promises to answer with the 'truth, whole truth and nothing but the truth'. Both can answer truthfully but, it seems, neither can answer with the whole truth. Can it be right, one wonders, to ask witnesses to swear to something they may not be able to do? Maybe the wording of the oath needs to be amended. Be that as it may, our focus is on the general point of whether Christians ought to take the oath before giving evidence in a court of law.

---

[54] NI Direct, 'Giving evidence in court'.
[55] See Bok, *Lying*, ch. 1: Is The "Whole Truth" Attainable?
[56] E.g. Stone, *Cross Examination in Criminal Cases* (2nd ed. 1995), 2. This footnote belongs to citation.
[57] Ashworth, 'Should the police', 110.

Jesus said: 'But I say to you, Do not swear at all . . . Let your word be "Yes, Yes" or "No, No"; anything more than this comes from the evil one' (Mt 5:34; 37).

Some Christians use these words of Jesus to support the view that oath-taking is prohibited absolutely. The Religious Society of Friends (Quakers) believe this, and some other Christian groups do too such as the Anabaptists. Quaker belief states:

> Throughout their history Friends have refused to take oaths; and they underwent much hardship before provision was made by statute allowing them to affirm. . . . The deeper meaning of simplicity can be seen in the stand of Friends against the taking of oaths. Friends believe that their word should be accepted at any time among all persons and thus [uphold] the right to stand simply on their own word rather than swearing on the Bible or before God, a witness which has gained recognition in modern legal practice.[58]

Anabaptist belief states:

> Christ, who teaches the perfection of the Law, prohibits all swearing to His [followers], whether true or false, -- neither by heaven, nor by the earth, nor by Jerusalem, nor by our head . . . [However] when one does not wish to understand, he remains closed to the meaning. Christ is simply Yea and Nay, and all those who seek Him simply will understand His Word. Amen.[59]

Scripture overall does not, however, seem to advocate an absolute prohibition of oaths. Ashley points out that in the Old Testament: the Law demanded that oaths be taken (Ex 22:10), Abraham both made an oath concerning Abimelech (Gn 21:23) and made his servant swear too (Gn 24:3), Jacob asked both Esau and Joseph to swear (Gn 25:32; 47:31), God swore by his own name (Gn 22:16; Dt 32:40); and that in the New Testament we hear that Paul used oaths too (Rom 1:9; Gal 1:20).[60] The *Catechism* points out that what the second commandment prohibits (Ex 20:7; Dt 5:11) is making a false oath (CCC 2150), and that it is our duty towards God not to do so (CCC 2151). The *Catechism* adds that all oaths must honour God and his truth and that '[d]iscretion in calling upon God

---

[58] Britain Yearly Meeting, *Quaker faith and practice*, ch. 20, paras. 48 and 50. Brackets belong to original text.
[59] Sattler, *The Schleitheim Confession of Faith*, Article 7. Brackets belong to original text.
[60] Ashley, *Living the Truth*, 392 and 394.

[in an oath] is allied with a respectful awareness of his presence, which all our *assertions* either witness to or mock.'[61] (CCC 2153)

Furthermore, the *Catechism* states: 'Following St Paul,[62] the tradition of the Church has understood Jesus' words as not excluding oaths made for grave and right reasons (for example, in court).'[63] (CCC 2154) The *Catechism* adds that an oath 'cannot be taken unless in truth, in judgement and in justice'. (CCC 2154) In other words, the oath must only be used to endorse truth, when necessary, and not for an evil purpose. The Church's qualified acceptance of the need at times to take an oath comes with concern that the utmost respect, caution and care accompany its use. The *Catechism* also states:

> The holiness of the divine name demands that we neither use it for *trivial matters*, nor take an oath which on the basis of the circumstances could be interpreted as approval of an authority unjustly requiring it. When an oath is required by illegitimate civil authorities, it may be refused. It must be refused when it is required for purposes contrary to the dignity of persons or to ecclesial communion. (CCC 2155 Emphasis added)

Since our concern is with legitimate authorities (e.g. the UK and the US) justly requiring the oath, our focus is with the *Catechism*'s point that the oath ought not to be used for trivial matters. Do legitimate authorities always use the oath for serious and proper reasons? While the necessity of the oath for serious cases is probably clear enough to most, this necessity might not exist for trivial offences. The giving of evidence in respect of offences such as urinating in a public place, parking on a double yellow line or allowing a dog to foul the pavement make the point that they are hardly the sort of subject matter in respect of which it is worthy of calling upon God to witness to one's truthfulness. On that basis, perhaps the approval of taking oaths ought not to extend to all cases that find themselves before a legitimate court of law.

---

[61] Emphasis added. Note, in passing, the *Catechism*'s use of the term assertion. This supports what was argued for previously when it was claimed that when the *Catechism* claims the purpose of speech is to reveal the truth, it is to be interpreted as applying to assertions, not other uses of speech. See sec. 4.3.2 Speech Acts and Assertions, and CCC 2485.

[62] Cf. 2 Cor 1:23; Gal 1:20. Footnote belongs to citation.

[63] Reference to Jesus' words is to Mt 5:33–34; 37.

7.4.2 Meaningless Oaths

The oath is meant to ensure witnesses speak the truth. Indeed, 'in all their disputes an oath is final for confirmation' (Heb 6:16). Sadly, assuring the truth by the oath is often not the case since the oath is frequently a mere formality in the criminal justice system; its religious significance largely insignificant to many, and hence the oath-taking process is, arguably, disrespectful to God. While one expects the post-mortem consequences of violating the oath to be a deterrent against perjury for religious people; for many witnesses, the oath seems to be of little deterrent. Grisez notes: 'Those who take oaths lightly show irreverence and seldom are careful enough about avoiding perjury.'[64] Watson concludes: 'For many defendants and other witnesses, the advantages of lying on oath greatly outweigh the disadvantages. Such people will continue to regard the oath as an empty formality until prosecutors and the courts begin to take the offence of perjury seriously.'[65]

Since the oath nowadays frequently fails to secure and act as confirmation of a witness' truthfulness, for the courts to continue requiring the oath in these circumstances is, arguably, an insult to God because it loses respect for God's name.[66] Is it, therefore, acceptable for courts to continue requiring the oath? Should Christians refuse to take the oath and choose to affirm instead? Herron comments: 'The lawgiver . . . should not lightly multiply demands for sworn statements; otherwise the oath can become a mere formality that is thus deprived of probative value, and the temptation to perjury is thereby increased.'[67] Using Catholic speak, one might say that the judicial system is therefore unjustly materially cooperating in the pervasive use of perjury by continuing to administer the oath in these circumstances.[68]

Some lawyers argue that all witnesses should affirm instead of taking the oath:

> We therefore think the time has come for the oath in its present form to be abolished and replaced by a form of undertaking which is more meaningful, more generally acceptable, and more likely to serve the cause of justice. All witnesses should be

---

[64] Grisez, *Way of the Lord Jesus, vol.2*, 75.
[65] Watson, 'Perjury, Prosecutors and the Courts'.
[66] Cf. CCC 2142.
[67] Herron, 'Perjury', 140.
[68] See sec. 3.8 Cooperation In The Evil Of Another.

required to make the same solemn affirmation so that there is no distinction in the respect that is accorded to them.[69]

Given the fact that the above sentiment was expressed over forty-five years ago (1973), it is, arguably, disappointing that, to date, no such changes have been made. Furthermore, the following warning given in this same text has indeed proven to be prophetic:

> If the oath is regarded by many witnesses as meaningless, and if it comes to be believed that only the most blatant instances of perjury are punished, then the climate of opinion must work against the maintenance of high standards of truth in our civil and criminal courts.[70]

It is not the purpose of this book to debate whether the oath should be abolished from our courts. Some argue it would be fairer if all witnesses take the same promise to speak the truth to avoid the possibility that one's religious affiliation might make one more credible in the eyes of the court. Others claim that moves to abolish the oath harbour a secular humanist agenda against the country's religious heritage. This book only seeks to highlight the meaningless way the oath is treated by many witnesses, that it is a significant problem within our legal system, and on this basis, the better option might be for Christians to affirm instead.

Nonetheless, let us consider a little further some of the views of those advocating the abolishment of the swearing of oaths in judicial proceedings. In 1998 Nicholas Price QC, a criminal law specialist, is reported to have said on the British Broadcasting Corporation (BBC) Radio 4 programme, *Law In Action*, that in our 'less God-fearing nation [Britain]', the oath should not mention God; instead, a new oath should be formulated which stresses a temporal punishment for perjury in preference to divine punishment.[71] In 2013, the Magistrates Association considered—though rejected—the proposal put forward by Bristol magistrate, Ian Abrahams, to end in England and Wales the swearing of oaths on the Bible and other sacred texts.[72] Arguments in favour of abolishing the oath have not, for all that, gone away. Writing in objection

---

[69] Hunter, *False Witness*, 23, para. 69. The distinction referred to is that the exercising of one's right to affirm can give cause for undermining one's perceived credibility before the court.

[70] Ibid., 21, para. 62.

[71] Price, *Law In Action*, as cited in Parry, 'Call for God', 5.

[72] Pigott, 'Motion to end Bible oaths'.

to the 2013 Magistrates' decision, David Pannick QC argues: 'Since the religious oath is . . . simply an expression of a binding commitment, why not simply ask witnesses to commit themselves to tell the truth without any religious element?'[73] He adds: 'Today, there are few people who would regard a religious oath as binding, and even fewer for whom a religious oath is the difference between giving honest evidence and perjury. Indeed, if a religious witness intends to give untrue evidence, they will no doubt choose to affirm.'[74] Hopefully, witnesses do not give false evidence. When it does happen, the fact remains, nevertheless, that affirming rather than taking the oath ensures that those who are intent on giving false evidence do not add to their sin by invoking God's truthfulness to witness to their untruthfulness.

All Christians should seriously consider the suggestion that, when giving evidence in judicial proceedings, it may very well be better for them to choose to affirm as an alternative to taking the oath.

7.4.3 Affirmation

A typical example of an affirmation used in a court of law is: 'I do solemnly, sincerely and truly declare and affirm that the evidence I shall give shall be the truth the whole truth and nothing but the truth.'[75] An affirmation is a solemn and formal declaration stating that one intends to speak the truth. It is an alternative to taking the oath. The law in England and Wales grants conscientious objectors the right to affirm. The Church calls false witness the speaking of a statement contrary to the truth in a court of law when not under oath.[76] While false witness is not perjury in an ecclesial sense, it is still punishable as perjury under criminal law.

The practice of affirming is not contrary to Catholic teaching. Grisez comments:

> In some cases, legal documents and procedures offer an alternative to taking an oath: affirming under the penalty for perjury. Since oaths are excluded generally, though not absolutely, one should take such an option when it is available. This is easily

---

[73] Pannick, 'Oaths, religious or not'.
[74] Ibid.
[75] NI Direct, 'Giving evidence in court'.
[76] Cf. CCC 2476. Peschke states: 'Statutory declarations [i.e. affirmations] in lieu of oath are forceful and explicit attestations of one's truthfulness, but they are not oaths in the strict sense.' (Peschke, *Christian Ethics, vol.2*, 595)

done, by forming the general intention of affirming rather than swearing in such cases.[77]

Grisez suggests one should affirm whenever the option is available. That may very well be a wise approach to take. This book only suggests the more limited approach of refusing the oath and opting to affirm as an alternative when one finds oneself in a judicial system in which many use the oath in a meaningless way.

There is also a point as to whether police officers should even be required to take an oath or affirmation before giving evidence in a court of law. At the beginning of their police career, police officers will have already made a declaration of their intent to, amongst other things, act with integrity, uphold fundamental human rights and carry out their policing duties in a lawful way. Non-police citizens have not made such a declaration regarding their integrity, respect for human rights and intent to be law-abiding. In England and Wales, the declaration police officers make upon appointment reads:

> I.................of.................do solemnly and sincerely declare and affirm that I will well and truly serve the Queen in the office of constable, with fairness, integrity, diligence and impartiality, upholding fundamental human rights and according equal respect to all people; and that I will, to the best of my power, cause the peace to be kept and preserved and prevent all offences against people and property; and that while I continue to hold the said office I will, to the best of my skill and knowledge, discharge all the duties thereof faithfully according to law.[78]

7.5 SUMMARY

Perjury is a problem within the judicial systems of the UK, US and no doubt elsewhere too. It is a problem that affects both the wider society and the police. The Magisterium of the Catholic Church condemns the act of perjury: it is an intrinsically evil act. Some good, sincere police officers, Christian or otherwise, are tempted at times to commit perjury based on the well-intentioned, yet misguided approach of noble-cause corruption.

---

[77] Grisez, *Way of the Lord Jesus, vol.2*, 75.

[78] The National Archives, Police Reform Act 2002, ch. 30, pt. 6, sec. 83 Attestation of Constable. Similar declarations are, no doubt, made by the police in other parts of the world.

The Catholic Christian general acceptance of the validity of taking oaths has been discussed, as well as the disapproval of oaths by Christian denominations, such as Quakers and Anabaptists. It has been argued that since the use of the oath nowadays in the UK and US criminal justice systems has become for many people a meaningless procedure, this disrespects the oath and thereby God, as is evidenced by the considerable amount of perjury that occurs. The suggestion made was that the most appropriate course of action for Christians might be to decline the oath and choose to affirm instead.

8

VIRTUOUS POLICING

Our study of police ethics has focussed on particular acts: lying, discreet language, perjury and oaths, as well as the issue of cooperating in the evil/wrongdoing of others. In this chapter, we focus on some of the desirable qualities of character a police officer should possess. In other words, we ask: what makes a virtuous police officer? To answer this, we first consider the thoughts on virtue by the ancient Greek philosopher Aristotle, whose ideas were adopted and adapted by Catholic Christianity.

8.1 VIRTUES: AN OVERVIEW

Aristotle's account of the virtues comes from his book, *Nicomachean Ethics*.[2] A virtue (Greek: *arête*) is an excellent human quality (a good habit), e.g. courage. He argues that we need virtues to live well, and in living a good moral life we become happy and flourish: in other words, we enjoy *eudaimonia*, our ultimate aim in life. Aristotle identified many virtues, and what counts as a virtue in one society may not count as a virtue in a different culture because individuals and communities might need different qualities to flourish. Aristotle identified four main virtues, and these have stood the test of time. They are prudence (ability to make good practical decisions), justice (being fair), temperance (self-control) and fortitude (courage).[3] These are known as the cardinal virtues because all other virtues are thought to be based/hinged around these four virtues.[4]

Moral virtue is a skill. Like all skills, one acquires moral virtues through corrected practice. For example, becoming excellent at playing the guitar

---

[1] CCC 1833. For the Christian, the more virtuous one becomes the more one conforms to God's will.

[2] Aristotle, *Nicomachean Ethics*.

[3] Plato, before Aristotle, also taught that these were the four key virtues.

[4] *'Cardo'* is the Latin word for 'hinge'.

requires practice, lots of it, thus cultivating good musical habits and eliminating bad ones. Similarly, a person acquires a moral virtue by putting that virtue into practice. Aristotle said that 'by doing just acts we become just, and by doing acts of temperance and courage we become temperate and courageous'.[5] To acquire the virtues of truthfulness and honesty, we need to practise being truthful and honest from day-to-day. So time and effort are required both to acquire virtue and then keep hold of it as part of one's character. Police recruits are drawn from the societies they serve and, one would have thought, should have already acquired the qualities their particular society consider to be virtues. Police culture will also seek to develop within its ranks, qualities of character in its officers that help promote the flourishing of the police community and eliminate bad qualities (vices) that are perceived to be a threat. Sadly, instances of corrupt police practice over the years suggest that vices sometimes win out over virtues.

An intuitively appealing aspect of the virtues is the place of role models in developing the virtues. Identifying excellent moral qualities in role models and emulating them in our own lives is the goal. Certainly, imitating the desirable qualities we see in others, whether they are moral qualities or sporting, academic or anything else, is part of the natural way we all learn new skills. In short, we need heroes, we need mentors, and we need examples of the qualities we seek to acquire. HMIC states: 'Any efforts to raise the level of integrity of junior staff will not succeed unless chief officers and other senior managers set the right example.'[6] The College of Policing's Code of Ethics states: 'All police personnel in leadership roles are critical role models. The right leadership will encourage ethical behaviour.'[7] Indubitably, for Christians, Jesus is the role model par excellence. However, there is a dark side to the use of role models too. That is to say, when people copy lousy role models, vices not virtues are developed. Policing has within its ranks both good and bad role models.

---

[5] Aristotle, *Nicomachean Ethics*, bk. 2, ch. 1.
[6] HMIC, *Police Integrity England, Wales, Northern Ireland*, 5, para. 16.
[7] College of Policing, *Code of Ethics*, 2, sec. 1.4.4.

8.2 CATECHISM ON VIRTUES

The *Catechism* states: 'A virtue is an habitual and firm disposition to do the good.' (CCC 1803) Furthermore, '[t]he moral virtues are acquired by human effort. They are the fruit and seed of morally good acts'. (CCC 1804) They are the seed because the virtues lead us to act correctly, and they are the fruit because by behaving correctly we develop the virtues. The *Catechism* then proceeds to briefly discuss the four cardinal virtues of prudence, justice, fortitude and temperance; which it emphasises are the hinge virtues because they are fundamental to all other virtues.

The *Catechism* states that the virtue of prudence enables us to:

> discern our true good in every circumstance and to choose the right means of achieving it . . . it guides the other virtues by setting rule and measure . . . guides the judgement of conscience . . . [and it helps us to] apply moral principles to particular cases without error and overcome doubts about the good to achieve and the evil to avoid. (CCC 1806)

The choosing of the right means to achieve our real good, resonates with the Magisterium's other teaching that the further end intended when acting (*why* one acts) and the circumstances within which one acts cannot justify an act that is evil (wrong) in itself. Put another way, for Catholicism the virtues work in harmony with the natural law, which, as we have seen, provides objective standards and contains moral absolutes. Talk of prudence helping one discern the right means to achieve the true good has a resonance too with the College of Policing's Code of Ethics where it speaks of 'doing the right thing in the right way'.[8] By making this link, one is not thereby suggesting the Code is endorsing the Catholic understanding of the sources of morality and its teaching on intrinsically evil acts.[9]

Justice, fortitude and temperance are then discussed. The *Catechism* states that the virtue of justice enables one to respect one's neighbours' rights and to be just to both neighbour and God (CCC 1807). It talks of fortitude (courage) as ensuring we are firm and constant in doing good, resisting temptation, overcoming fear and able to withstand 'trials and persecutions'. (CCC 1808) Moral courage to resist the temptation to corruption, noble or otherwise, is possibly a significant challenge for a police officer if he or she is working within a culture that condones

---

[8] Ibid., 3, sec. 2.1.
[9] See sec. 3.3.1 Human Act: Traditionalist Approach (Magisterium's Approach).

malpractice of one shape or another and expects others to do likewise. In respect of temperance, the *Catechism* says that it enables the control of instincts and desires, thus channelling them to the good (CCC 1809). In short, it relates self-control to the control of human desires so that one does not become a slave to them, but use them instead to praise God. Speaking more generally, temperance (self-control) enables one not to be a slave to emotions and passions. The *Catechism* also reminds us that, although one acquires human virtues through education, deliberate acts and perseverance, they are 'purified and elevated by divine grace'. (CCC 1810) In other words, we need God's help in becoming virtuous, in the fostering of good character.

The *Catechism* then discusses the three theological virtues of faith, hope and charity (love). First, it teaches that these theological virtues underpin the human virtues (e.g. cardinal virtues), they incline 'Christians to live in a relationship with the Holy Trinity . . . [and] are the foundation of Christian moral activity'. (CCC 1812 & 1813) The role of the theological virtues endorses the point made in Chapter 2 that for the Christian police officer, his or her embedding of the Code of Ethics into his police decision making is underpinned by his relationship with Jesus as he or she seeks to do God's will in all things. Concerning the virtue of faith, it teaches that Christians 'must not only keep the faith [in God] and live on it, but also profess it, confidently bear witness to it and spread it'. (CCC 1816) For a Christian police officer, he or she is a Christian in uniform and, in harmony with fulfilling his policing duties, must also be true to his Christian duty to bear witness to his faith in Jesus. Then in respect of the virtue of hope, the *Catechism* says it involves 'placing our trust in Christ's promises and relying not on our own strength, but on the help of the grace of the Holy Spirit' (CCC 1817); powerful words for a Christian police officer struggling to live out the implications of being a Christian in uniform. Indeed, as St Paul testifies: 'Therefore I am content with weaknesses, insults, hardships, persecutions, and calamities for the sake of Christ; for whenever I am weak, then I am strong.' (2 Cor 12:10) Also, 'I can do all things through him [Christ] who strengthens me.' (Ph 4:13)

The virtue of charity is the 'virtue by which we love God above all things for his own sake, and our neighbour as ourselves for the love of God'. (CCC 1822) As Jesus told us: 'This is my commandment, that you love one another as I have loved you.' (Jn 15:12) The *Catechism* also reminds us: 'Christ died out of love for us, while we were still "enemies" [sinners].'[10] (CCC 1825) The sacrificial death of Jesus is certainly worth keeping at the forefront of one's mind for the Christian police officer striving to bring the love of Christ to lawbreakers and the rest of society through the fulfilment of one's policing duties. For the Christian police officer this command to love as Christ has loved us can be a reminder that in the exercising of policing powers, in the detection of crime, maybe too in ambition to progress in rank or status within the police organisation, if it is not couched in love (charity) it counts for nothing. Charity is the most important of all the virtues, quoting St Paul, 'If I . . . have not charity [love] I am nothing'. (CCC 1826)[11]

Police officers can lack love—act selfishly—when they fail to put the needs of the community they serve before their own interests. On the other hand, well-intentioned officers can also be said, so to speak, to overdo their love of the community too when they neglect to love themselves by asking too much of themselves or by allowing others to ask too much of them. The truly loving police officer properly loves the community he serves when he also loves himself, which involves being true to his moral principles while applying the relevant police code of ethics to his decision making. Moreover, for the Christian police officer, this love for his community is enveloped within his love for God: a love which is a response to God's love for him.

8.3 POLICE VIRTUES

What qualities of character should police officers possess and/or seek to develop? The short answer to this question is whatever virtues are necessary for the flourishing of society, the police and the individual police officer. The longer answer involves identifying specific virtues that police officers need. From the Catholic Christian perspective, the previous discussion of the cardinal virtues and theological virtues apply to the moral life whether one is functioning within the role of a police officer or not. It is not the purpose of this book to offer a comprehensive list of virtues that police officers should possess. It is for the police themselves, though not in isolation from the wider community, to articulate a developed set of virtues they wish to see present in the

---

[10] Citing Rom 5:10.
[11] Citing 1 Cor 13:1–3.

character of their officers.[12] The principles in the College of Policing's Code of Ethics point police officers in the right direction; but how these principles are interpreted and applied in practice is affected by the virtues of the moral agent. For example, while a person of honest character will embrace the principle of honesty, what this veracious quality requires of him in the nitty-gritty of life is correctly ascertained when the virtue of honesty finds the correct balance in any given situation between being too honest and being too secretive. Recall the *Catechism*'s teaching: 'The virtue of truth gives another his just due. Truthfulness keeps to the just mean between what ought to be expressed and what ought to be kept secret: it entails honesty and discretion.' (CCC 2469)

The table below suggests three more virtues, as well as their excess and deficiency, that have relevance to policing in our consideration of lying, loyalty and the place of rules in the moral life:

Vice of deficiency	Virtuous mean	Vice of excess
Unjustly deceptive	Truthfulness	Unjustly truthful
Unfaithfulness	Loyalty	Misplaced loyalty
Fanatical rule-following	Discretion	Anarchy

The virtue of truthfulness, which we have referred to already, has been put between being unjustly deceptive and unjustly truthful; and underpinning this approach is an acknowledgement of the circumstance of the right or no right of another to the truth. Whether the virtue of

---

[12] The following resource may be of interest to the reader: The Jubilee Centre for Character and Virtues at the University of Birmingham, United Kingdom. On its website, The Jubilee Centre states:

> The Jubilee Centre is a pioneering interdisciplinary research centre focussing on character, virtues and values in the interest of human flourishing. The Centre promotes a moral concept of character in order to explore the importance of virtue for public and professional life. The Centre is a leading informant on policy and practice in this area and through its extensive range of projects contributes to a renewal of character virtues in both individuals and societies. . . . The Jubilee Centre for Character and Virtues will address critical questions about character in Britain. The Centre will promote, build and strengthen character virtues in the contexts of the family, school, community, university, professions, voluntary organisations and the wider workplace. . . . We believe that the virtues that characterise a distinctly human form of life influence how we think and act in the particular situations that confront us.

(University of Birmingham. 'About the Jubilee Centre').

truthfulness permits the use of falsehood with intent to deceive—without lying—depends upon one's definition of a lie and/or the context within which one understands the rule (norm) against lying is supposed to operate. The virtue of truthfulness does, nevertheless, permit the use of wide mental reservation (WMR)—without lying—to evade an answer directly, though possibly not if there is an intent to deceive present. Bent-for-oneself police officers suffer from a deficiency of the virtue of truthfulness as they unjustly deceive others, while the police officer who has not mastered the art of being appropriately deceptive when necessary (hence unjustly truthful) is likely to be incompetent at his job and a liability to his colleagues. Correctly judging an appropriate means of being deceptive and when to use it will be the preserve of the officer who has acquired the virtue of truthfulness.[13]

We saw in our discussion of police culture that loyalty amongst police officers is highly valued. This loyalty is a virtue when used correctly, and is necessary for the flourishing of both the police as an organisation and individual police officers. The notion of the virtuous mean and its excess and deficiency is abundantly evident in respect of police loyalty. An officer who does not support his colleagues, one whom they cannot count upon in the hour of need, is a liability to himself and others, and his unfaithfulness is destructive to successful policing. Here the virtue of loyalty still guards against the temptations from police peer pressure which might demand support for unacceptable police practices. Precisely what the virtue of loyalty will support is affected by the operation of other virtues too, such as the virtue of justice and the virtue of truthfulness. We should also remember that the virtue of loyalty applies to a police officer's other relationships as well, such as duty to family, commitment to one's religious faith and the society whom one serves. It is the rudder virtue of prudence that makes the practical judgement of what action conforms to acceptable police loyalty.

Police officers use their discretion every day. They frequently operate on their own, during which time they have to make on the spot decisions, such as whether to perform a stop and search, offer a warning instead of a traffic ticket, or make an arrest. Indeed, if a police officer booked every violation of the law he encountered, he would not get very far on patrol

---

[13] In accord with the Magisterium's teaching, this treatment of the virtue of truthfulness has not sought to justify the act of lying. In contrast, many would claim that the virtue of truthfulness can, as an exception, accommodate the use of lies in certain circumstances.

due to being overwhelmed with work and thereby fail to be available to deal with more serious violations of the law. As well as this, an overzealous approach to policing, lacking appropriate discretion, will not help foster the support of the general public by whose consent the police do their job. Of course, if the police never held people to account then anarchy would ensue. As such, the virtue of discretion is key to successful policing, both for individual officers and also for police policy in how they deal with certain types of crime and offences. The discretion now shown towards the possession of cannabis is a case in point.

As might be expected, the police are not supposed to use discretion over whether they police by the book or cut corners to get the job done. That said, many would say that only a fanatical rule-follower would never break *any* rule regardless of the circumstances.[14] Arguably, the virtue of discretion might need to come into play on occasions to ascertain what rule-bending, if any, can be morally done in the cause of justice. A cavalier approach to rules can give an officer a sense of being above the law even though he is subject to the law as well as being its enforcer, possibly leading to a disregard of the rights of others. Then at the other end of the spectrum, there is the danger of blind obedience to rules without any concern for the unjust consequences resulting from an absolute observance of these rules. It is, no doubt, when rules are perceived to fail in ensuring people get their just due, that some police officers in the grip of a noble-cause corruption mindset, apply the due justice model to their work rather than follow the due process model.

8.4 SPIRIT OR LETTER

In this book, we have acknowledged that there has been a considerable challenge in recent years to the Magisterium's approach (traditionalist approach) to the moral evaluation of human acts.[15] The challenge was to the way the Magisterium understands the sources of morality whereby the object (what you do) of a human act is deemed to be the primary constituent in an act's moral evaluation; together with its teaching that an act whose object is intrinsically evil is always treated as morally wrong

---

[14] Some rules can be broken without breaking the law. See also sec. 7.3.1 Noble-cause Corruption?

[15] See: Chapters 1 and 3 and *Appendices 2* and *3*.

regardless of intention or circumstances. We saw too that the proportionalist school of thought has been central to this challenge.

Further reflection on the recent work of Joseph Selling in his book, *Reframing Catholic Theological Ethics* is now appropriate.[16] Selling, as we saw, seeks to encourage a teleological approach to the moral evaluation of human acts (i.e. via the intended goals of one's action and life) rather than the traditionalists' absolutist normative object (what you do) based perspective which, he believes, has led to a legalist approach to the adherence of the moral law. Selling argues that Catholic ethics needs to 'regain a focus on the meaning and purpose of any moral law, its "spirit" rather than merely its letter'.[17] He states: 'If the literal interpretation of commandments and rules is the deepest level of insight that one can master, we have a simple, black and white, all or nothing paradigm.'[18]

Selling's considerations about the spirit and letter of the law are, one suggests, echoed within the policing context too in respect of the selective use of falsehoods with intent to deceive ('lies') by the police at the investigative and interrogatory stages of police work. It also exists in respect of one's approach to testimonial deception, regardless of how it is construed and by whom committed. It just so happens that Selling uses the eighth commandment ('thou shall not bear false witness against thy neighbour') as an example of what it means to focus on the spirit rather than the letter of the moral law. He argues that once we appreciate the 'meaning or purpose' of this commandment is 'to protect and promote interpersonal and social relationships' then we can also appreciate that there are times when one ought not to reveal the truth.[19] He argues that the application of the virtues is one contributory factor in one's discernment of what the spirit of the law requires; and in the case of the eighth commandment, the specific virtues of truthfulness and discretion.[20]

---

[16] Discussed previously in sec. 3.3.2 Human Act: Proportionalist Approach.
[17] Selling, *Reframing*, 44.
[18] Selling, *Reframing*, 42.
[19] Ibid. It seems, for Selling, this may require the use of a lie.
[20] It is beyond the purpose of this book to explore Selling's distinctive approach to the virtues in any depth. One notes, nonetheless, that Selling postulates the existence of many complementary virtues that are situated between their respective two extremes. Hence, in respect of the eighth commandment, Selling states that 'there needs to be a continuum between truthfulness and discretion, the virtues that avoid the extremes of bluntness and mendacity respectively' (Ibid.).

There is a further parallel between Selling's musings and ethical issues within policing. Selling refers to what he calls the goal-oriented approach of Catholic social teaching over the past 150 years, and compares (contrasts) this with the absolutism of the Catholic traditionalist normative approach.[21] My understanding is that Selling is arguing that the teleological and normative approaches to moral evaluation within Catholic ethics can find a consensus when one focuses upon the spirit not the letter of the law; in other words, by adopting a method of using norms to guide us in living virtuously towards the goals of our ethical lives.[22] Relating this to our consideration of lying within the different stages of policing, it might suggest the following. An absolute proscription of all instances of an individual police officer's use of falsehoods with intent to deceive ('lies') needs to be tempered by an appreciation of the social goal of the criminal justice system: which, put simply, is the application of the law for the achievement of justice in pursuance of the common good of society. From this perspective, what is deemed to lead to ethical living is determined collectively by the virtues of society as a whole, the virtues within society's smaller communities (e.g. police force) and the virtues of its citizens themselves (e.g. civilians and police officers alike).

Furthermore, when society permits the police use of falsehood with intent to deceive in some areas of their work and not others, what is going on is, in effect, an appeal to the *spirit* of the moral law (norm) against lying, rather than adherence to the *letter* of the moral law. Society thus appears to be exhibiting what, one suggests, Selling would describe as an appreciation that the purpose of the eighth commandment 'is to protect and promote interpersonal and social relationships' rather than having 'a simple, black and white, all or nothing paradigm'.[23]

8.5 CASE STUDY

The following case study, containing some extreme scenarios, allows the reader an opportunity to test his or her ethical viewpoint and associated reasoning. When engaging with the different situations, reflect upon whether or not the police officers' actions are morally justified. Consider:

---

[21] Ibid., 200.

[22] I apologise to Selling if this interpretation fails to adequately capture the essence of his position.

[23] Ibid., 42.

(i) the moral basis of your reasoning, e.g. is it based on the morality of the act in itself and/or the likely consequences derived from the action? (ii) does the moral basis of your reasoning change between scenarios, and if so, why?[24]

Stage 1: Police officers have a hunch, but no evidential basis, to stop a car that is occupied by four persons. The police search the vehicle, discover possible bomb-making equipment, and arrest the car's four occupants. The police are concerned to avoid potential problems regarding the grounds for their stop and search and its risk of making their evidence inadmissible in court. As a result, two of the *police officers lie (falsehood with intent to deceive)* in their written statement, saying they had received a tip-off from an unnamed source about the car and its four occupants and, on that basis, stopped and searched the vehicle. *A third officer uses WMR* in his written statement so as not to contradict the evidence of the officers who lie.

Stage 2: One of the officers who lied in the scenario above subsequently becomes a Christian, leading him *in court to speak the truth* about the reason why the car was stopped and searched. The case is thrown out of court, and the car's four occupants (who are, in fact, terrorists) walk free. The freed terrorists set about planning their next bombing campaign.

Stage 3: At a later date, other police officers on both sides of the Atlantic are interviewing members of a terrorist organisation. These are the four persons referred to in the stages above: two of the terrorists are in the United States (US), the other two are in the United Kingdom (UK). The terrorists have planted two large bombs: one in London, the other in New York. The US and UK police are in constant communication with each other, and the terrorists have made it abundantly clear that the New York bomb will detonate in one hour and the London bomb in two. Despite repeated questioning, the terrorists refuse to reveal the location of the bombs—and are bragging about the carnage and devastation these bombs will soon inflict upon US and UK soil.

If the bombs detonate, hundreds of innocent people will be killed and seriously injured, including many women and children. (The reader should also assume that close members of his or her own family, such as spouse, parents, children, are included in those that would be murdered

---

[24] Before considering the case study, it would be useful to refer back to the notes you were asked to make about identifying the moral principles/values you live by (or believe you live by). See sec. 2.1.2 Corruption, p. 14, fn. 28.

by these bombs). To prevent the New York bombing, in desperation, some US police officers (ex-military) *waterboard one of the terrorists, but are stopped* by another police officer (a Catholic as it happens). Within the hour the bomb is detonated, and the anticipated carnage of hundreds of innocents takes place, including members of *your* family.

Stage 4(i): The UK police are fully aware of the events in the US (as set out in stage 3 above). The London bomb is less than one hour away from detonation. In the desperate effort to stop another catastrophe, police officers *hit the terrorists several times, causing black eyes, and threaten more violence* if the terrorists do not cooperate. In fear and to stop themselves from being hit further, the terrorists reveal the bomb's precise location. The police subsequently defuse the bomb, thus saving the lives of hundreds of innocent members of the public, including members of your family.

Stage 4(ii): Everything else is the same as in stage 4(i) above, except instead of hitting the terrorists, *police officers lie (falsehood with intent to deceive) to the terrorists* and thereby succeed in finding out the bomb's location. The police subsequently defuse the bomb, thus saving the lives of hundreds of innocent members of the public, including members of your family.

Stage 5: Following on from stage 4(i) above, the police officers are subsequently in court giving evidence. To avoid the prosecution case being put in jeopardy, as well as incriminating themselves for their hitting of the terrorists, one police officer *commits perjury* by denying he hit the terrorist, while another uses *WMR under oath* to avoid revealing the truth.

In the various stages of this case study, in your opinion, which, if any, of the police officers' actions, are morally justified (i.e. morally upright/praiseworthy)? What is the moral basis of your reasoning? Some of the police officers' actions are illegal, while others are not. If you approve of any of the police actions in these scenarios, does what you approve of conform to the College of Policing's Code of Ethics? If you were a police officer in these scenarios, would you be prepared to defend your action or decision in public?[25] If the reader is a Christian, Catholic or otherwise, you should also ask yourself: what would Jesus do? If your evaluation in any of these scenarios leads to a different conclusion from what you believe Jesus would do, then you may need to think a little more.

---

[25] Cf. College of Policing, *Code of Ethics*, 17, sec. 4.1.7.

8.6 SUMMARY

The virtuous police officer habitually does the right thing in the right way. We have seen how the virtues function in the moral life. The Catholic Christian understanding of the virtues, both cardinal and theological, has been considered, and their link to the natural law and God's will has been acknowledged. An exploratory and suggestive compilation of a few other virtues that may form the character of a virtuous police officer has been made. Through engagement with the various stages of the case study, the reader has engaged in ethical thinking from within a policing context. The College of Policing's Code of Ethics' principle of accountability states: 'You are answerable for your decisions, actions and omissions.'[26] In respect of their actions and decisions, all police officers will, therefore, need to consider whether they would be comfortable in explaining themselves to their supervisors as well as being prepared to defend themselves in public.[27] Catholic Christian police officers and other theists will also need to consider whether their actions and decisions are pleasing to God.

---

[26] Ibid., 3, sec. 2.1.
[27] Ibid., 17, sec. 4.1.7.

*[A]nd you will know the truth,
and the truth will make you free.*
—Jn 8:32

9

CONCLUSION

The focus of this book has been on a number of ethical issues that present challenges for police officers. We have concerned ourselves primarily with responding to the problems of lying, perjury, oath-taking, noble-cause corruption and misplaced loyalty.

The issue of lying has been a key focal point of the book. It was noted that the circumstance of whether or not one's interlocutor has a right to the truth has relevance to the issue of lying for: the proportionalist approach; Grotius' definition of a lie; a lie being an assertion *contra mentem*; Guevin's concern about the relevance of ethical context; as well as the use of discreet language (mental reservation).

The main goal has been to articulate ethical guidance from within the Catholic Christian tradition. This book has not sought to find ways of dodging the ramifications of the Catholic Church's teachings; instead, it has tried to understand better, interpret and apply these teachings to various ethical issues within policing.

Throughout the book, the Magisterium's teaching has been made clear. Differences of perspectives within Catholic Christianity and the broader parameters of Christianity have been acknowledged. For all Christian police officers, it is one's relationship with Jesus that underpins everything.

Religious communities, Catholic or otherwise, can make a significant contribution to the further development of police ethics. In the introduction to this book, we noted Sherman's question of whether a Christian can be a police officer. The answer to this question is a resounding 'yes', but one must be prepared to face up to the challenges of the policing role. It is worth remembering that for evil to triumph, it is only necessary that good men do nothing.[1]

---

[1] The origin of this saying is often attributed to the eighteenth-century Irish political philosopher, Edmund Burke, though its true origin is uncertain.

In facing up to the various challenges of policing, police officers can and should call upon the help and support of St Michael the Archangel: Patron Saint of Police Officers, whose feast day is 29 September. The prayer to St Michael reads:

> St. Michael the Archangel, defend us in battle; be our defense against the wickedness and snares of the devil. May God rebuke him, we humbly pray; and do you, O prince of the heavenly host, by the power of God, thrust into hell Satan and the other evil spirits who prowl about the world for the ruin of souls. Amen.[2]

While there is a dearth of Catholic Christian academic material devoted to the genre of police ethics, the Catholic and broader Christian community's pastoral engagement with policing is, however, more promising. For example, in 1914 the Metropolitan and City Catholic Police Guild was formed for police officers in the Metropolitan Police and City of London Police. Then in 1974, the Guild became national in that it opened up its membership to police officers throughout England and Wales. It thus became known as the Catholic Police Guild of England and Wales (CPG).[3] The stated objectives of the Guild's Constitution are:

> [T]o provide a fraternal environment through which members may *exercise their professional roles and duties within the teachings of the Roman Catholic faith*; to provide a focal point of opportunity for all employees of the police service of England & Wales to refer when in need of spiritual guidance in respect of their professional duties; to foster respect and love within the family; to *foster the belief in justice and loyalty*; to *encourage integrity, sincerity, truthfulness, kindliness and strength of character*[4]

It is encouraging to see that areas of interest discussed in this book are similar to some of the objectives in the Guild's Constitution, namely: policing in accordance with Catholic teaching, concern to develop a belief in justice and loyalty, and the encouragement of integrity, sincerity, truthfulness and character. I wholeheartedly encourage Catholic police officers to join organisations such as the Catholic Police Guild. Support from organisations like this will help Catholic police officers as they journey through their police career. Hopefully, these sorts of organisations will become more proactive in the promotion of Catholic

---

[2] See Loyola Press, 'Prayer to St. Michael'.
[3] The Catholic Police Guild of England and Wales website is: www.catholicpoliceguild.co.uk (accessed 08 December 2018).
[4] Catholic Police Guild of England and Wales, 'CPG Constitution', sec. 2: Objects. Emphasis added.

academic material specifically dedicated to the policing role and the challenges it presents. There are also other Catholic organisations around the world that support Catholic police officers, such as various branches of the Police Holy Name Society in the United States (US).[5]

For Christian police officers in the United Kingdom (UK), there also exists the Christian Police Association (CPA).[6] Again, I would encourage Catholic police officers as well as all Christian police officers to join Christian organisations like this. Indeed, it is most heart-warming to visit the CPA website and listen to how its members bring together their police duties with their Christian faith commitment. Moreover, there also exists the International Christian Police Fellowship (ICPF),[7] an umbrella organisation supporting regional and national Christian police groups all over the world.

Within his homily to the Gendarmerie Corps (the Vatican police), Pope Francis gave this advice:

> In your work, you have a somewhat difficult task . . . Pray often so that, with the intercession of St Michael the Archangel, the Lord may safeguard you from giving in to every temptation . . . And, like Jesus, the more humble, the more humble your service is, the more fruitful and the more useful it will be for us all.[8]

---

[5] For example: Police Holy Name Society of Nassau County (www.policeholyname.org (accessed 08 December 2018)); the Police Holy Name Society of Suffolk County (www.scpdholyname.org (accessed 08 December 2018)); and the Brooklyn and Queens Police Holy Name Society (www.bqholyname.org (accessed 08 December 2018)).
Note in passing the following comments made in 2015 by a Catholic police officer serving in the New York City Police Department (NYPD):

> During my fifteen years as a New York City Police Officer, I have witnessed the almost complete disintegration of Catholic adherence and piety on this once-devout job . . . As I became more and more frustrated with the lack of a true Catholic culture and identity on my job, I began to speak to many people about why there wasn't a serious Catholic identity on a job that is 35,000 strong — 75 percent of whom are baptized Catholics. To think that out of a pool that large that you are hard-pressed to find a Catholic who does the minimum by going every Sunday and Holy Day is a truly sobering experience.

(Reid, 'NYPD Catholic').
[6] The Christian Police Association website is: www.cpauk.net (accessed 01 March 2018).
[7] The International Christian Police Fellowship website is: www.internationalcpf.org (accessed 01 March 2018).
[8] Francis, 'Homily'.

This book ends with a message to all Christian police officers. With all your goodwill, inform your conscience properly and follow it as you face up to the challenges of the policing role. Have the courage of your convictions, seek God's will in all things, and remember that the God whom you worship and serve is a just, loving and forgiving God. He understands you perfectly and knows the challenges you face within policing. Jesus looks at your heart and whether you try to do what you sincerely believe is pleasing to Him. When you police in this way, I imagine Sir Robert Peel will be looking down approvingly too.

That is natural which has the same validity everywhere,
and does not depend on our accepting or rejecting it;
—Aristotle[1]

Appendix 1

NATURAL MORAL LAW – AN OUTLINE

In the fourth century BCE, the Greek philosopher Aristotle spoke of finding and fulfilling our purpose in life, and if we do, we will lead a fulfilled life on earth, known as *eudaimonia*. In the thirteenth century CE, Thomas Aquinas placed natural law thinking within a Christian context.[2] For Aquinas, our purpose is to do God's will, and by following God's law via natural law we grow towards perfection, and thus become more and more the persons God intends us to be. The precepts (rules) of natural law lead us to become closer to God and ultimately being at one with Him in the afterlife, known as *beatitudo*. Natural law is deontological (duty to follow the natural law), but it has a teleological character too (a focus on the consequences of acts) since it leads to human flourishing, which Christians believe leads ultimately to God.

The start of morality, the fundamental principle of natural law, is that we are to do good and avoid doing evil. Aquinas set out a structured way of understanding the natural law by using what he called primary precepts and secondary precepts.

The five primary precepts of natural law are: to protect innocent life, to reproduce, to educate the young, to live in an ordered society, and to worship God. Doing good and avoiding evil means living in ways that are in harmony with the primary precepts. There is an absolute obligation to do so.

The primary precepts are very general, so we derive more specific rules—aka the secondary precepts—from these primary precepts to provide further guidance on how to live. For example, the moral norm

---

[1] Aristotle, *Nicomachean Ethics*, bk. 5, ch. 7. The universal validity of natural law, in season as well as out, challenges the relativism often found in much of modern-day society.
[2] Aquinas, *STh*, I–II, q. 94.

(secondary precept) against murder (do not murder) is derived from the primary precepts to protect innocent life and live in an ordered society. Secondary precepts must always uphold (respect/honour/be in harmony with) all the primary precepts, which in turn uphold the fundamental principle of morality: doing good and avoiding evil.

There is, at times, some flexibility in secondary precepts—provided any change to a secondary precept continues to uphold the primary precepts and hence the fundamental principle of morality. For example, while the secondary precept that prohibits murder would not admit of exceptions, the secondary precept prohibiting killing human life admits of exceptions, such as during times of justified war. The Magisterium does not permit exceptions to the moral norm (secondary precept) prohibiting falsehood with intent to deceive ('lie').

We must choose good acts and do them with good intention. When we choose acts that are in harmony with the natural law, we are choosing what are referred to as real goods because they lead us towards fulfilment in God; but when we choose acts not in harmony with the natural law, we are choosing what are referred to as apparent goods because they do not lead us towards such fulfilment. For example, speaking the truth is a real good, lying is an apparent good. However, to develop good character, one must also have a good intention when acting. So, for example, speaking the truth is a good act, but if done to harm another we do not improve our character by so acting.

In more recent times, some Catholic moral theologians speak of basic human goods (values), this being a development of Aquinas' treatment of natural law theory. We cannot, however, pursue these developments in this outline.

*[T]here are times when a man has to push
his principles aside and do the right thing.*
—Fletcher[1]

Appendix 2

SITUATION ETHICS – AN OUTLINE

In his book, *Situation Ethics: The New Morality* (1966), Joseph Fletcher set out his approach. He claims situation ethics is not a new theory because, he says, it goes back to the heart of Christian morality, namely love (agape). In the New Testament, agape is used to describe the love God has for us and the love we should have in return for both God and our neighbour. In situation ethics, each situation is key in determining what will constitute the morally right and morally wrong action to take.

Fletcher saw his approach as avoiding the strict following of rules (legalism) in ethics, which, in his view, was the case with natural law thinking and biblical commandments. Situation ethics does, all the same, follow the rules and principles of one's society and tradition but abandons them if, by following the rules, one does not best serve love. For situation ethics, in any situation, the morally correct action is that which is the most loving thing to do in those particular circumstances. Agape love is the supreme principle governing all our actions.

In setting out his theory, Fletcher said there are four presuppositions (assumptions) one must make. He called them his four working principles, which are:[2]

- Pragmatism: the correct response to an ethical situation must work in bringing about the most loving outcome. An action based on any other criteria is wrong.

- Relativism: there are no absolute rules; judge acts in all situations relative to love.

---

[1] Fletcher, *Situation Ethics*, 13. Originally printed in 1966. The above words were spoken to Fletcher by a St Louis cab driver who, says Fletcher, is the hero of his book: *Situation Ethics*.

[2] Ibid., 40–52.

- Positivism: One must choose in faith both that God is love and that love is the best option; one cannot prove this but only accept it in faith.

- Personalism: people come before the following of rules, laws or principles. In other words, do not follow a rule if it is damaging (unloving) to people.

Agape love (the same self-sacrificing, unconditional love that God has for humanity) is the supreme principle that must govern all our actions. He then explains what this agape love amounts to by reference to what he calls the six fundamental principles.[3] They are:

- 'Only one "thing" is intrinsically good; namely, love: nothing else at all.'[4] Acts are only good if they lead to the most loving outcome (i.e. acts are only *extrinsically* good).

- 'The ruling norm of Christian decision is love: nothing else.'[5] Rules need only be followed if they serve the spirit of love; blind rule-following (legalism) is wrong.

- 'Love and justice are the same, for justice is love distributed, nothing else.'[6] In other words, to act justly is to love; if we are not acting justly, we are not acting lovingly.

- 'Love wills the neighbor's good whether we like him or not.'[7] We should love everyone, even our enemies; our attitude must be to do what is best for them.

- 'Only the end justifies the means; nothing else.'[8] The morality of an act (means) is only correct if it leads to love; a teleological approach, so no intrinsically wrong acts.

- 'Love's decisions are made situationally, not prescriptively.'[9] One cannot decide before a situation has happened (e.g. by a rule, law or principle) what acts are wrong/right.

Situation ethics' situationally based and teleological approach to the moral evaluation of human acts is at odds with an act-based approach to morality, especially one that involves the notion of some acts being intrinsically evil and hence absolutely prohibited. Situation ethics is also

---

[3] Ibid., 57–145.
[4] Ibid., 57.
[5] Ibid., 69.
[6] Ibid., 87.
[7] Ibid., 103.
[8] Ibid., 120.
[9] Ibid., 134.

at odds with both a natural law approach to ethics and an approach that emphasises the authority of the Bible's commandments and teachings.

*[P]roportionalism encouraged a reappraisal of the
methodology for evaluating moral action in a
direction that was more hospitable to concerns
about the particularity and context of the agent.*
—Kalbian[1]

Appendix 3

PROPORTIONALISM – A CONTEXT

In the thirteenth century, Thomas Aquinas discussed the moral evaluation
of human acts.[2] Both traditionalists and proportionalists find within
Aquinas' work, material to buttress their respective positions. Joseph
Selling teaches that, despite the impression given by some that the *fontes
moralitatis* are '"traditional", even ancient' within the Church, the
nineteenth-century manuals are the real catalyst for the *fontes moralitatis*
approach to the moral evaluation of human acts.[3] Selling adds: 'The aim
of these handbooks was not to develop a theory of Christian ethics, but
rather to train men preparing for the priesthood in how to administer the
sacrament of reconciliation.'[4]

Slater's, *A Manual of Moral Theology* is one example of an English
manual of moral theology, and it addresses the *fontes moralitatis* in a way
that echoes Aquinas' previous contribution. *Veritatis Splendor* (VS) also
refers to Aquinas' teaching on the primacy of the object in the moral
evaluation of human acts.[5]

From the 1960s onwards, the so-called moral crisis within the Church,
sparked by Pope Paul VI condemnation of artificial contraception in his
encyclical *Humanae Vitae* (1968), led to further debate concerning the
moral evaluation of human acts. In short, the proportionalist school of
thought attacked the traditional concept of the *fontes moralitatis*. From the
time of *Humanae Vitae* 'there would be two "camps" of moral theology

---

[1] Kalbian, 'Where Have All The Proportionalists Gone?', 3.
[2] Aquinas, *STh* I–II, q.q. 6–21.
[3] Selling, 'The Context', 52–53.
[4] Ibid., 52.
[5] John Paul II, *Veritatis Splendor,* 78. See Aquinas, *STh* I–II, q. 18, a. 6.

within the Roman Catholic Church, the "revisionists" and the "traditional" moral theologians."[6]

The 1993 Papal Encyclical *Veritatis Splendor* endorsed the traditionalist approach to the moral evaluation of human acts and, thereby, rejected the type of evaluation offered by proportionalist theologians. In response to *Veritatis Splendor*, a cumulative response in the form of a collection of articles appeared from the proportionalist school of thought in *The Spendor of Accuracy: An Examination of the Assertions made by Veritatis Splendor.*[7] Another cumulative response in the form of a further collection of articles also appeared, but this time from the traditionalist school of thought, namely *Veritatis Splendor and the Renewal of Moral Theology.*[8]

The recent work by Joseph Selling, *Reframing Catholic Theological Ethics*, is a product of the proportionalist school of thought.

---

[6] Selling, 'The Context', 15. The so-called revisionists are essentially those who adopt a proportionalist approach, whereas the so-called traditionalists are those who take a deontological approach to the moral evaluation of human acts in line with magisterial thinking.

[7] Selling and Jans, *The Splendor of Accuracy.*

[8] DiNoia, and Cessario, *Veritatis Splendor and the Renewal.*

*[W]hile Jewish texts regard lying as prohibited, certain lies,
and especially those told to preserve the peace
of the household, are regarded as exceptions*
—Bok[1]

Appendix 4

JUDAISM AND LYING

Rabbi Passamaneck offers what he says is a possible Jewish approach to police lying, based on the theoretical arguments he makes in his book, *Police Ethics and the Jewish Tradition*:

> From the point of the three-fold typology of deception in law enforcement, the Jewish tradition suggests that forms of pre-trial deceptive tactics would be generally acceptable, although deceit as a feature of ordinary human intercourse and certainly where innocents might come to harm through it would be unacceptable. . . . [W]hen one is dealing with criminals, deception, lying, undercover agents, and so forth appear to be justified, and even under certain circumstances, laudable tactics . . . Deceptive tactics, however, have no place in a court of law. Lying to the court, dissembling, and the manufacture of evidence find no support whatsoever in Jewish tradition.[2]

It is, therefore, reasonable to conclude that the Jewish tradition, as understood nowadays, does not rule out the use of lying within police work. This conclusion also finds support from the point by Bok, cited above, concerning the Jewish approach to lying in general. It might be beneficial for Christians to explore different Jewish approaches to the issue of lying, especially as Jesus was a Jew.

---

[1] Bok, *Lying*, 45. This Jewish viewpoint challenges the Catholic absolute proscription of lying. Bok adds to the cited text a footnote reference to Lewis Jacobs, *Jewish Values* (London: Vallentine, Mitchell, 1960).

[2] Passamaneck, *Police Ethics and the Jewish Tradition*, 154 and 163. The late Rabbi Dr Stephen M. Passamaneck was Professor of Rabbinics at the Hebrew Union College–Jewish Institute of Religion, Los Angeles, and a former Police Chaplain with the Los Angeles County Sheriff Department. As a sworn and trained line Reserve Duty Sheriff, Professor Passamaneck has had patrol and detective assignments and served with an elite surveillance and apprehension unit. Professor Passamaneck was also a former Secretary in the International Conference of Police Chaplains.

Three things can be said with confidence about perjury.
It is a serious crime.
It is committed very frequently.
Offenders are rarely convicted.
—Watson[1]

Appendix 5

REALITY OF PERJURY

The information in this appendix is offered to help demonstrate the prevalence of perjury within the United Kingdom (UK) and United States (US) judicial systems:

- US: 'Mounting evidence suggests that the broad public commitment to telling the truth under oath has been breaking down, eroding over recent decades, a trend that has been accelerating in recent years . . . Perjury has infected nearly every aspect of society'.[2]

- US: 'Police officers also sometimes lie under oath because of the "blue wall of silence," an unwritten code in many departments which prohibits disclosing perjury or other misconduct by fellow officers, or even testifying truthfully if the facts would implicate the conduct of a fellow officer.'[3]

- UK: Writing in 1986, Barrister David Wolchover, from his experience of practice at the Bar, almost totally in London, estimates that 30% of trials involve police perjury, and claims he is not the only barrister to take this view.[4]

- US: Reporting in 1986, a study by Kittel found that 57% of the 277 attorneys surveyed believe that police perjury occurs frequently or very frequently.[5]

- UK: Seabrook, a former London Metropolitan police officer, discusses the difficulties, at times, of administering the requirement of

---

[1] Watson, 'Lying On Oath', 169 JPN 548. Watson has a UK focus.
[2] Stewart, *Tangled Webs*.
[3] Chin and Wells, 'The Blue Wall of Silence', 237.
[4] Wolchover, 'Police Perjury in London', 183.
[5] Barker and Carter, *Police Deviance*, 146. Study referred to is by N.G. Kittel, 'Police Perjury: Criminal Defense Attorneys' Perspective', *American Journal of Criminal Justice* 11 (1) (Fall 1986), 11–22.

the law to caution a suspect immediately after arrest. He notes how this difficulty leads to perjured police testimony in court when officers routinely lie to say that the caution was so given: '[V]irtually every policeman giving evidence of an arrest made in the street perjures himself in the box, with everybody in the court knowing full well that he is doing it'.[6]

- US: Kleinig states:

    [I]t is well known that police have often engaged in testimonial deception. In one of the few empirical studies of police testimonial deception – a series of comparisons of police reports before and after the Supreme Court's 1961 decision in *Mapp v. Ohio*, – there was strong evidence that, in order to comply with the constraints of *Mapp*, police regularly fabricated elements of their testimony.[7]

Kleinig acknowledges that some police officers claim it was not a case of tailoring evidence; instead, it was a case of a change in the *modus operandi* of narcotic possessors.[8]

- For further evidence of perjury, see Chapter 2, section 2.1.4 Perjury.

---

[6] Seabrook, *Coppers*, 60.
[7] Kleinig, *Ethics of Policing*, 145. A footnote from the citation has been removed.
[8] Ibid., 305, fn. 83.

Abbreviations

BBC	British Broadcasting Corporation
BWC	body-worn camera
CCC	*Catechism of the Catholic Church*
CCC1	*Catechism of the Catholic Church* (provisional edition)
CCC2	*Catechism of the Catholic Church* (definitive edition)
CCE	Catholic Christian ethics
CCTV	closed-circuit television
CSPL	Committee on Standards in Public Life
CIA	Criminal Intelligence Agency
CPA	Christian Police Association
CPG	Catholic Police Guild
GWC	God-worn camera
HHS	Health and Human Services
HMIC	Her Majesty's Inspectorate of Constabulary
ICPF	International Christian Police Fellowship
IPCC	Independent Police Complaints Commission
JWT	just war tradition
MI6	Secret Intelligence Service
NCE	New Catholic Encyclopedia
NDM	National Decision Model
NFP	natural family planning
NYPD	New York City Police Department
PDE	principle of double effect
STh	*Summa Theologiae*
UK	United Kingdom
US	United States (of America)
VS	*Veritatis Splendor*
SMR	strict mental reservation
WMR	wide mental reservation

Bibliography

The bibliography contains four sections: Church/Magisterial Documents, Moral Theology, Policing, and Other Relevant Texts.

CHURCH/MAGISTERIAL DOCUMENTS

Benedict XVI, Pope. 'Message of His Holiness Pope Benedict XVI for the Twenty-Sixth World Youth Day (2011)'. 6 August 2010. http://w2.vatican.va/content/vatican/en.html (accessed 20 December 2018).

Benedict XVI, Pope. 'Angelus: Courtyard of the Papal Summer Residence, Castel Gandolfo'. 4 September 2011. http://w2.vatican.va/content/benedict-xvi/en.html (accessed 22 November 2018).

Congregation for the Doctrine of the Faith. *Donum Veritatis*: On The Ecclesial Vocation Of The Theologian. 24 May 1990. http://w2.vatican.va/content/vatican/en.html (accessed 22 November 2018).

Congregation for the Doctrine of the Faith. 'Letter to the Bishops regarding the new revision of number 2267 of the Catechism of the Catholic Church on the death penalty'. 2 August 2018. http://w2.vatican.va/content/vatican/en.html (accessed 22 December 2018).

Francis, Pope. 'Homily of His Holiness Pope Francis'. Holy Mass celebrated for the Gendarmerie Corps of Vatican City State, 3 October 2015, Chapel of the Governorate. http://w2.vatican.va/content/vatican/en.html (accessed 03 December 2018).

John Paul II, Pope. *Catéchisme De L'Église Catholique*. French edition (Cittá del Vaticano: Libreria Editrice Vaticana, 1992). Online copy available on the Vatican website: http://w2.vatican.va/content/vatican/en.html (accessed 22 November 2018).

John Paul II, Pope. Apostolic Constitution *Fidei Depositum*. 11 October 1992. http://w2.vatican.va/content/vatican/en.html (accessed 22 November 2018).

John Paul II, Pope. *Veritatis Splendor*. English translation (Sherbrooke: Editions Paulines, 1993). Online copy available on the Vatican website: http://w2.vatican.va/content/vatican/en.html (accessed 22 November 2018).

John Paul II, Pope. *Catechism of the Catholic Church*, English translation (London: Geoffrey Chapman, 1994).

John Paul II, Pope. *Catechismus Catholicae Ecclesiae*. Latin edition (Cittá del Vaticano: Libreria Editrice Vaticana, 1997). Online copy available on the Vatican website: http://w2.vatican.va/content/vatican/en.html (accessed 22 November 2018).

John Paul II, Pope. *Catechism of the Catholic Church: Corrigenda*. Amendments to the 1992 Edition. Vatican translation. Libreria Editrice Vaticana, 1997 (Oxford: Family Publications, 1997).

John Paul II, Pope. Apostolic Letter *Laetamur Magnopere*. 15 August 1997. http://w2.vatican.va/content/vatican/en.html (accessed 02 December 2018).

John Paul II, Pope. *Catechism of the Catholic Church*. Popular and definitive edition, English translation (London: Geoffrey Chapman, 2000). Online copy available on the Vatican website: http://w2.vatican.va/content/vatican/en.html (accessed 22 November 2018).

Paul VI, Pope. *Lumen Gentium* (1964), Second Vatican Council. http://w2.vatican.va/content/vatican/en.html (accessed 22 November 2018).

Paul VI, Pope. *Dignitatis humanae* (1965), Second Vatican Council. http://w2.vatican.va/content/vatican/en.html (accessed 22 November 2018).

Paul VI, Pope. *Humanae Vitae* (1968). http://w2.vatican.va/content/vatican/en.html (accessed 01 March 2019).

Pius XII, Pope. 'Instruction Of The Holy Office On "Situation Ethics"' (1956). In J. Neuner and J. Dupuis, (eds), *The Christian Faith in the Doctrinal Documents of the Catholic Church*, 6th revised and enlarged edition (New York: Alba House, 1996).

Ratzinger, Cardinal Joseph. 'Mass Pro Eligendo Romano Pontifice: Homily of His Eminence Card. Joseph Ratzinger Dean of the College of Cardinals. 18 April 2005, Vatican Basilica. http://w2.vatican.va/content/vatican/en.html (accessed 20 December 2018).

MORAL THEOLOGY

Aquinas, Thomas. *Summa Theologiae*, 2nd and revised edition, 1920. Translated by the Fathers of the English Dominican Province (Online edition: New Advent, 2017). http://www.newadvent.org/summa/ (accessed 22 November 2018).

Ashley, Benedict M. *Living the Truth in Love: A Biblical Introduction to Moral Theology* (New York: Alba House, 1996).

Ashley, Benedict M. and Kevin D. O'Rourke. *Health Care Ethics: A Theological Analysis*, 4th edition (Washington, DC: Georgetown University Press, 1997).

Augustine, Saint. *De mendacio.* Translated by H. Browne from *Nicene and Post-Nicene Fathers First Series*, Vol. 3. Edited by Philip Schaff (Buffalo, NY: Christian Literature Publishing Co, 1987). Revised and edited for New Advent by Kevin Knight (Online edition: New Advent, 2017). http://www.newadvent.org/fathers/1312.htm (accessed 22 November 2018).

Augustine, Saint. *Contra mendacium.* Translated by H. Browne from *Nicene and Post-Nicene Fathers First Series*, Vol. 3. Edited by Philip Schaff (Buffalo, NY: Christian Literature Publishing Co, 1987). Revised and edited for New Advent by Kevin Knight (Online edition: New Advent, 2017). http://www.newadvent.org/fathers/1313.htm (accessed 22 November 2018).

Augustine, Saint. *The Enchiridion on Faith, Hope and Love.* Translated by J.F. Shaw from *Nicene and Post-Nicene Fathers First Series*, Vol. 3. Edited by Philip Schaff (Buffalo, NY: Christian Literature Publishing Co, 1987). Revised and edited for New Advent by Kevin Knight (Online edition: New Advent, 2017). http://www.newadvent.org/fathers/1302.htm (accessed 22 November 2018).

Barnes, Peter. 'Was Rahab's Lie a Sin?'. *Reformed Theological Review* 54 (1) (Jan–Apr 1995), 1–9.

Bonhoeffer, Dietrich. *Ethics*, 2nd Impression (London: Collins, Fontana Library, 1968). First published in Germany under the title '*Ethik*' by Chr. Kaiser Verlag, 1949.

Bracken, Jerome W. 'What should be one's moral response to the HHS "contraceptive mandate"?'. *The Linacre Quarterly* 80 (1) (2013), 63–73.

Britain Yearly Meeting. *Quaker faith and practice*, 5th edition (London: The Yearly Meeting of the Religious Society of Friends (Quakers) in Britain, 2013). https://qfp.quaker.org.uk/ (accessed 28 August 2018).

Cole, Darrell. 'Whether Spies Too Can Be Saved'. *Journal of Religious Ethics* 36 (1) (2008), 125–154.

Curran, Charles E. (ed.). *Conscience: Readings in Moral Theology, No. 14* (New York: Paulist Press, 2004).

Delany, Joseph F. 'Perjury'. In *The Catholic Encyclopedia*, Vol.11 (New York: Robert Appleton Company, 1911). http://www.newadvent.org/cathen/11696a.htm (accessed 22 November 2018).

Di Camillo, John A. (National Catholic Bioethics Center, US). 'Understanding Cooperation with Evil: Forging Collaborative Arrangements'. *Ethics & Medics* 38 (7) (July 2013). https://www.ncbcenter.org/ (accessed 22 November 2018).

DiNoia, J.A. and Romanus Cessario (eds). *Veritatis Splendor and the Renewal of Moral Theology: Studies by Ten Outstanding Scholars* (Chicago, IL: Midwest Theological Forum, 1999).

Dixon, Paul. 'The Principle of Objectified Circumstances (POC): Clarifying the Proximate End'. *The Heythrop Journal* 56 (4) (2015), 570–583.

Dorszynski, Julius A. *Catholic Teaching about the Morality of Falsehood. S.T.D. Dissertation* (Washington, DC: Catholic University of America Press, 1948).

EWTN News: Catholic News Agency. 'Live Action President Responds To Controversy Over Group's Tactics', 23 February 2011. http://www.ewtn.com/v/news/getstory.asp?number=111752 (accessed 02 December 2018).

Finnis, John. *Aquinas: Moral, Political and Legal Theory* (Oxford: Oxford University Press, 1998).

Fleming, Julia. 'By Coincidence or Design?: Cassian's Disagreement with Augustine Concerning the Ethics of Falsehood'. *Augustinian Studies* 29 (2) (1998), 19–34.

Fleming, Julia. 'The Ethics of Lying in Contemporary Moral Theology: Strategies for Stimulating the Discussion'. *Louvain Studies* 24 (1999) 57–71.

Fletcher, Joseph. *Situation Ethics: The New Morality* (Philadelphia: Westminster Press, 1975).

Fuchs, Josef. 'The Absoluteness of Moral Terms'. In Charles E. Curran and Richard A. McCormick (eds), *Readings in Moral Theology, No. 1: Norms and Catholic Tradition* (New York: Paulist Press, 1979) 94–137.

Fuchs, Josef. *Personal Responsibility and Christian Morality* (Washington, DC: Georgetown University Press, 1983).

Griffiths, Paul J. 'The Gift and the Lie: Augustine on Lying'. *Communio* 26 (Spring 1999), 3–30.

Grisez, Germain. *The Way of the Lord Jesus, vol.1, Christian Moral Principles* (Chicago, IL: Franciscan Herald Press, 1983).

Grisez, Germain. *The Way of the Lord Jesus, vol.2, Living a Christian Life* (Chicago, IL: Franciscan Herald Press, 1993).

Grisez, Germain. *The Way of the Lord Jesus, vol.3, Difficult Moral Questions* (Chicago, IL: Franciscan Herald Press, 1997).

Grotius, Hugo. *On the Law of War and Peace*. bk. 3, ch. 1, XI–XV, The Character of Falsehood, trans. by Francis W. Kelsey (New York: Bobbs-Merrill Co., 1925). In Sissela Bok, *Lying: Moral Choice in Public and Private Life*, 2nd edition (New York: VintageBooks, 1999) 263–267.

Guevin, Benedict M. 'When A Lie Is Not A Lie: The Importance Of Ethical Context'. *The Thomist* 66 (2002), 267–274.

Härring, Bernard. *The Law of Christ, vol.3, Moral Theology for Priests and Laity* (Cork: Mercier Press, 1967).

Herron, M. 'Perjury'. In *New Catholic Encyclopedia*, Vol. XI (London: McGraw-Hill, 1967).

Hoose, Bernard. 'Towards the Truth about Hiding the Truth'. *Louvain Studies* 26 (2001), 63–84.

Hoose, Jayne. 'Conscience in *Veritatis Splendor* and the *Catechism*'. In Charles E. Curran (ed.), *Conscience: Readings in Moral Theology, No. 14* (New York: Paulist Press, 2004) 89–94.

Hughes, D. 'Lying'. In *New Catholic Encyclopedia*, Vol. VIII (London: McGraw-Hill, 1967).

Hughes, D. 'Mental Reservation'. In *New Catholic Encyclopedia*, Vol. IX (London: McGraw-Hill, 1967).

Hughes, Gerard J. 'Our Human Vocation' In Michael J. Walsh (ed.), *Commentary on the Catechism of the Catholic Church'* (London: Geoffrey Chapman, 1994) 336–356.

Janssens, Louis. 'Ontic Evil and Moral Evil'. In Charles E. Curran & Richard A. McCormick (eds), *Readings in Moral Theology, No.1: Norms and Catholic Tradition* (New York: Paulist Press, 1979) 40–93.

Janssens, Louis. 'Teleology and Proportionality: Thoughts about the Encyclical *Veritatis Splendor*'. In Joseph A. Selling and Jan Jans (eds), *The Splendor of Accuracy: An Examination of the Assertions Made by Veritatis Splendor* (Kampen, the Netherlands: Kok Pharos Publishing House, 1994) 99–113.

Jonsen, Albert R., and Stephen Toulmin. *The Abuse of Casuistry: A History of Moral Reasoning* (Berkeley, CA: University of California Press, 1988).

Kalbian, Aline H. 'Where Have All The Proportionalists Gone?'. *Journal of Religious Ethics* 30 (1) (2002), 3–22.

Kaveny, Cathleen. 'Truth or Consequences: In Ireland, Straying Far From The Mental Reservation'. *Commonweal*, 15 January 2010.

Kelly, Francis D. '*The Catechism of the Catholic Church*: Its literary form, authority and Catechetical implications'. *Communio* 21 (1994), 399–408.

Kemp, Kenneth W., and Thomas Sullivan. 'Speaking Falsely and Telling Lies'. *Proceedings of the American Catholic Philosophical Association* 67 (1993), 151–170.

Leo XIII, Pope. 'Prayer to St. Michael'. Available on the Loyola Press website: www.loyolapress.com (accessed 01 March 2019).

MacIntyre, Alasdair. 'Truthfulness, Lies, and Moral Philosophers: What Can We Learn from Mill and Kant?'. *The Tanner Lectures on Human Values*. Delivered at Princeton University 6th and 7th April 1994. https://tannerlectures.utah.edu/_documents/a-to-z/m/macintyre_1994.pdf (accessed 23 August 2018).

MacIntyre, Alasdair. *Ethics and Politics: Selected Essays, Volume 2* (Cambridge:Cambridge University Press, 2006).

May, William E. *An Introduction to Moral Theology*, 2nd edition (Huntington, IN: Our Sunday Visitor, Inc., 2003).

McCormick, Richard A. 'Notes on Moral Theology: 1981'. *Theological Studies* 43 (1) (1982), 69–124.

McCormick, Richard A. '*Veritatis Splendor* in focus: Killing the Patient'. *The Tablet,* 30 October 1993, 1410–1411.

Miller, Robert T. 'The HHS Mandate, Cooperation with Evil, and Coercion'. *Public Discourse,* Online Journal of the Witherspoon Institute, 22 February 2012. http://www.thepublicdiscourse.com/2012/02/4817/ (accessed 24 August 2018).

Molinski, Waldemar. 'Truthfulness'. In Karl Rahner (ed.), *Encyclopedia of Theology: A Concise Sacramentum Mundi* (London: Burns and Oates, 1975), 1776–1782.

Newman, John Henry. *A Letter Addressed To His Grace The Duke Of Norfolk On Occasion Of Mr Gladstones Recent Exposition* (London: Pickering, 1875). https://archive.org/details/letteraddressedt00newm (accessed 24 August 2018).

Newman, John Henry. *Apologia pro Vita Sua* (London: Longmans, 1890). Online copy available at the Project Gutenberg website: www.gutenberg.org (accessed 13 January 2019).

O'Rourke, Kevin D., and Philip Boyle. *Medical Ethics: Sources of Catholic Teachings*, 3rd edition (Washington, DC: Georgetown University Press, 1999).

Peschke, C. Henry. *Christian Ethics, vol.1, A Presentation of General Moral Theology in the Light of Vatican II* (Alcester and Dublin: C. Goodliffe Neale, 1981).

Peschke, C. Henry. *Christian Ethics, vol. 2, A Presentation of Special Moral Theology in the Light of Vatican II* (Alcester and Dublin: C. Goodliffe Neale, 1981).

Pruss, Alexander R. 'Lying and Speaking your Interlocutor's Language'. *The Thomist* 63 (1999), 439–453.

Ramsey, Boniface. 'Two Traditions on Lying and Deception in the Ancient Church'. *The Thomist* 49 (1985), 504–533.

Ratzinger, Cardinal Joseph. 'The *Catechism of the Catholic Church* and the optimism of the Redeemed'. *Communio* 20 (1993), 469–484.

Ratzinger, Cardinal Joseph, and Christoph Schönborn. *Introduction to the Catechism of the Catholic Church* (San Francisco: Ignatius Press, 1994).

Sattler, Michael. *The Schleitheim Confession of Faith*, trans. J.C. Wenger (1527). Reprint from *The Mennonite Quarterly Review* Vol. 19 (4) (October 1945), 247–253. https://courses.washington.edu/hist112/ SCHLEITHEIM%20CONFESSION%20OF%20FAITH.htm (accessed 28 August 2018).

Selling, Joseph A. 'You Shall Love Your Neighbour: Commandments 4–10'. In Michael J. Walsh (ed.), *Commentary on the Catechism of the Catholic Church* (London: Geoffrey Chapman, 1994) 367–394.

Selling, Joseph A. 'The Context and the Arguments of *Veritatis Splendor*'. In Joseph A. Selling and Jan Jans (eds), *The Splendor of Accuracy An Examination of the Assertions Made by Veritatis Splendor* (Kampen, the Netherlands: Kok Pharos Publishing House, 1994) 11–70.

Selling, Joseph A. *Reframing Catholic Theological Ethics* (Oxford: Oxford University Press, 2016).

Selling, Joseph A. and Jan Jans (eds). *The Splendor of Accuracy: An Examination of the Assertions Made by Veritatis Splendor* (Kampen, The Netherlands: Kok Pharos Publishing House, 1994).

Slater, Thomas. 'Mental Reservation'. In *The Catholic Encyclopedia*, Vol.10 (New York: Robert Appleton Company, 1911). Transcribed for New Advent by Simon Parent. http://www.newadvent.org/cathen/ 10195b.htm (accessed 23 November 2018).

Slater, Thomas. *A Manual of Moral Theology for English Speaking Countries, Vol.1*, 5th revised edition (London: Burns Oates and Washbourne Ltd, 1925).

Smith, Janet E. 'Moral Terminology and Proportionalism'. In Thomas Hibbs and John O'Callaghan (eds), *Recovering Nature: Essays in Natural Philosophy, Ethics, and Metaphysics in Honor of Ralph McInerny* (Notre Dame, IN: University of Notre Dame Press, 1999) 127–146.

Smith, Janet E. 'Fig Leaves and Falsehoods'. *First Things: A Monthly Journal of Religion and Public Life*, Issue 214 (June/July 2011), 45–49. https://www.firstthings.com/article/2011/06/fig-leaves-and-falsehoods (accessed 25 August 2018).

Tollefsen, Christopher O. *Lying and Christian Ethics* (Cambridge: Cambridge University Press, 2018. First published 2014.).

POLICING

Alpert, Geoffrey P., and Jeffrey J. Noble. 'Lies, True Lies, and Conscious Deception: Police Officers and the Truth'. *Police Quarterly* 12 (2) (June 2009), 237–254.

Ashworth, Andrew. 'Ethics and Criminal Justice'. In Ross Cranston (ed.), *Legal Ethics and Professional Responsibility* (Oxford: Clarendon Press, 1995) 145–174.

Ashworth, Andrew. 'Should the Police be Allowed to use Deceptive Practices?'. *The Law Quarterly Review* 114 (Jan 1998), 108–140.

Barker, Thomas and David L. Carter. *Police Deviance*, 3rd edition (Cincinnati, Ohio: Anderson Publishing, 1994).

Burke Jr., Francis V. 'Lying During Crisis Negotiations: A Costly Means to Expedient Resolution'. *Criminal Justice Ethics* 14 (1) (1995), 49–62.

Caldero, Michael A., and John P. Crank. *Police Ethics: The Corruption of Noble Cause*, 3rd edition (Oxon: Routledge, 2015).

Catholic Police Guild of England and Wales. 'CPG Constitution'. https://www.catholicpoliceguild.co.uk (accessed 23 November 2018).

Chin, Gabriel J., and Scott C. Wells. 'The "Blue Wall of Silence" as evidence of bias and motive to lie: A new approach to police perjury'. *University of Law Review Pittsburgh* 59 (1998), 223–299.

Christian Police Association (CPA). http://www.cpauk.net (accessed 23 November 2018).

City of New York. *The Knapp Commission Report on Police Corruption* (New York: George Braziller, 1973). Otherwise known as the 'Knapp Commission'.

City of New York. *Commission Report: Commission to Investigate Allegations of Police Corruption and the Anti-Corruption Procedures of the Police Department* (Milton Mollen, Chair), 7 July 1994. Otherwise known as the 'Mollen Commission'.

College of Policing, *Code of Ethics: A Code of Practice for the Principles and Standards of Professional Behaviour for the Policing Profession of England and*

Wales (Coventry: College of Policing Limited, July 2014). http://www.college.police.uk (accessed 23August 2018).

College of Policing, *The Code of Ethics – Reading list.* http://www.college. police.uk (accessed 29 November 2018).

College of Policing, 'How we developed the Code of Ethics'. http://www.college.police.uk (accessed 29 November 2018).

Committee on Standards in Public Life (CSPL). *The 7 principles of public life* (London: CSPL, 31 May 1995). https://www.gov.uk/government/ publications/the-7-principles-of-public-life (accessed 24 August 2018).

Cunningham, Larry. 'Taking on Testilying: The Prosecutor's Response to In-Court Police Deception'. *Criminal Justice Ethics* 18 (1) (Winter/Spring 1999), 26–40.

Davis, David. 'Police culture needs root and branch reform'. *The Times*, 23 October 2013. https://www.thetimes.co.uk (accessed 26 August 2018).

Dixon, Paul. 'Police Lies and the Catechism on Lying'. *Irish Theological Quarterly* 78 (2) (2013), 162–178.

Duncan, Roderic (Judge). 'Lying in Court'. (California: Nolo Press, 1992). Available at Nolo on TenantNet: http://tenant.net/Court/nolo/ nn102.html (accessed 31 August 2018).

Eleftheriou-Smith, Loulla-Mae. 'Plebgate: The timeline of events that left Andrew Mitchell's career in tatters'. *Independent*, 28 November 2014. https://www.independent.co.uk (accessed 06 December 2018).

Foley, Michael Oliver. 'Police Perjury: A Factorial Survey', (PhD dissertation for The City University of New York: Graduate Faculty of Criminal Justice, 2000). https://www.ncjrs.gov/pdffiles1/nij/ grants/181241.pdf (accessed 27 August 2018).

Goldstein, Joseph. '"Testilying" by Police: A Stubborn Problem'. *The New York Times*, 18 March 2018. https://www.nytimes.com/2018/03/18/ nyregion/testilying-police-perjury-new-york.html (accessed 01 October 2018). A version of the article in print, 19 March 2018, p. A1 called '"Testilying" by Police Persists As Cameras Capture Truth'.

Goldstein, Joseph. 'Promotions, Not Punishments, for Officers Accused of Lying'. *The New York Times*, 19 March 2018. https://www.nytimes. com/2018/03/19/nyregion/new-york-police-perjury- promotions.html (accessed 01 October 2018). A version of the article in print, 20 March 2018, p. A1 called 'Caught in Lie, Then Getting Away With It'.

Goldstein, Joseph. 'Police "Testilying" Remains a Problem. Here Is How the Criminal Justice System Could Reduce It'. *The New York Times*, 22 March 2018.https://www.nytimes.com/2018/03/22/nyregion/police-lying-new-york.html (accessed 01 October 2018). A version of the article in print, 23 March 2018, p. A25 called 'How the System Could Reduce Police "Testilying"'.

Graef, Roger. *Talking Blue: The Police in their Own Words* (London: Collins Harvill, 1989).

Hillsborough Independent Panel. *Hillsborough: The Report of the Hillsborough Independent Panel* (London: The Stationary Office, 12 September 2012). https://www.gov.uk/government/publications/the-report-of-the-hillsborough-independent-panel (accessed 31 August 2018).

HMIC, *Police Integrity England, Wales, Northern Ireland: securing and maintaining public Confidence* (London: Home Office Communication Directorate, June 1999). https://www.justiceinspectorates.gov.uk/hmicfrs/media/police-integrity-19990601.pdf (accessed 23 August 2018).

Home Office. *Policy Paper PACE Code G 2012*. https://www.gov.uk/government/publications/pace-code-g-2012 (accessed 03 December 2018).

Home Office. *Definition of policing by consent*. Freedom of information (FOI) release 25060, 10 December 2012. https://www.gov.uk/government/publications/policing-by-consent/definition-of-policing-by-consent (accessed 25 August 2018).

Hopson, Justin. *Breaking the Blue Wall: One Man's War Against Police Corruption* (Bloomington, IN: WestBow Press, 2012).

House of Commons Home Affairs Committee. *Independent Police Complaints Commission, Eleventh Report of Session 2012–2013*, HC 494 (London: The Stationery Office, 1 February 2013). https://publications.parliament.uk/pa/cm201213/cmselect/cmhaff/494/494.pdf (accessed 06 December 2018).

House of Commons Home Affairs Committee. *College of Policing: three years on (Fourth Report of Sessions 2016-2017)*, HC 23 (London: The Stationary Office, 9 July 2016). https://publications.parliament.uk/pa/cm201617/cmselect/cmhaff/23/23.pdf (accessed 23 August 2018).

Hunt, Jennifer, and Peter K. Manning. 'The Social Context of Police Lying'. *Symbolic Interaction* 14 (1) (1991), 51–70.

Independent Police Commission (Ben Bradford, Jennifer Brown, and Isabell Schuster), *Results of a survey on the state of the police in England and Wales* (December 2012). http://library.college.police.uk/docs/Police-officer-report-final-2013.docx (accessed 28 November 2018).

Independent Police Complaints Commission (IPCC). *Corruption in the police service in England and Wales, Second report – a report based on the IPCC's experience from 2008 to 2011* (London: The Stationery Office, May 2012). https://assets.publishing.service.gov.uk/government/uploads/syste m/uploads/attachment_data/file/243479/9780108511622.pdf (accessed 23 August 2018).

Khasin, Irina. 'Honesty Is the Best Policy: A Case for the Limitation of Deceptive Police Interrogation Practices in the United States'. *Vanderbilt Journal of Transnational Law* 42 (2009), 1029–1061.

Kleinig, John. 'Ethical Questions Facing Law Enforcement Agents'. In Brenda Almond (ed.), *Introducing Applied Ethics* (Oxford: Blackwell, 1995), ch. 14.

Kleinig, John. *The Ethics of Policing* (Cambridge: Cambridge University Press, 1996).

Kleinig, John. 'Rethinking noble cause corruption'. *International Journal of Police Science and Management* 4 (4) (2002), 287–314.

Klockars, Carl B. 'The Dirty Harry Problem'. *Annals of the American Academy of Political and Social Science* 452 (November 1980), 33–47.

Klockars, Carl B. 'Blue Lies and Police Placebos: The Moralities of Police Lying'. *American Behavioral Scientist* 27 (4) (Mar/Apr 1984), 529–544.

Koepke, J.E. 'The Failure To Breach The Blue Wall Of Silence: The Circling Of The Wagons To Protect Police Perjury'. *Washburn Law Journal* 39 (2001), 211–242.

Maguire, M., and T. John. 'Covert and Deceptive Policing in England and Wales: Issues in Regulation and Practice'. *European Journal of Crime, Criminal Law and Criminal Justice* 4 (1996), 316–334.

Mass, Peter. *Serpico: The cop who defied the system* (New York: The Viking Press, 1973). Later publications are available.

McConville, Mike, and Dan Shepherd. *Watching Police, Watching Communities* (London: Routledge, 1992).

Miller, Joel. *Police Corruption in England and Wales: An assessment of current evidence* (London: Home Office Research, Development and Statistics Directorate, Online Report, 11 March 2003). https://pdfs. semanticscholar.org/0b25/cd356d69a8e897a921d9e32196f5cd33049 8.pdf (accessed 23 August 2018).

Miller, Seumas. 'Integrity Systems and Professional Reporting in Police Organizations'. *Criminal Justice Ethics* 29 (3) (2010), 241–257.

Montaldo, Charles. 'Miranda Warning and Your Rights', ThoughtCo, 17 March 2017. https://www.thoughtco.com/miranda-warning-and-your-rights-972921 (accessed 03 December 2018).

Moore, Nicholas J. 'Ten (10) Ways Police Can Legally Lie To You', The Law Office of Nicholas J. Moore, Esq. blog, 14 September 2015. https://www.njmoorelaw.com/10-ways-police-can-lie-to-you (accessed 02 December 2018).

Morton, James. *Bent Coppers: A Survey of Police Corruption* (London: Warner Books, 1994). First published in 1993 by Little Brown and Company.

Murphy, Patrick V. *Commissioner: A View from the Top of American Law Enforcement* (New York: Simon and Schuster, 1977).

Nathan, Christopher. 'Liability to Deception and Manipulation: The Ethics of Undercover Policing'. *Journal of Applied Philosophy* 34 (3) (2017), 370–388.

Newburn, Tim. *Understanding and preventing police corruption: lessons from the literature*, edited by Barry Webb. Police Research Series Paper 110 (London: Home Office, Policing and Reducing Crime Unit, Research, Development and Statistics Directorate, June 1999). http://citeseerx.ist.psu.edu/viewdoc/download?doi=10.1.1.431.1012&rep=rep1&type=pdf (accessed 24 August 2018).

Newburn, Tim. *Literature review – Police integrity and corruption* (London: HMIC, January 2015). https://www.justiceinspectorates.gov.uk/hmicfrs/wp-content/uploads/pic-literature-review.pdf (accessed 23 August 2018).

Panzarella, Robert, and Joanna Funk. 'Police Deception Tactics and Public Consent in the US and Great Britain'. *Criminal Justice Policy Review* 2 (2) (June 1987), 133–149.

Passamaneck, Stephen M. *Police Ethics and the Jewish Tradition* (Illinois: Charles C. Thomas, 2003).

Peel, Robert Sir. *Sir Robert Peel's Principles of Law Enforcement, 1829*. Available in the College of Policing's *The Code of Ethics – Reading List*, p.5. https://www.college.police.uk (accessed 01 March 2019).

Reid, Matthew. 'NYPD Catholic: The Story of the Patrolman's Fraternity of St Michael'. *Regina* Magazine, 4 June 2015. https://reginamag.com/nypd-catholic/ (accessed 08 December 2018).

Richards, Neil. 'A Question of Loyalty'. *Criminal Justice Ethics* 12 (1) (1993), 48–56.

Richards, Neil. 'Police Loyalty Redux'. *Criminal Justice Ethics* 29 (3) (2010), 221–240.

Ross, Tim. 'Keith Vaz calls for Royal Commission into policing'. *The Telegraph,* 30 December 2012. http://www.telegraph.co.uk/news/politics/9771532/Keith-Vaz-calls-for-Royal-Commission-into-policing.html (accessed 06 December 2018).

Seabrook, Mike. *Coppers: An Inside View of the British Police* (London: Harrap, 1987).

Sherman, Lawrence. 'Learning Police Ethics'. *Criminal Justice Ethics* 1 (1) (1982), 10–19.

Sherman, Lawrence W. *Ethics in Criminal Justice Education* (New York: The Hastings Centre, 1982).

Skolnick, Jerome H. 'Deception by Police'. *Criminal Justice Ethics* 1 (2) (Summer/Fall 1982), 40–54.

Slobogin, Christopher. 'Testilying: Police Perjury and What to do About It'. *University of Colorado Law Review* 67 (1996), 1037–1060.

The National Archives. 'Police and Criminal Evidence Act 1984'. https://www.legislation.gov.uk/ukpga/1984/60/contents (accessed 23 August 2018).

The National Archives. 'Police Reform Act 2002'. https://www.legislation.gov.uk/ukpga/2002/30/section/83 (accessed 29 August 2018).

University of Cambridge Institute of Criminology. 'Use of body-worn cameras sees complaints against police "virtually vanish", study finds'. https://www.cam.ac.uk/research/news/use-of-body-worn-cameras-sees-complaints-against-police-virtually-vanish-study-finds (accessed 28 November 2018). Full findings of the study are published in Barak, Ariel, and Alex Sutherland et al. '"Contagious Accountability": A Global Multisite Randomized Controlled Trial on the Effect of Police Body-Worn Cameras on Citizen Complaints Against the Police'. *Criminal Justice and Behavior* 44 (2) (February 2017), 293-316.

Vatican City State. 'Gendarme Corps'. http://www.vaticanstate.va/content/vaticanstate/en/stato-e-governo/struttura-del-governatorato/corpo-della-gendarmeria.html (accessed 07 December 2018).

Villiers, Peter. *Better Police Ethics: A Practical Guide* (London: Kogan Page, 1997).

Warwick University Interdisciplinary Ethics Research Group (Department of Politics and International Studies). 'College of Policing Draft Code of Ethics: Comments: Interdisciplinary Ethics Research Group'. https://warwick.ac.uk/fac/soc/pais/research/

researchcentres/ierg/news/ierg_warwick_comments_on_draft_code _of_police_ethics.pdf (accessed 24 August 2018).

Westmarland, Louise. 'Police Ethics and Integrity: Breaking the Blue Code of Silence'. *Policing and Society* 15 (2) (2005), 145–165.

Westmarland, Louise, and Michael Rowe. 'Police ethics and integrity: can a new code overturn the blue code'. *Policing and Society* 28 (7) (2018), 854–870.

Winright, Tobias L. 'The Perpetrator as Person: Theological Reflections on the Just War Tradition and the Use of Force by Police'. *Criminal Justice Ethics* 14 (2) (1995), 37–56.

Wolchover, David. 'Police Perjury in London'. *New Law Journal* 136 (28 February 1986), 181–184.

OTHER RELEVANT TEXTS

Aristotle, *Nicomachean Ethics,* 5th edition, trans. by F.H. Peters (London: Kegan Paul, Trench, Trübner and Co., 1893). Available at Online Library of Liberty. http://oll.libertyfund.org/titles/aristotle-the-nicomachean-ethics (accessed 21 February 2018).

British Broadcasting Corporation (BBC). 'A Week Without Lying – The Honesty Experiment'. BBC2 Horizon. First screened 29 August 2018.

Bok, Sissela. *Secrets: On the Ethics of Concealment and Reconciliation* (New York: Vintage Books, 1989). First published by Pantheon Books, 1983.

Bok, Sissela. *Lying: Moral Choice in Public and Private Life*, 2nd edition (New York: Vintage Books, 1999).

Carson, Thomas. 'The Definition of Lying'. *Noûs 40* (2) (2006), 284–306.

Cecil, Henry. *Brief Tales from the Bench* (London: BBC Publications, 1968).

Curriden, Mark. 'The Lies Have It'. *A.B.A.J.* (May 1995) 69. As cited in Harris, Lisa C. 'Perjury Defeats Justice'. *The Wayne Law Review* 42 (1996), 1755–1803, at 1784, fn.120.

Green, Stuart P. 'Lying, Misleading, and Falsely Denying: How Moral Concepts Inform the Law of Perjury, Fraud, and False Statements'. *Hastings Law Journal* 53 (1) (Nov 2001), 157–211. https://repository.uchastings.edu/hastings_law_journal/vol53/iss1/2 (accessed 27 August 2018).

Harris, Lisa C. 'Perjury Defeats Justice'. *The Wayne Law Review* 42 (1996), 1755–1803.

Harris, Sam. *Lying* (United States: Four Elephants Press, 2013).

Hunter, Muir QC. *False Witness – The Problem of Perjury, A Report by Justice* (London: Stevens and Sons, 1973).

Ipsos MORI. 'Politicians remain the least trusted profession in Britain'. 30 November 2017. https://www.ipsos.com/ipsos-mori/en-uk/ politicians-remain-least-trusted-profession-britain (accessed 02 March 2019).

Kant, Immanuel. 'Appendix 1: On a Supposed Right to Lie from Benevolent Motives'. In *Kant's Critique of Practical Reason and Other Works on the Theory of Ethics,* 5th edition, revised, trans. by Thomas Kingsmill Abbott (London: Longmans, Green and Co., 1898). Available at Online Library of Liberty. https://oll.libertyfund.org/ titles/kant-kants-critique-of-practical-reason-and-other-works-on- the-theory-of-ethics--3 (accessed 24 August 2018).

NI Direct. 'Giving evidence in court'. https://www.nidirect.gov.uk (accessed 07 December 2018).

Pannick, David QC. 'Oaths, religious or not, are a statement that you are telling the truth'. *The Times*, 24 October 2013. https://www.thetimes. co.uk/article/oaths-religious-or-not-are-a-statement-that-you-are- telling-the-truth-dq7qb8x956b (accessed 29 August 2018).

Pickover, David. 'False Witness'. *Police Review,* 4 July 1997, 26–28.

Pigott, Robert. 'Motion to end Bible oaths in court defeated'. BBC News (UK), 19 October 2013. https://www.bbc.co.uk (accessed 07 December 2018).

Price, Nicholas QC. *Law In Action.* BBC Radio 4, as cited in Parry, Marie. 'Call for God to be dropped from courts' witness oath'. *Universe Catholic weekly newspaper*, 25 October 1998.

Saul, Jennifer Mather. *Lying, Misleading, and What is Said: An Exploration in Philosophy of Language and in Ethics* (Oxford: OUP, 2012).

Stewart, James B. *Tangled Webs: How False Statements Are Undermining America: From Martha Stewart to Bernie Madoff* (Penguin, 2011). As cited by Jeffrey Rosen. 'Is There a Perjury Epidemic?'. *The New York Times*, 15 July 2011. http://www.nytimes.com/2011/07/17/books/review/ book-review-tangled-webs-by-james-b-stewart.html (accessed 07 March 2018).

The National Archives. 'Perjury Act 1911'. http://www.legislation. gov.uk/ukpga/Geo5/1-2/6 (accessed 26 August 2018).

Thornton, Robert J. *The Lexicon of Intentionally Ambiguous Recommendations (L.I.A.R.)*, 2nd edition (Illinois: Sourcebooks, 2003).

University of Birmingham. 'About the Jubilee Centre'. https://www.jubileecentre.ac.uk/355/about (accessed 08 December 2018).

Watson, Michael. 'Perjury, Prosecutors and the Courts'. *Criminal Law and Justice Weekly* 30, 26 July 2003, 167 JPN 567.

Watson, Michael. 'Lying On Oath: New Light on Perjury'. *Criminal Law and Justice Weekly* 29, 16 July 2005, 169 JPN 548.

Weber, Max. 'Politics as a Vocation'. Reprinted from Max Weber. *Essays in Sociology*, edited and trans. by H.H. Gerth and C. Wright Mills (New York: Oxford University Press, 1946). Moulin digital editions 2014, available at Internet Archive. https://archive.org/details/weber_max_1864_1920_politics_as_a_vocation/page/n0 (accessed 12 October 2018).

Index

accountability, 22, 24, 49, 158

affirmation, 134, 142, 144–145

Anabaptists, 140

Aquinas, St. Thomas, 95–97, 113n10, 165–166

Aristotle, 147–148

assertions, *see* speech acts and assertions

Augustine of Hippo, St., 73, 75, 94–95

Barker, Thomas, 71

bent-for-oneself, *see* corruption, bent-for-oneself

bent-for-the-job, *see* corruption, noble-cause

blue wall of silence, 15–16, 28, 55–57, 173

Bocca della Verità, 120

Bok, Sissela, 69n19, 172

Bonhoeffer, Dietrich, 79, 109, 111n1, 123

cameras, body-worn/God-worn, 1, 21

case study, 156–158

Catechism of the Catholic Church,
    authority, 37, 46–48
    conscience, 44, 46–48
    discreet language, 112
    lying, 73–77, 77–85, 103–104
    perjury, 128–129
    virtues, 149–151

Catholic ethics, 36–42

challenging and reporting, 28–30

Christian ethics, 34–36

Christian Police Association, 1, 162

code of ethics, *see* College of Policing, code of ethics

College of Policing,
    code of ethics, 4, 9, 10n6, 18–30, 26n70, 39, 49n53, 53, 148, 149
    National Decision Model, 19–22
    policing principles, 22–25
    standards of professional behaviour, 25–30

conscience, 4–5, 43–63
    additional Catholic guidance, 49–53, 55–63
    Catholic teaching, 37, 44–49
    invincible and vincible, 45–46
    police, 53–54
    views on, 43–44

cooperating in evil/wrongdoing, 55–63
    material or formal, 57–61
    misplaced loyalty, 55–57
    scandal, 61–63

corruption, 12–14
    bent-for-oneself, 12, 16
    noble-cause, 13–14, 14n26, 35, 39, 51–52, 59–61, 129–138

covert, *see* undercover

CPA, *see* Christian Police Association

culture, police, *see* police, culture

deceive, intent to (re lying), 73, 95–96, 116–118, 118–119

deceptive practices, 10–12, 69–73

deontology, 2, 10n5, 32, 52n57, 165

dilemma, 43, 61, 65, 134–135

dirty hands, 135–136

Dirty Harry, 14, 61

discreet language, *see* mental reservation

dissent, issue of, 4, 47–48

double effect, principle of, 49–50

due justice, 15, 131, 154

due process, 15, 130–131, 154

duress, 60n81, 131n23

Early Church Fathers, 93

eighth commandment, 24, 34, 74, 92–93, 155

end justifying the means, 14, 15, 39, 54, 69, 130

epikeia, 52–53

equivocation, 98, 112, 115, 118–119

ethical context, 78–80

ethics,
    Catholic, 36–42

Christian, 34–36
  overview, 31–33
  police, 18–30
eudaimonia, 147, 165
evil,
  intrinsic, *see* intrinsic evil
  ontic, 101–103
  physical, *see* evil, ontic
  pre-moral, *see* evil, ontic
examples,
  courtroom testimony, 96n20, 113,
    121–123, 129–131
  lie to Gestapo, 66, 73n41, 75, 78–79,
    82
  police moral scenarios, *see* police,
    moral scenarios
  World Trade Centre, 65

false witness, 128–129, 144 (*see also*
  eighth commandment)
falsehood, 118–119
Fletcher, Joseph, 35, 167
fontes moralitatis, *see* morality, sources of
force, use of, 10, 13n21, 27, 59, 104–
  108, 130n20
Fuchs, Josef, 52n57

God's will, 4, 18n46, 20, 21, 32, 34–35,
  36, 38, 43, 44, 54, 150, 163
Golden Rule, 24, 46, 111
Grisez, Germain, 51, 60nn81–82, 94,
  116–117, 117n18, 130, 144
Grotius, Hugo, 82, 89n96, 97–98, 101,
  103, 132n25
Guevin, Benedict, 78–80

Hebrew midwives, 92–94
honesty and integrity, 22, 24, 25–27,
  56–57, 72–73, 100, 145
human act, 37–42, 101–102, 154–155,
  170–171
  Magisterium, 37–40
  proportionalist, 40–42
human flourishing, 147, 151, 152n12,
  165

ignorance,
  invincible and vincible, 45–46

infallibility, 37n12, 46–47, 47n47
intrinsic evil, 4, 38–40, 41, 137n48,
  154–155
IPCC, 12, 17

Janssens, Louis, 101–103
Jesus Christ, 4, 20, 24, 28, 29, 34–35,
  36, 140, 150, 163
Joshua spies, *see* Rahab
just war tradition, 104–108

Kant, Immanuel, 40–41, 68, 99–100
Kemp, Kenneth W., 80–88, 90,
  132n24
Kleinig, John, 134–138

law enforcement, *see* police
lesser of two evils, principle of, 51–52
loyalty, *see* police, loyalty
lying,
  absolute proscription, 68–69, 74–75,
    77, 80, 88, 93n3, 96, 99–100,
    130n20
  Aquinas, 95–97
  Augustine, 94–95
  Catechism, 73–77, 77–85, 103–104
  Christian Tradition, 92–104
  Grotius, Hugo, 97–98
  internal and social character, 79, 84,
    97, 100
  MacIntyre, Alasdair, 99–101
  marital act analogy, 84
  Newman, Cardinal John Henry,
    98–99
  police, 68–73, 85–90, 105–108, 109–
    110
  proportionalism, 40–41, 101–103,
    155
  scripture and Early Church Fathers,
    92–94
  society, 66–68
  war and spies, 66n6, 81–82, 106

MacIntyre, Alasdair, 66–67, 68, 83n79,
  99–101, 130n20
Magisterium, 46–49
McCormick, Richard A., 40–42
mental reservation, 112–123

court, 121–123
police, 114–115
responsible parenting analogy, 114
strict and wide, 112–114
WMR and assertions, 119–121
WMR and falsehood, 118–119
WMR and intent to deceive, 116–118
Miranda warning, *see* police caution
misconduct, 13n21, 29n78, 55–57, 64
(*see also* corruption)
morality, (*see also* ethics)
Kleinig, John, 137–138
moral law, spirit or letter, 154–156
natural law, 45n43, 47, 165–166
proportionalism, 40–42, 101–103, 170–171
situation ethics, 35–36 167–169
sources of, 37–40, 134
morals, absolute, 10, 44, 138 (*see also* intrinsic evil)

National Decision Model, 19–22
natural law, 32, 45n43, 47, 52, 165–166
New York City Police Department, 3, 13n23, 16, 53n60, 126, 127, 162n5
Newburn, Tim, 12, 14, 56–57
Newman, Cardinal John Henry, 98–99
noble-cause corruption, *see* corruption, noble-cause
norms, moral, 36, 41, 52n57, 102, 107, 155–156

oaths,
false, 128
meaningless, 141–144
validity, 139–141
obsequium religiosum, 47n47

pacifism, 109–110
Peel, Sir Robert, 23, 44, 99, 163
Perjury Act 1911, 125
perjury,
Church teaching, 128–129
phenomenon, 16–18, 125–127, 173–174

police, 13n23, 17–18, 56, 110, 126–127, 129–138, 131n23, 173–174
Police and Criminal Evidence Act, 1
police,
caution, 87n91
corruption, *see* corruption
culture, 5, 9–10, 10–18, 23, 43, 55–57, 62–63, 126–127, 130, 131n23, 148
ethics, 18–30
loyalty, 15–16, 55–57, 152, 153
lying and JWT, 105–108
lying and pacifism, 109–110
moral scenarios, 16, 33, 40, 50, 51–53, 54, 55–57, 58, 59–61, 61–63, 69–70, 86, 107, 114–115, 122, 132–133, 136–137, 153–154, 156–158
probationer, 5, 15, 43, 56
policing,
assertion-making contexts, 85–90
by consent, 21–22, 44, 89–90
principles, 22–25
undercover, *see* undercover
proportionalism, 40–42, 52n56, 101–103, 137n48, 154–156, 170–171

Quakers, 105, 140

Rahab, 92–94
relativism, 20n52, 35–36, 39, 165n1, 167
Religious Society of Friends, *see* Quakers
role models, 24, 34, 148
rookie, *see* police, probationer

Saul, Jennifer Mather, 68, 73n41, 81n68, 96n20, 106, 122
scandal, 61–63, 64
secular, 10, 20, 32n2, 44, 143
Selling, Joseph A., 42, 155–156, 170
Sherman, Lawrence, 1, 43, 53
sin,
mortal, 74n42, 128
social, 62–63. 64
venial, 74n42

situation ethics, 35–36, 44n42, 138n51, 167–169
Skolnick, Jerome H., 71, 86, 130
Smith, Janet, 76–77
speech acts and assertions, 80–85, 141n61
  court, 131–133
  mental reservation, 119–121
  police, 85–90
St. Michael, prayer to, 161
standards of professional behaviour, 25–30

teleology, 2, 10n5, 42, 155–156, 165
Ten Commandments, 10, 18n46, 34
testilying, 3n8, 17
testimonial deception, 86–87, 109–110, 133–135
Tollefsen, Christopher O., 69n19
truth, right to,
  assertion making, 82–83, 83
  Catechism, 75–77, 78n51, 83, 112
  in court, 86–87, 121–123, 131–133
  discreet language, 112, 115n14, 120, 121–123
  ethical context, 79–80
  Grotius, 97–98
  imperfect world, 94
  MacIntyre, 101n43
  policing, 86–90, 89n96
  proportionalism, 103

undercover, 11, 25–26, 26n70, 70, 79n60, 114–115

values, 10, 14n28, 18–19, 23, 44, 54, 62
Veracity Index, Ipsos MORI, 67
virtues,
  case study, 156–158
  Catechism, 149–151
  overview, 147–148
  police, 151–154
  Selling, Joseph, 155–156

Weber, Max, 134–135
whistle-blowing, 16, 28–30, 53
wide mental reservation, *see* mental reservation

WWJD, 4, 158

- There is no moral reference point

- Moral Goodness b/c if moral goodness is only a social construct based on what is good for society then it is not objective

- US law uphold an absolute probition against lying by police
  - False

- Moral decision - Making
  - abt God's will
  - primarily obeying laws
  - acceptable behavior depends on the consequences of the behavior
  - doing what feels right

Aquinas
  - intent to decieve is irrevelant
  - when one communicates on asserts what one believes to be true
  - when you aren't being truthful you ruin your personal authenticity

Grotus
  - Lie is saying what is fake with an intention to decieve another who has a right to truth
  - lie conflicts w/ another's right to the truth
  - person you are lying to has right to truth

lying to aggressors:
  - protect truthful relationship least harmful ways to afford effective defense against aggression

Ch. 4

- permitting some lies (broadly) depending on motivations & consequences

- premitting no lies (narrowly)
    - what cathesism embraces

Stable society requires truthful relationships
    - use deception to achieve justice; not having to tell full truth

Investigation + Interrogation -> more acceptable police deception

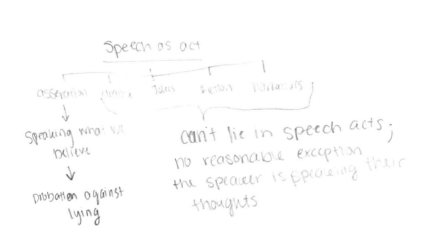

Speech as act

assertion / drama / Jokes / fiction / narratives

↓
Speaking what we believe
↓
probation against lying

can't lie in speech acts; no reasonable exception the speaker is speaking their thoughts

Ch. 6
- two options for protecting a legitimate secret
    - silence + discreet language

- perjury - intrensically evil

- due process may be more highly valued by the public than outcome

Catholic teaching pertaining to conscience
- must follow conscience
- various sources
- must inform conscience

oath = asking God
affirmation: you swear to tell the truth
w/o God

Made in United States
Orlando, FL
06 January 2024

42134659R00115